RADICAL SYDNEY

The authors met at the University of Sydney in the 1960s and have worked together on historical projects since. In various capacities – academic (Irving), freelance journalist (Cahill) – and as independent scholars, the authors have collectively spent decades researching, and writing about, aspects of Australia's radical and dissident past, at times recording it first-hand, and participating in its making.

Radical educationist and historian **Dr Terry Irving** taught history and politics at the University of Sydney. He was one of the founders of the Free University (Sydney) in the 1960s and a prominent New Left figure in the labour history movement. Continuing the tradition of radical history found in the work of Gordon Childe, Brian Fitzpatrick and Bert Evatt, he writes about class analysis, youth politics, labour intellectuals, and radical democracy. His most recent book is *The Southern Tree of Liberty* (2006). He is currently Visiting Professorial Fellow at the University of Wollongong.

Rowan Cahill was prominent in the anti-war, student, and New Left movements during the 1960s and early 1970s. He has worked as a teacher, freelance writer, agricultural labourer, and for the trade union movement as a journalist, historian and rank-and-file activist. Currently a part-time academic at the University of Wollongong, he has published extensively in labour movement, radical and academic publications. His most recent book (as co-editor) is *A Turbulent Decade: Social Protest Movements and the Labour Movement, 1965–1975* (2005).

RADICAL SYDNEY

PLACES, PORTRAITS AND UNRULY EPISODES

TERRY IRVING AND ROWAN CAHILL

UNSW
PRESS

A UNSW Press book

Published by
University of New South Wales Press Ltd
University of New South Wales
Sydney NSW 2052
AUSTRALIA
www.unswpress.com.au

10 9 8 7 6 5 4 3 2 1

National Library of Australia
Cataloguing-in-Publication entry
　　Author: Irving, Terry, 1938-
　　Title: Radical Sydney: places, portraits and unruly episodes/Terry Irving, Rowan Cahill.
　　ISBN: 978 174223 093 1 (pbk.)
　　Notes: Includes index.
　　　　　Bibliography.
　　Subjects: Social change – New South Wales – Sydney – History.
　　　　　　Labor movement – New South Wales – Sydney – History.
　　　　　　Sydney (N.S.W.) – Social conditions – History.
　　Other Authors/Contributors: Cahill, Rowan J., 1945-
　　Dewey Number: 994.41

Design Josephine Pajor-Markus
Cover Author Kylie Tennant mischievously hams it up for the camera at a fancy dress party. Tennant was a fiery advocate for the International Labour Defence organisation in the 1930s (National Library of Australia, MS 7574).

This book is printed on paper using fibre supplied from plantation or sustainably managed forests.

All reasonable efforts were taken to obtain permission to use copyright material reproduced in this book, but in some cases copyright holders could not be traced. The authors welcome information in this regard.

The authors are grateful to the State Library of New South Wales for waiving reproduction fees associated with their images.

STATE LIBRARY™
NEW SOUTH WALES

CONTENTS

Acknowledgments   viii
Alphabetical table of sites for maps   xi
Suburbs of Sydney map   xiv
City of Sydney map   xvi

 1   Introduction: A different Sydney   1

 2   Dawes Point: Moral dilemmas   7

 3   Observatory Hill: Remembering Vinegar Hill   13

 4   Touring hell: Hyde Park Barracks   21

 5   Johann Lhotsky, Revolutionary   28

 6   Tumult in paradise: The watch houses of Sydney   36

 7   The Mutual Protection Association –   46
        The Customs House

 8   Cabbage tree and tricolour   54

 9   The 8-hour day and the Holy Spirit – Garrison   61
        and Mariners' churches, The Rocks

10   Lucien Henry, Communard – Victoria Street,   67
        Kings Cross

11   John Norton and the democratic riots of 1887   75

12   The Henry Lawson statue: Iconic Henry and 'faded'   83
        Louisa

13   A 'democratic rendezvous': The bookshops of radical   89
        Sydney Bruce Scates

14   A convict legend of the 1890s – Bulletin Place   97

15	'Gone bung': The terror of 1893 – The Savings Bank in Barrack Street	105
16	Defending free speech: On the stump in 1915 – Speakers' corners	114
17	The Battle of Central	121
18	Vere Gordon Childe and the pacifists – The Friends' Meeting House, Devonshire Street	130
19	Merv Flanagan, Labour martyr – The Mortuary Station, Regent Street *Lucy Taksa*	136
20	A nerve centre of revolution – Rawson Place	144
21	The Trades Hall Reds versus the Domain Fascists	151
22	Australia for Australians: Fred Maynard makes progress – St David's Hall, Surry Hills	161
23	Joy and rough music on the picket line	168
24	The death of *The World*	175
25	The Venerable Boote – *The Worker* Building, Castlereagh Street *Peter Kirkpatrick*	181
26	Defending Darlinghurst from the Reds – Angel Place	186
27	The anti-eviction war – Union Street, Erskineville	196
28	The defence of Dhakiyarr Wirrpanda	204
29	The New Theatre *Michelle Arrow*	210
30	The day of mourning – The Australian Hall, 150–52 Elizabeth Street	216
31	Welcoming the Nazi tourist – Sydney Town Hall, 1938	223
32	Ken Cook and the Japanese collaborators – The Grace Building, 77–79 York Street *Drew Cottle and Shane Cahill*	231
33	The Battle of Bligh Street	238

34	Fred Wong and the Chinese Seamen's Union – 175 Hay Street	244
35	'Barging' at the GPO: Imperialism at bay	251
36	Margaret Street riot, 1947	257
37	Dorothy Hewett and the Redfern Reds – Lawson Square	265
38	The Waterside Workers' Cultural Committee *Lisa Milner*	273
39	Youth Carnival defies Menzies: The city of the left in the 1950s	279
40	P&O wall fountain – Hunter Street	285
41	Nestor's cellar: Lefties in the sky with diamonds – 72 Oxford Street, Paddington	292
42	Political bolt-cutting – Sydney University's front lawn	298
43	The siege of Victoria Street – Kings Cross	305
44	The conspiracy against Ananda Marga	314
45	Combating the 'greatest social menace' – Darlinghurst Police Station	321
46	Survival Day, 26 January 1988, Koori Redfern – The Empress Hotel, Regent Street	328
47	The 'invisible' maritime worker – Memorial at the National Maritime Museum	335
Recommended reading		348
Index		359

ACKNOWLEDGMENTS

Belying the history it reveals, this book is the result of the goodwill and collaboration of many people and organisations; to all of them we extend our warmest thanks. Ian Syson suggested we write the book, and Lucy Taksa participated in our early discussions. We drew on the expertise of guest contributors Michelle Arrow, Shane Cahill, Drew Cottle, Peter Kirkpatrick, Lisa Milner, Bruce Scates and Lucy Taksa. Their chapters are identified in the Contents, and their biographies appear below.

Ideas for, or comments on, our chapters were provided by Tim Anderson, Damien Cahill, Erin Cahill, Clem Gorman, Cecil Grivas, Alistair Hulett (now deceased), Michael Matteson, John Maynard, Lyndall Ryan and Warren Smith. Permission to reproduce images was given by Robert Cameron, Kate Lilley and Richard Neville.

From many libraries, archives and organisations we received professional help and, importantly for independent scholars like us, the waiving of reproduction fees. In this regard we would like to express our particular gratitude to the State Library of New South Wales, whose collections provided the largest number of images used in our book. For assistance with the illustrations we would like to thank David Atfield of the National Film and Sound Archive, Helen Benacek of the State Library of New South Wales, Gillian Dooley of the Flinders University Library, Jill Farish of the City of Sydney Archives, Iwona Hetherington of the Powerhouse Museum, Sian Jenkins of Currency Press, Wayne Johnston and Lynda Kelly of the Sydney Harbour Foreshore Authority, Scott Krafft of Northwestern University Library, Kevin Leamon of the State Library of New South Wales, Sarah Lethbridge of the Australian National University Archives Program, Nga Nguyen of the State Library of Victoria, Neale Towart of UnionsNSW, Crystal Wang of the Chinese

Youth League of Australia, and Katie Wood of the University of Melbourne Archives.

Robert Irving and Nick Irving provided contemporary photographs of radical sites in Sydney.

At a crucial moment in our preparation of the book, the SEARCH Foundation came to the rescue with a grant to cover the cost of digitising the images. Thank you, Peter Murphy and the members of the Foundation's Left and Labour Movement Sub-Committee.

Early versions of Chapters 9, 17 and 31 by Rowan Cahill have appeared in *Workers Online* and *Overland*; parts of Chapter 47 appeared in the pamphlet *The Hungry Mile and 'Maritime Invisibility'*, published in 2006 by the Sydney Branch of the Maritime Union of Australia. We acknowledge with gratitude the interest in independent scholarship of the various editors and organisations involved.

Robin Derricourt of UNSW Press took us on board when we were looking for a sympathetic publisher. His suggestions materially improved the book. The staff of the Press, especially Heather Cam, Chantal Gibbs, Phillipa McGuinness and Di Quick provided helpful and friendly support. Sarah Shrubb was our expert editor.

Throughout the long gestation of this book, the unconditional support, encouragement and many contributions of Sue Irving and Pam Cahill have been crucial. And speaking finally of each other, we are pleased to report that there have been no unruly episodes; quite the contrary. Writing together has been a rewarding and comradely experience.

NOTES ON GUEST CONTRIBUTORS

Michelle Arrow is a senior lecturer in the Department of Modern History, Politics and International Relations at Macquarie University (Sydney). She has presented Australian history on television, and published widely on media issues, Australian theatre and popular culture in Australia.

Shane Cahill has held a range of senior positions in public relations and communications; he has a research interest in the influence of Japan in Australia from 1901 to 1945.

Drew Cottle is a senior lecturer in politics at the University of Western Sydney. He has published widely on the political and social history of Australia, and has an abiding interest in capital history.

Peter Kirkpatrick is a poet, and a senior lecturer in English at Sydney University. He has published widely in the areas of Australian literature and literary criticism, and has a specialist historical interest in Sydney as a site of literary production.

Lisa Milner teaches at Southern Cross University (Lismore, NSW) in the School of Arts and Social Sciences. She has worked on community projects involving video production and theatre restoration. Her research interests include Australian film and television production, documentary filmmaking and national cinema, trade union films and community exhibition.

Bruce Scates holds the Chair of History and Australian Studies at Monash University (Melbourne) and is the Director of the National Centre for Australian Studies. He has published widely on Australian radicalism and on the Australian experience of war.

Lucy Taksa is Professor and Head of the Department of Business at Macquarie University (Sydney). She has published widely on labour history issues and has a specialist interest in railway history/heritage.

ALPHABETICAL TABLE OF SITES FOR MAPS

No.	Description	Map
1	Angel Place (Ch 26)	city
2	Australian Hall, Elizabeth Street (Ch 30)	city
3	Bligh Street, site of Adyar Hall (Ch 33)	city
4	Bulletin Place (Ch 14)	city
5	167 Castlereagh Street, site of New Theatre (Ch 29)	city
6	Central Station (Ch 17)	city
7	Cumberland Street watch house (Ch 6)	city
8	Customs House, Circular Quay (Ch 7)	city
9	Darlinghurst Police Station, Oxford Square (Ch 45)	city
10	Dawes Point (Ch 2)	city
11	The Domain (Ch 21)	city
12	Empress Hotel, Regent Street, Redfern (Ch 46)	suburb
13	Exhibition Building, Prince Alfred Park (Ch 11)	city
14	Fountain on the P&O Building, Hunter Street (Ch 40)	city
15	Friends' Meeting House, Devonshire Street (Ch 18)	city
16	Front lawn at Sydney University (Ch 42)	suburb
17	Garrison Church, The Rocks (Ch 9)	city
18	General Post Office, Martin Place (Ch 35)	city
19	Grace Building, King and York Streets (Ch 32)	city
20	175 Hay Street (Ch 34)	city
21	Henry Lawson statue, The Domain (Ch 12)	city
22	Hudson's timber yard, Bridge Road, now Sydney Secondary College, Blackwattle Campus (Ch 23)	suburb
23	The Hungry Mile, Sussex Street & Hickson Road (Ch 47)	city

24	Hyde Park Barracks, Macquarie Street (Ch 4)	city
25	Ironworkers' Building, 188 George St (Ch 39)	city
26	Lawson Square, Redfern (Ch 37)	suburb
27	Lucien and Juliette Henry's salon, Victoria Street, Kings Cross (Ch 10)	city
28	Macdonnell House, Pitt Street (Ch 24)	city
29	Margaret Street, site of Kembla Building (Ch 36)	city
30	Mariners' Church, The Rocks (Ch 9)	city
31	65 Marriott Street, Redfern (Ch 37)	suburb
32	McNamara's Bookshop, Castlereagh Street (Ch 13)	city
33	Memorial to merchant seamen, National Maritime Museum, Darling Harbour (Ch 47)	city
34	Mortuary Station, Regent Street (Ch 19)	city
35	Mrs Macquarie's Chair, the Domain (Ch 46)	city
36	New Theatre, King Street, Newtown (Ch 29)	suburb
37	Observatory Hill (Ch 3)	city
38	72 Oxford Street, Paddington (Ch 41)	city
39	Paddington Town Hall, Oxford Street (Ch 39)	suburb
40	Queen's Square (Ch 16)	city
41	Queen Street, Newtown (Ch 44)	suburb
42	Rawson Place (Ch 20)	city
43	Roma House (Ch 28)	city
44	Royal Equestrian Circus and Adelphi Hotel, York Street (Ch 8)	city
45	Royal Hotel, George Street, now site of Dymock's Book Arcade (Ch 5)	city
46	Saving's Bank, Barrack Street (Ch 15)	city
47	St David's Hall, Arthur Street, Surry Hills (Ch 22)	city
48	St James watch house, Elizabeth Street (Ch 6)	city

49 Sydney Town Hall, George Street (Ch 31)   city

50 Trades Hall, Goulburn Street (Ch 21)   city

51 Union Street, Erskineville (Ch 27)   suburb

52 Victoria Street, Kings Cross (Ch 43)   city

53 Wharfies' Hall, Sussex Street (Ch 38)   city

54 *The Worker* Building, Castlereagh Street (Ch 25)   city

SUBURBS OF SYDNEY

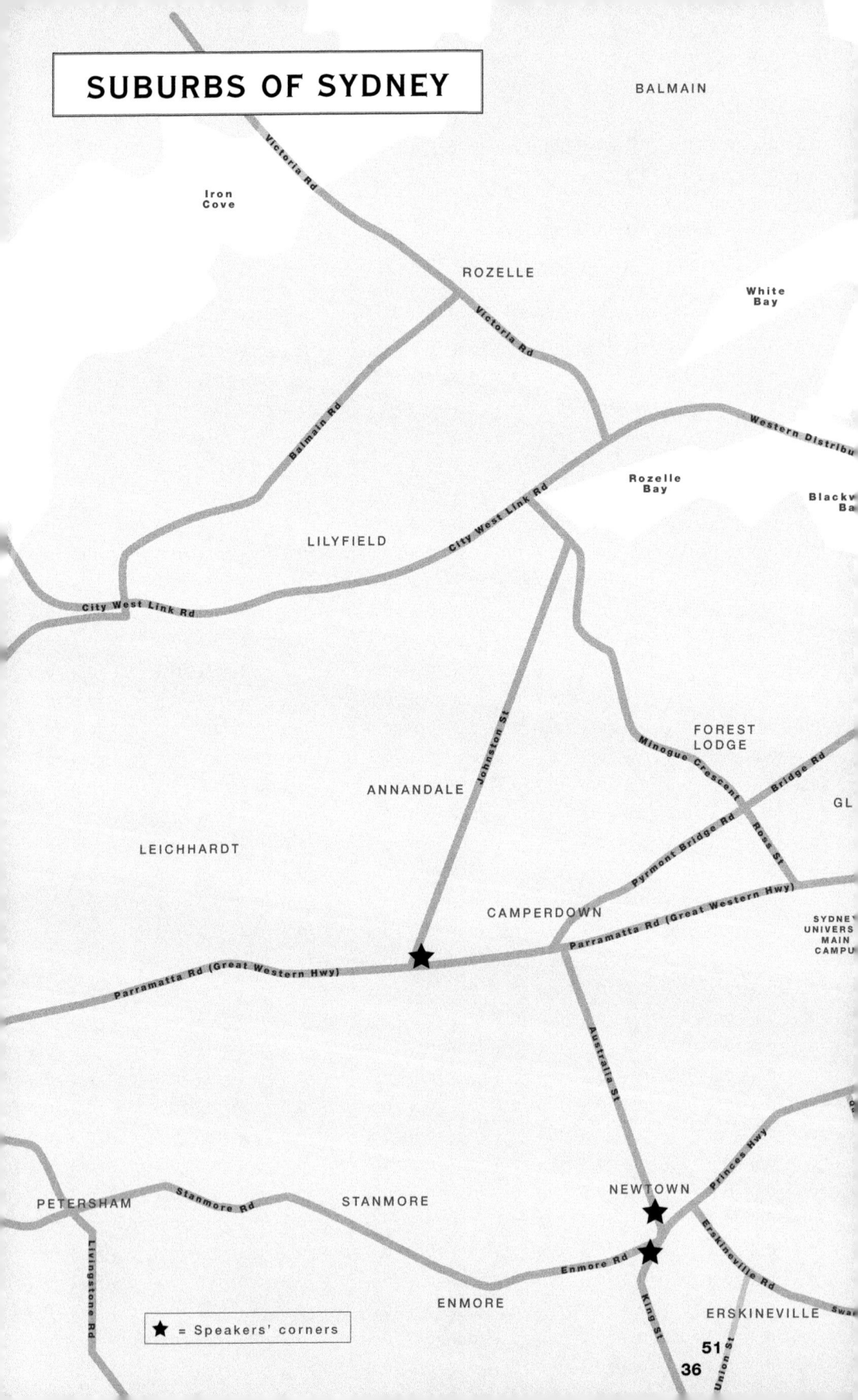

BALMAIN

Victoria Rd

Iron
Cove

ROZELLE

Victoria Rd

White
Bay

Balmain Rd

Western Distribu

Rozelle
Bay

Blackw
Ba

City West Link Rd

LILYFIELD

City West Link Rd

FOREST
LODGE

Minogue Crescent

Bridge Rd

GL

Johnston St

ANNANDALE

Pyrmont Bridge Rd

Ross St

LEICHHARDT

CAMPERDOWN

Parramatta Rd (Great Western Hwy)

SYDNE
UNIVERS
MAIN
CAMPU

Parramatta Rd (Great Western Hwy)

★

Australia St

Princes Hwy

PETERSHAM

Stanmore Rd

STANMORE

NEWTOWN ★

Erskineville Rd

Livingstone Rd

Enmore Rd

★

ENMORE

ERSKINEVILLE

Swa

King St

Unton St

★ = Speakers' corners

51
36

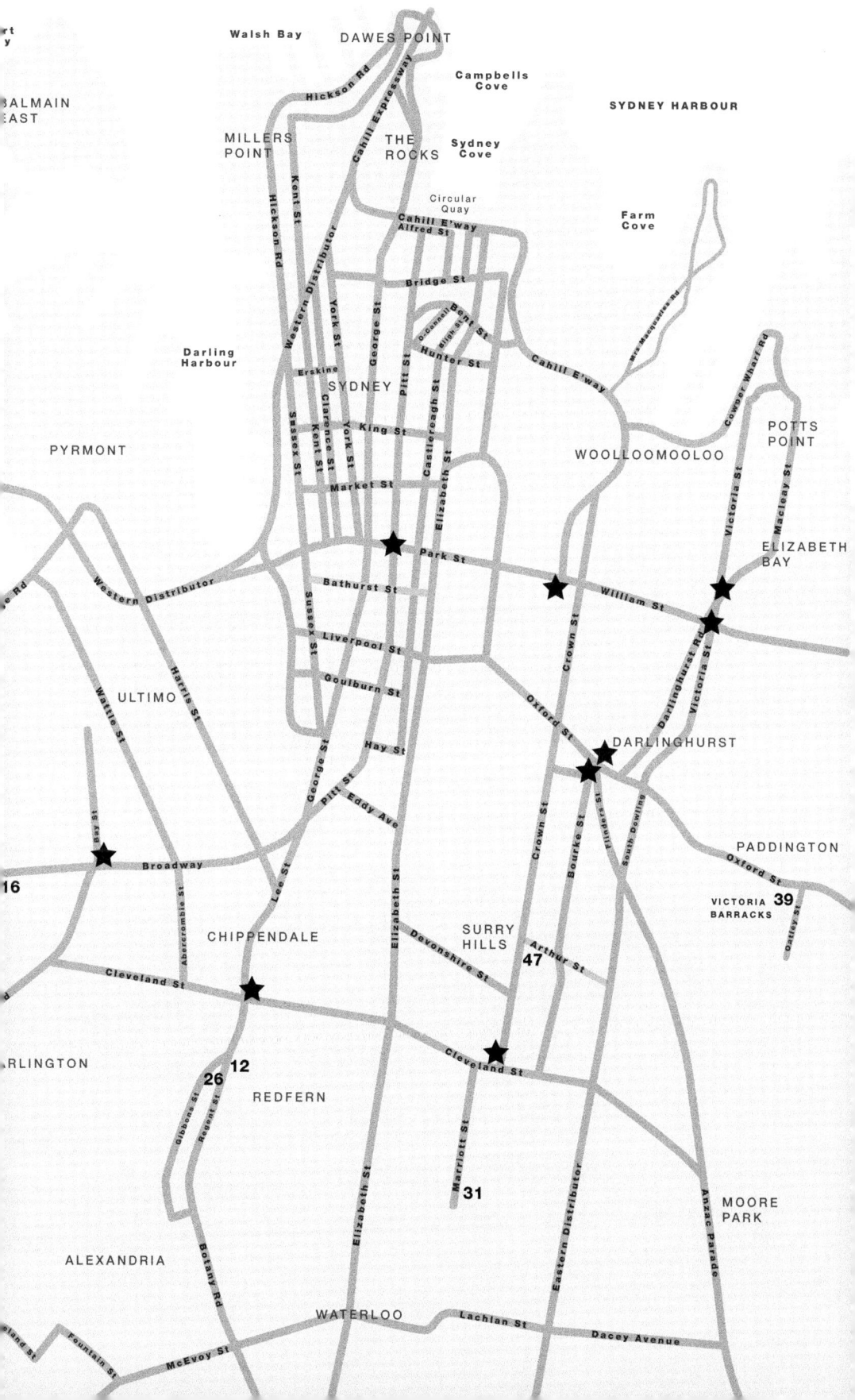

Walsh Bay DAWES POINT Campbells Cove SYDNEY HARBOUR

BALMAIN EAST

Hickson Rd Cahill Expressway

MILLERS POINT THE ROCKS Sydney Cove

Hickson Rd Kent St Western Distributor

Circular Quay Farm Cove

Cahill E'way Alfred St

Bridge St

O'Connell St Bent St Pitt St High St

Darling Harbour Erskine George St Hunter St Cahill E'way

SYDNEY Clarence St York St King St Castlereagh St Elizabeth St

PYRMONT Sussex St Kent St Market St WOOLLOOMOOLOO POTTS POINT

Park St ELIZABETH BAY

William St Crown St Victoria St Macleay St

Bathurst St Western Distributor

Harris St Ultimo Liverpool St Sussex St

Goulburn St Oxford St DARLINGHURST

Wattle St Bay St Hay St George St Pitt St Crown St Bourke St Riley St Forbes St Darlinghurst Rd Victoria St

Eddy Ave Lee St PADDINGTON

16 Broadway Oxford St

Abercrombie St Elizabeth St Devonshire St SURRY HILLS Arthur St VICTORIA BARRACKS 39

CHIPPENDALE Cleveland St 47

Cleveland St Crown St

26 12 Cleveland St Anzac Parade

DARLINGTON REDFERN Gibbons St Regent St Marriott St MOORE PARK

31 Eastern Distributor

ALEXANDRIA Botany Rd WATERLOO Lachlan St Dacey Avenue

Fountain St McEvoy St

Mrs Macquaries Rd Cowper Wharf Rd

CITY OF SYDNEY

10

30

Hickson Rd

Cahill Expressway

17

Argyle St

37
OBSERVATORY PARK

7

35

Cahill Expressway
Alfred St

8

25

4

Bridge St

23

Hickson Rd

Kent St

Western Distributor

Margaret St

29

Pitt St

3
Hunter St

Bligh

14

53
Erskine St

Carrington St

George St

1
ANGEL PL

Martin Place

18

Phillip St

Macquarie St

11
THE DOMAIN

21
Mrs Macquaries Rd

Lime St

Kent St

Clarence St

York St

46

King St

19

King St

44

QUEENS SQUARE

24

48

40

33 Pyrmont Bridge

Darling Drive

Sussex St

Market st

45

George St

Pitt St

Castlereagh St

Elizabeth St

College St

52
Brougham St

Victoria St

Western Distributor

Druitt St

49

Park St

5

Park St

Crown St

Bourke St

Forbes St

Eastern Distributor

28

Bathurst St

William St

(Cross City Tunnel)

Harris St

Pyrmont St

32

54

Elizabeth St

College St

Bourke St

Forbes

Crown St

Liverpool St

Liverpool St

Oxford St

Bellevue Rd

Pier St

43

Dixon St

50

Pitt St

Castlereagh St

Nithsdale

Alberta

2

Goulburn St

Goulburn St

Crown St

9
Forbes

Darlinghurst Rd

Victoria St

Wattle St

Harris St

Darling Drive

Sussex St

Hay St

20

42

George St

REGENT ST

Hay St

Campbell St

TAYLOR SQUARE

Oxford St

Boundary St

Comber St

Hopewell

38

6
CENTRAL STATION

Eddy Ave

Elizabeth St

Albion St

Bourke St

Flinders St

South Dowling

Broadway

Foveaux St

Regent St

34

13
PRINCE ALFRED PARK

15

47 Arthur St

Devonshire St

★ = Speakers' corners

1

INTRODUCTION

A DIFFERENT SYDNEY

Sydney is variously promoted to the world by commercial and political PR-spinners as 'a cosmopolitan city', 'a global city', 'an economic powerhouse', 'the business gateway to Australia'. In a forest of glossy publications and on a deluge of websites, attendant photographs reduce the city to the Opera House, the Harbour Bridge, and the concrete and glass eyries of the Central Business District, all drenched in sunlight and framed by the digitally enhanced blues of Sydney's harbour and sky.

True in part, but it is also a city of disappearances. As Marele Day's Claudia Valentine observed in *The Life and Crimes of Harry Lavender* (1988), the city sometimes looks 'like a huge building site' where the present annihilates the past and sweet-talks the future, a city in which memories can be short. Post-World War II, a combination of road, petrol, automobile and development interests coalesced to variously rip out people-friendly infrastructures and ruthlessly, at times corruptly, develop the city skywards, a *carte blanche* obliteration of the past and the creation of a canyon environment with arteries that would later choke. It was a process of 'forgetting', one halted and forced into compromise only by the Green Bans movement of the 1970s, with the result that uneasy dialogues continue, between the present and the future, between memory and forgetting.

Beyond postcard Sydney is a city its rulers are not fond of. We get a glimpse of it in the media-created images of today's Redfern, western Sydney, and the 'Shire', all of which are combustible, unpredictable places, with social problems and uncertain voting. Stigmatised when they are not the objects of condescending attention, the people of this other Sydney are rarely heard from. Many of them actually have a positive view of the city they inhabit. They see it as a place of challenge and opportunity, where new ideas can be tested, politics invigorated, power contested.

This book is about the history of that other Sydney, as both a place on a map and a product of the radical imagination. Ranging from the convict era through to the recent past, we provide glimpses of lives and stories that have largely been marginalised or ignored in mainstream accounts of the city. We reconstruct sites of a politics that challenged the political elites and dominant ideologies of their day, and enable some rebel voices to be heard again. We restore clamour and disturbance to politics, refusing to ignore the violence underlying the social order, violence that is actual as well as threatened, overt as well as covert, violence which, when not employed by the state and its supporters, is regarded as a political aberration.

In the mainstream of white, masculine, middle-class history, the voices of Aboriginal fighters, convict poets, feminist journalists, democratic agitators, bohemian dreamers, and revolutionaries are rarely heard. As historian Eric Fry once explained (*Rebels & Radicals*, 1983), the past and the present involve contradictory and conflicting social/historical forces; rebels and radicals are indispensable agents, helping shape the future by opposing and restricting society's rulers, paving the way for social change, opening doors to reformers, giving birth to what, at the time, might appear 'unthinkable'. And in the process, empowering themselves and others.

Sydney is a huge geographical and demographic entity. It is the largest city in Australia, its metropolitan area covering some 12,000 square kilometres, and has a population of about 4.3 million people living in over 640 suburbs (as determined by postal authorities), administered as 40 local government areas. Given these statistics, and the millions of people who have lived in the area over time, it stands to reason that the extent of radical Sydney is vast, compelling choice when it comes to writing its history. It is certainly more than the small canon of individuals, organisations and ideas preferred by some historians, more than the limited geography we deal with, and more than the sampling of stories we have chosen to recover from what has been allowed to drop through the cracks of history.

In the social imagination of the city's rulers, the negative image of radical Sydney has changed little over time. From 1850, when a Society for the Protection of Life and Property was formed, the respectable and propertied citizens have imagined the 'other' Sydney as a bubbling stew of discontent. Constantly worried about crime and the disrespectful behaviour of Cabbage Tree Hat mobs, larrikin pushes and bodgie gangs, Sydney's rulers feared most of all the onset of political crisis, when the mob, be it organised by Irish disloyalists, Labor demagogues or Communist agitators, would break out of its ghetto slums and enclaves and threaten the social order.

The fear of Sydney's menacing 'other' has left its traces in the buildings whose function is to defend law and order. After the convict uprising at Vinegar Hill in 1804, Governor Philip King ordered the construction of Fort Phillip at Millers Point, to protect the city. He was worried as much by the seditious Irish who were already present as by an unlikely future French invasion. Over the next century, in gaols and courthouses, the law was used not only to resist the tides of criminality but also, as delinquency and radical activity increased, to mop up the spillage of failed attempts at social control. The military too would play a part, as its Commanding Officer recognised in 1892 when he recommended the formation of a flying column to combat militant trade unionists. He wrote from the imposing Victoria Barracks at Paddington, which had been completed in the 1870s. It was both the headquarters of imperial military power in the colony and a base from which to confront internal civil disruption; its intimidating gun-slits overlooked the working-class area to the south and east of the business centre of the city.

From the 1880s to the 1950s, the radical Sydney we deal with remained virtually unchanged, a large and explosive space of marginalised ideas and peripheral places surrounding the centre of the city, a subversive and threatening arc of overcrowded working-class suburbs, bohemian neighbourhoods, dissident politics and contentious action. Starting in The Rocks, we can trace the inner ring of radical Sydney along the waterfront's notorious 'hungry mile' south to Darling Harbour. Our route takes in the warehouses of Pyrmont and the tenements of Ultimo and Chippendale, then turns across the southern end of the city through the factories of Darlington and the railway yards of Redfern, before swinging north through Surry Hills and Darlinghurst to the waterfront again at Woolloomooloo, on the eastern side of the city.

As Sydney grew, this semicircle broadened to take in adjoining suburbs: west to Balmain and Leichhardt, southwest through Sydenham and Marrickville to Bankstown, south to Botany and east to Paddington. Partly enclosed by the arc, always within its menacing reach, was official and commercial Sydney, a city of substantial and imposing buildings where government decisions were made and business power was concentrated. Here were the symbolic buildings of church and state – the Town Hall, the cathedrals, Government House and Parliament. Close by were the engine rooms of capitalism – the head offices of the great trading companies, the banks and finance houses, the stock exchange, the newspaper editorial rooms, and the retail emporia. Here too were the open spaces where people could recognise each other as citizens, mingling in democratic leisure along the harbour shore, in the public gardens and on the streets as they made their way to theatres and hotels.

These public spaces were important to radical Sydney. The working people of Sydney had been claiming their rights as citizens for 100 years or more, so they naturally wanted their chance to enjoy its pleasures. More than that, they wanted to demonstrate the only kind of power they had, the power of numbers. That is why the streets of the city became political battlefields. Getting a crowd together was a central tactic of electoral politics from the 1840s until long after the introduction of the secret ballot; radical agitators used people power as a weapon, particularly if the action occurred at a site of symbolic importance to the governing elites. When the labour movement was formed, its annual procession made a similar point, marching with banners of craft pride and class solidarity through the main streets of the city, ostentatiously passing sites such as the Town Hall and Parliament.

The need to express radical ideas on the streets was especially important because the commercial daily newspapers were closed to radicals. Street-corner meetings were characteristic of radical politics, and those held in the city were particularly valued because so much effort was needed to stage them in the face of the determination of the police and city authorities to prevent, or at least strictly regulate, them. From the perspective of the government, a safety valve already existed in the Sunday afternoon speakers' corner in the Domain. Here as well, the impact of a wave of organised radicalism in the 1880s was felt, transforming the Domain from desultory crankiness into a continuing, vital democratic forum. Crowds were regular and large, in times of crisis reaching over 100,000.

One such crisis was during World War I, when the federal Labor government tried to introduce conscription but was twice defeated at referenda. Christian socialist Lewis Rodd, growing up in Surry Hills at this time, was just emerging into political awareness. In his memoir of these years (*A Gentle Shipwreck*, 1975) he recalled his political education in the Domain and the great arc of radical Sydney that it served. On Sundays, with his older brother, he would join the crowd walking down Oxford Street:

> It was not so much a pleasant Sunday afternoon stroll as an army on the march, an army of men and women, bitter, disillusioned, most of them elderly, whose political idols, the Holmans and the Hugheses, had proved to have feet of brass ... At the corner of Hyde Park where the new Wentworth Avenue joined with College Street came another steadily marching, almost silent group from Ultimo, Glebe and Redfern. More straggled across Hyde Park and at the Domain gates joined with two more, one surging up from Woolloomooloo and the other coming across the city from the Rocks.

In many accounts of Sydney's history, the Domain is an iconic, sentimental, political favourite, forming both part of a spatial/visual representation of democracy and proof of its existence; the eccentric, cranky, agitational crucible at one end of Macquarie Street, within strolling distance of both Parliament, citadel of the lawmakers, and the courts, entrusted with arbiting and enforcing those laws. However, for the Sunday army of people trooping in to the Domain from all points across the city, politically angry, disillusioned, bitter people, the grist of radical Sydney, democracy was a response to lived, daily experience, a response more pervasive and extensive than a weekly gathering in one officially sanctioned safety valve.

Although the state and business stamped their authority on the city by making it the centre of their operations, radicals defined a different political zone in Sydney, a space where a tradition of challenging ruling power took hold. After two centuries, the shape of radical Sydney has hardly altered. The Domain, it is true, has succumbed to the banalities of corporate entertainment, but the new middle-class radicals who appeared in the 1970s and 1980s slipped easily into the transgressive space created by their working-class and bohemian predecessors. The rise of mass media, itself also exploited vigorously by the new middle-class radicals, has not disrupted this pattern of resistance, for it was in the central business district, and in Darlington, Redfern, Paddington, Kings Cross, Glebe and other inner suburbs where radicals had dissented and defied since the 1840s, that the activists of Black Power, resident action, sexual liberation, cultural rebellion, nuclear disarmament, green bans and peace have raised their banners, eyed the TV cameras, and set up their alternative living and organising spaces since the 1970s.

This book is about remembering, and about restoring some of the radicals, some of the unruly, to the history of Sydney. It discovers the street corners where they spoke, their union offices and lecture halls, and the pubs and cafés in which they socialised. It follows their marches into the city and the battles they fought with police. It goes into the studios where the posters, banners and films were produced, and the theatres where political skits lambasted the powerful. It remembers the writers, printers and editors of radical Sydney, and the pamphlets and journals that carried their ideas of justice, equality and the common good. It tells of lives lived in politics, and honours a politics that places the betterment of society and the pursuit of social justice before self-interest.

2

DAWES POINT

MORAL DILEMMAS

The southern pylon of the Sydney Harbour Bridge rises from Dawes Point, named after Lieutenant William Dawes (1762–1836), a First Fleet officer of marines, engineer, surveyor, mapmaker, astronomer, ethnologist and botanist. Until the 1970s Dawes was primarily remembered as an astronomer. Then, as more sources became available to researchers and as political imperatives changed, he became celebrated as a linguist, radicalised as a conscientious objector, and depicted as a symbol of nascent racial understanding/harmony, harbinger of a type of race relations that failed to develop in Australia. Unlike some of his officer peers, Dawes published no account of his Antipodean years. Many of his personal papers were destroyed or lost post-mortem. This biographical void has been conducive to imaginative, and agenda-motivated, reconstructions.

During his stay at Port Jackson, from 1788 to 1791, Dawes established an observatory on the peninsula that now bears his name. Away from the campfire brightness of the main settlement the observatory allowed him uncontaminated observation of the southern skies, which he needed in order to fulfil a scientific brief from the Astronomer Royal. In his capacity as ordnance officer Dawes established batteries around the harbour, including on the peninsula.

Born in 1762 in the naval port of Portsmouth, England, Dawes was the son of a clerk of works in the local Ordnance Office. Like many teenage boys of his time who had a classical education but no wealthy family behind them, he joined one of the services, in his case the marine corps. He became a Second Lieutenant in 1779. Two years later, during the War of American Independence, he was wounded in action. Mathematics and astronomy were two of his passions, and it seems more than likely that these skills played a part in the success of his application to join the First Fleet to New South Wales.

William Dawes contributed a great deal to the fledgling colony. From March 1788 onwards he was ashore in Sydney, carrying out engineering and surveying work, whilst at the same time setting up the observatory on what is now known as Dawes Point and carrying out his scientific work. He fortified Sydney Cove, laid out the first streets and farm allotments in Sydney and Parramatta, and was part of many exploration expeditions; his surveying and mapmaking skills were highly regarded. In 1789 he led the first European expedition into the precipitous ravines of the Blue Mountains region.

In Sydney, Dawes lived in a hut near his observatory, in relative isolation from the main settlement. This isolation and privacy gave him the opportunity to establish contact with the local Aborigines. They were initially wary of the main settlement, but began to frequent it late in 1790. Dawes met a young Aboriginal woman, aged about 15, called Patyegarang or Patye, and a close relationship developed. Patye was variously his companion, language informant, possibly lover. Dawes began to learn about the local Aboriginal language from her, and he began to teach her English.

Glimpses of this encounter, the inspiration for Kate Grenville's novel *The Lieutenant* (2008), are contained in two small notebooks now in the School of Oriental and African Studies at the University of London (also online at http://www.williamdawes.org). More than the compilation of a vocabulary, the notebooks indicate that Dawes was using his exploration of Aboriginal vocabulary and grammar as a means of understanding Indigenous society and culture, and how the people thought and felt. Extracts from the notebooks were published in 1834, but it was not until 1972 that they were 'rediscovered', and not until 1999 that substantial extracts were published.

Trouble came in December 1790 when Governor Arthur Phillip ordered Dawes to participate in the first punitive expedition against Aboriginal people, an exercise in state terrorism. The task was to capture two Aboriginal males, kill and decapitate 10 others, and bring their heads back to the settlement. This was reprisal for the spearing of the brutish John McIntire, a convict employed as a personal game shooter by Phillip. McIntire was one of only three convicts allowed to carry a musket, and was free to wander the bush in pursuit of meat. He was feared by some Aboriginal people, hated by others, as he had shot and wounded one of them; he may have killed and raped others. He died from his wound.

Since the arrival of the First Fleet there had been resistance to the invaders by the Aboriginal people; at least 17 invaders had been seriously wounded or killed. It was irregular, improvised, spur of the moment resistance. For the most part the Aboriginal people maintained a standoffish distance from the invaders, whose muskets instilled at least caution, and often plain fear. But reasons for hostility were increasingly present: competition for land and food through the disruption of traditional food-gathering processes as food-rich areas, especially waterways, were appropriated by the invaders, resulting in famine for the Aboriginal people during the winter of 1788; the smallpox epidemic of 1789 that decimated the Aboriginal people from Botany Bay to Pittwater, smallpox being a disease they had never before experienced; the theft of Aboriginal weapons and artifacts by the invaders for souvenirs; and Phillip's attempt to create dialogue between the two civilisations by kidnapping Aboriginal people and using them as cultural bridges. Initially Phillip acted with restraint. However, the spearing of McIntire was the last straw: it was no more Mr Nice Guy, and hello Zero Tolerance.

Lieutenant Watkin Tench, Dawes' colleague and friend, was placed in charge of the expedition. He was disgusted with his orders. In a meeting with Phillip he managed to change the assignment to the capture of six Aborigines, some to be executed, the others to be imprisoned. Like Dawes, Tench was establishing contact with the Aboriginal people and coming to respect and know them individually; language study was also at the centre of his relationship, though he acknowledged Dawes' superiority in this regard.

The punitive action flew in the face of Dawes' developing understanding of the Aboriginal people and his understanding of Christian principles. He refused to comply with the order. Governor Phillip threatened legal consequences. Following counsel and prayer with the settlement's chaplain, Dawes was coaxed into complying. He participated in the expedition but publicly told Phillip he regretted his compliance, and would never obey a similar order in the future. The expedition spent three days in the field and failed to capture or kill anyone, much to the relief of Tench and Dawes.

The line had been drawn. Phillip demanded an apology from Dawes for his open display of defiance. Dawes refused, which further enraged the Governor. The result was that despite his wish to stay, he was forced to leave New South Wales in December 1791 and return to England when the marine corps completed its tour of duty. Dawes never set foot in the Antipodes again, though he applied to do so in order to resume his scientific and language studies. Also, a well-supported appeal to the Colonial Office in 1826 for extra remuneration for the surveying and engineering work he had done in New South Wales, beyond his original job description, was refused.

The Tench punitive expedition marked the beginning of a rapidly deteriorating relationship between the invaders and the Aboriginal people. Large-scale Aboriginal armed resistance over the next 26 years generated large-scale military responses, as well as brutal, indiscriminate vigilante activity by armed civilians. By 1801 the situation had deteriorated so much that Governor King all but declared a state of war against the Aboriginal people in the area around Parramatta, Prospect Hill and the Georges River. It was not until 1816, during the administration of Governor Lachlan Macquarie, that Aboriginal resistance in the Sydney area finally was finally quelled.

Dawes spent most of the rest of his life campaigning against the international slave trade and working to ameliorate the human damage slavery left in its wake. It was a commitment that brought him into close contact with anti-slavery crusader William Wilberforce (1759–

Map of Sydney Cove, 1788, showing the military camp of the invaders and the moorings of their naval fleet, the tents of the convicts, and the site of Dawes' observatory – lower right (attributed to First Lieutenant William Bradley; Mitchell Library, State Library of New South Wales, ML Safe 1/14).

Sydney Cove, Port Jackson.

The position of the encampment & buildings are as they stood 1st March 1788. The Transports are placed in the Cove as Moored on their Arrival.

Surveyed by Capt. Hunter

1833), and took him for long periods to West Africa and the West Indies. He died in Antigua in 1836 under strained financial circumstances, and after a long period of ill-health.

In 2009 historian Cassandra Pybus, drawing on primary sources, challenged the depiction of Dawes as a 'saintly' hero. Focusing on his NSW career as an officer/disciplinarian, and later as an administrator of Sierra Leone, a colony for liberated slaves, she raised serious, and credible, allegations of harsh discipline, corruption, sexploitation, the encouragement of infanticide, and oppressive administration, against Dawes:

> If Australians are to find an impeccably moral and humane man as
> a founding hero, we will have to look further afield than Lieutenant
> Dawes.

In West Africa and the West Indies, Pybus argued, Dawes presented himself as an anti-slaver, but in practice he was not an anti-racist and may have hypocritically and immorally corrupted, exploited and compromised his cause. If so, how then should we understand his attitude to Aborigines in Sydney? Given the role contemporary historians are developing for Dawes as the first recorded European defender of Aboriginal rights, a comprehensive and critical biography of the man is essential.

3

OBSERVATORY HILL

REMEMBERING VINEGAR HILL

Observatory Hill, overlooking The Rocks, is associated with scientific endeavour. Between 1858 and 1982 the observatory on the hill, Sydney's highest natural vantage point, was a scientific research unit of international repute, its usefulness only terminated when the growth of the city, bright lights and smog cruelled astronomical observation. The observatory building and the surrounding Moreton Bay fig trees have inspired generations of artists. The gentle appeal of scientific curiosity, observation and reason, and the legacy of their architectural expression among the huge old trees, endow the modern site with peace and tranquillity.

But this was not always so, and before science and the picturesque, the hill was the site of Fort Phillip, a link to a radical and bloody past. In 1802 a small French scientific expedition paid a surprise visit to Sydney - Britain and France were at peace as there was a lull in the Napoleonic Wars (1799-1815). The Governor of New South Wales, Philip Gidley King, was a suspicious man; he feared the French were engaged in activity inimical to the British Empire, such as looking to strike at the Empire by linking up with unruly Irish convicts. What sealed the matter was an uprising two years later by said Irish convicts. Stressed by the demands of his job, in poor health, overweight, paranoid, at times verging on breakdown, ruling over a colony of what he described as 'people who sold rum and people who drank it', part of King's response was the construction of Fort Phillip.

Britain transported an estimated 160,000 convicts to the Australian

Prepared for insurrection or invasion: view of Sydney Cove, 1810, with flag flying on Fort Phillip on the centre horizon (by John Eyre; Mitchell Library, State Library of New South Wales, XV1/1808/9).

colonies between 1788 and 1868; some 26,500 of these were despatched directly from Ireland. In 1804 there were 2000 Irish convicts in New South Wales; of these, over 600 had been transported for political activity – riot and sedition. This was the result of their involvement in the rebellion in Ireland in 1798.

In Ireland, late in May 1798, long-festering Irish antagonism and opposition to English colonisation broke out in armed rebellion. Inspiration was drawn in part from the American colonists some 20 years earlier, who had carried out a successful armed struggle for independence from English rule, in part from the French Revolution (1789), and in part from the clarifying arguments of Thomas Paine's tract *The Rights of Man*, which ran to at least seven Irish editions between 1791 and 1792. The rebellion lacked co-ordination and was improvised in many ways: weaponry often consisted of little more than farming tools and homemade pikes. Despite this, the English authorities were traumatised as the rebels displayed unexpected military prowess and chalked up a string of early victories. An atmosphere of confusion, chaos and hysteria was generated; there were mass atrocities by the forces of law and order, and by the rebels. In the end English military power, martial law, and the assistance of enthusiastic, vengeful, loyalist militias, triumphed. Rebel forces were finally routed at the bloody Battle of Vinegar Hill, County Wexford, in June 1798. The rebellion brought about the deaths of an estimated 30,000 men, women and children. In subsequent trials of accused rebels, death sentences, and penal transportation to New South Wales, were liberally meted out.

During the early penal years, Irish convicts in New South Wales, irrespective of their crimes, were regarded with suspicion. Collectively they were regarded as a threat. Anxiety spread among administrators and free settlers alike. There were also some in authority who considered the Irish convicts an inferior species, ignorant and stupid, hardly warranting human classification.

On the receiving end of this, resentment stewed among Irish convicts. Racist attitudes, suspicion, fear and anxiety did not make for enlightened penal practice. There was the sense among some Irish convicts that they were victims twice over of colonialism – first the homeland experience and now New South Wales. There was the belief also that commanders of convict transport ships were authorised to ensure a higher than normal death rate among prisoners of Irish origin, a belief rooted in the abnormally high Irish death rates on some of the early convict transports. Catholics among the Irish convicts also chafed at the refusal by authorities to allow them access to Catholic priests and rites, a situation that continued until a reluctant policy change in 1803.

Penal servitude encouraged escapist dreams in some, dreams of finding passage on a passing friendly vessel. After all, the Scottish political prisoner Thomas Muir, sentenced to 14 years for radical democratic activism, had successfully escaped from New South Wales in 1796 on an American fur-trading vessel, eventually finding sanctuary in Revolutionary

France. Others, with little or no formal education, entertained beliefs that they could walk to China, or find a utopia in the Australian interior where they would be welcomed. These beliefs had the persistence, authority and popularity of modern urban myths. And others had more ambitious thoughts, of rebellion in the spirit of 1798, of seizing a vessel and sailing to freedom.

At 7 pm on Sunday, 4 March 1804, rebellion it was. On the Government Farm at Castle Hill, on the fringe of Sydney, convicts rushed from their quarters, heeding the prearranged and unauthorised ringing of the farm bell. The farm had been established in 1802, and some 200 convicts, the majority of them Irish Catholics, had been assigned to clear and cultivate the land.

Overpowering their guards and seizing weapons, the rebel convicts torched a house, the signal for others in the district to join the rebellion. They located the official scourger who had shredded their backs over time, and paid him in kind. Then they headed for the Hawkesbury River region to enlist the support of Irish convicts who had been sent to labour there, and of a citizenry generally regarded as independent/unruly. The plan was to gather a large force of rebels, collect weapons and supplies from farms and settlements along the way, then move on and capture the regional stronghold of Parramatta, prior to marching on Sydney, where escape vessels could be commandeered.

It was not a foolish plan; the majority of the non-Indigenous population of the colony were men, women, and children who were either convicts or of convict origin. The colonial state relied on the questionable military strength of the NSW Corps (1790–1810), which had never seen military action as a unit. Specially recruited for the task of protecting the colony, the Corps had abused its power, established monopoly control over the extremely profitable rum and alcohol trade, and through this controlled the colony's economy. It consistently challenged the power of governors, while its officer clique, in effect a junta, largely engaged in personal wealth accumulation, and was rent with jealousies.

But the rebel plan was flawed. It failed to correctly estimate the response time of the authorities, overestimated the combat abilities of the rebels, and assumed access to reliable weapons and ammunition. It also failed to appreciate the difficulties of organising and moving a large number of untrained and emotionally charged people at night, difficulties exacerbated by the consumption of looted alcohol. When it came to the crunch, the NSW Corps rose to the occasion; after all, it was defending its own spheres of political and economic interest, and its own assets.

News of the revolt reached authorities in Sydney by 11.30 pm, and King responded quickly. Sydney was put on alert: defence preparations were made and weapons distributed to militia volunteers. King had long regarded the Irish as a problem and did not mince words in official reports: 'seditious people', capable of 'diabolical' plots was his summation. Anticipating trouble, he had formed volunteer militia units in Sydney and Parramatta, and had responded harshly to any Irish convict threat, real or imagined, with savage corporal punishments, and with exile to the isolation and torturous cruelties of what was known in convict slang as 'the old hell', the Norfolk Island penal colony.

Prior to personally taking command of the situation in Parramatta, King despatched a fully equipped and armed military detachment of 55 men under the command of Major George Johnston to the trouble area, to bolster the Parramatta defence establishment and spearhead suppression. Johnston was a military veteran, having fought against American rebels during the War of Independence, where he had shown considerable courage under fire. After an overnight forced march, his detachment arrived in Parramatta around 6 am on Monday. King and his party had arrived earlier on horseback. Martial law was proclaimed in the outlying region of Sydney, stretching from Parramatta to the Hawkesbury River, and Johnston was sent after the rebels.

He found them on a strategic knoll, en route for the Hawkesbury. About 260 rebel convicts, some with firearms, but lacking adequate ammunition, others bearing farm implements or big sticks, confronted armed loyalists and the firepower and bayonets of the NSW Corps. Later the site became known as Vinegar Hill, after the last battle of the 1798 Irish Rebellion.

Before the commencement of hostilities, Major Johnston, using an Irish Catholic priest as intermediary, suckered two of the rebel leaders into coming forward for discussions, as a means of avoiding bloodshed. He then captured them at gunpoint, and gave the order to open fire:

initially nine rebels were killed and many were wounded. Return fire was scattered and ineffective, reports indicating that there were faults with the rebels' weapons, or with their loading. There were no casualties among the soldiers or volunteers. The rebels broke ranks and fled into the bush and across the countryside; troops moved forward with what was later reported as great 'zeal and activity'.

Mopping up operations continued during the next few days, with Johnston and his troops and volunteers moving across country to the Hawkesbury River. Over 300 rebels were eventually hunted down and rounded up, including some who had not managed to join up with the main rebel force. Convict stonemason Philip Cunningham, a veteran of the 1798 rebellion in Ireland and one of the two rebel leaders personally 'arrested' by Major Johnston, was wounded during the original attack; he was executed without trial, strung from the staircase of a government store in the Hawkesbury settlement. On Sunday night he had

‖ The remains of Fort Phillip today on Observatory Hill (Robert Irving).

This plaque commemorates the bicentenary of the Battle of Vinegar Hill, which took place
on 5 March 1804 following an uprising by mostly Irish prisoners at the Castle Hill Government farm
the previous evening. The battle, between the poorly-armed rebels and the New South Wales Corps,
supported by armed settlers, resulted in some twenty prisoners being killed, after their leaders were
taken prisoner while negotiating under a flag of truce. Nine prisoners were later hanged. Many of the rebels
were sentenced to floggings of up to 500 lashes, and some were sent to the coal mines at Coal River
(Newcastle). The original Battle of Vinegar Hill took place in County Wexford Ireland on 21 June 1798.
The nine rebels executed were:

Philip Cunningham
hanged without trial at Green Hills (Windsor) 5 or 6 March 1804
The remaining eight were court-martialled at Parramatta and sentenced to death
Charles Hill, Samuel Humes, John Place
hanged at Parramatta 8 March 1804
William Johnson, John Neale, George Harrington
hanged at Castle Hill 9 March 1804
John Brannon, Timothy Hogan
hanged at Sydney 10 March 1804
"DEATH OR LIBERTY"

This plaque was erected by the Irish community in NSW, the Mineworkers' Trust, the Blacktown City Council
and the Government and People of Ireland.
Donated by Castlebrook Memorial Park.

One of the few Australian memorials to rebellion and resistance: the
'Death or Liberty' plaque at the Vinegar Hill memorial, Castlebrook
cemetery (Nick Irving).

told the convicts who followed him off the penal farm that the enterprise they were embarking on was a matter of 'Liberty or Death', the
slogan of the 1798 Rebellion.

King ruthlessly set about smashing the spirit of rebellion. Three days
after the battle, 10 rebels deemed leaders were tried and sentenced to
be executed and hung in chains, the traditional treatment for the truly
infamous. The process of bodily decay was left on public display for
months, sending an unambiguous political message to all and sundry
about the results of challenging the power of the British state. Two of
the rebels managed to have their sentences commuted; the remaining
executions took place in Castle Hill, Parramatta and Sydney. Other
punishments were meted out as well: nine rebels received floggings, of
between 200 and 500 lashes; 34 were sent to mine coal in the Hunter

River seams – this was sweated, brutally enforced, deadly labour. Those regarded as 'less culpable' were dispersed to forced labour on chain gangs, building roads, hewing and crushing rocks, on the fringes of the colony.

As part of the control process, the construction of Fort Phillip began. However, it was never completed, nor was a shot ever fired in anger from it. After King finished up as Governor the Fort was cannibalised for other projects – it became a vegetable garden for a time – before science took over, leaving behind only the stone ramparts that led to the Fort. In December 1854, when Ballarat gold miners, many of them Irish, took up arms against the colonial government in Victoria and formed the Eureka Stockade in the general cause of democracy and the redress of goldfield injustices, the rebel password was 'Vinegar Hill', homage to both the 1798 rebellion in Ireland and the 1804 uprising in New South Wales.

Today the name Vinegar Hill is not a Sydney place name, although a road near the battle site bears the name, and Observatory Hill is all about science. The convict revolt of 1804 is regarded as an oddity rather than what it was, the desperate expression of important ideas, testament to the tenacious human spirit of resistance against oppression. In the grounds of Castlebrook Lawn Cemetery, by the Windsor Road, Rouse Hill (NSW), near where the battle took place, is a dignified memorial to the rebel uprising, unveiled on the anniversary of the event 184 years later.

4

TOURING HELL

HYDE PARK BARRACKS

On board the 11 ships of the First Fleet in 1788 were some 1400 people, half of whom were convicts. By 1840, when the transportation of convicts to New South Wales ceased, 80,000 convicts had been despatched to the colony by Britain. The colony's remoteness – it was a 24,000 kilometre dangerous sea voyage from Britain – amounted to a form of marooning for the convicts; Robinson Crusoe in penal garb. This, in conjunction with the well-armed administration and a reward system that could dispense a variety of leniencies and work and land packages, tended to keep convicts in line as they carried out their often menial and labour-intensive work duties.

For convicts who challenged/defied the system there were punishments, at times pathologically and torturously dispensed: sweated labour under hellish conditions as lime burners and hewers of coal; increased sentences; flesh-stripping floggings with the cat-o'-nine-tails; the wearing of crippling leg irons and chains and spiked iron collars; mind-destroying periods of solitary confinement; bread and water diets; the treadmill; and execution.

Hyde Park Barracks was a key part of the penal system. It was built between 1817 and 1819 to a design by architect Francis Greenway, a former convict. Its purpose was to accommodate, and punish when necessary, 600 male convicts, a function it served until its closure in 1848. The Georgian-style building was commissioned by Lachlan Macquarie, Governor of New South Wales from 1810 to 1821. He intended it to be an architectural showpiece, part of his paternalistic, radical missionary-style program of civic recasting and rebuilding.

Hyde Park Barracks in the 1840s. The Barracks played a significant role in the incarceration of Frank the Poet. From the 1840s, the front of the Barracks became a favourite rallying point for protests by Sydney radicals (Mitchell Library, State Library of New South Wales, PX*D 123/5b).

After 1788 the settlement developed into an economically thriving, chaotic, alcohol-soaked, polluted, jerry-built town. According to Macquarie, it was 'in most ruinous decay'. Streets were dusty and impassable in times of rain; the main road was potholed; and unwanted children, pigs and goats roamed streets littered with offal, garbage and human excrement. Many buildings that were not yet 20 years old were already rotting, warping or collapsing. By 1819, at the height of his civic program, Macquarie had allocated 80 per cent of the skilled convicts to work on his civic schemes, much to the chagrin of private enterprise.

As with the town, so too with the convict system. Under previous administrations convicts tended to be used for private gain rather than for public works and the common good. At night, having completed their work, many convicts were left to their own devices, which included arranging their own accommodation. 'Night Robberies and Burglaries' became problems; The Rocks and Hyde Park were convict haunts; the non-convict population was concerned. The Barracks was built to accommodate and secure male convicts at night, lower the crime rate, house those convicts engaged in Macquarie's civic schemes, and generally introduce a sense of order and control to the penal system.

Eventually up to 1400 convicts were crammed into the Barracks at night. In his memoirs, written whilst awaiting execution in 1844 on the Sydney gallows, former naval captain and convicted murderer John Knatchbull wrote of his convict experience in the Georgian showpiece:

> I was horrorstruck, not only by the dirty, miserable inmates, but by the dirty, lousy, filthy state of the place, a disgrace ... where you might pick off your body and clothes lice of full-grown size, as big as grains of barley, at all and every moment.

Homosexuality was rife. New arrivals to the colony were sent to the Barracks prior to being assigned work duties. Youths in particular were taken over by older convict men, given female names, and forced to exchange sex for protection.

Hyde Park Barracks became noted for the skill with which the cat-o'-nine-tails was administered there. Superintendent Ernest Slade (1833–34) thought 'the cat' was a most effective form of punishment, capable of breaking the spirit of any convict when vigorously applied by a skilled scourger. It was widely believed that Barracks scourgers had developed a knack of inflicting extra pain, a 'peculiar art in the flourish of the scourge' as one magistrate observed.

Francis MacNamara was an educated Irish convict who spent the best part of five years in Hyde Park Barracks, receiving there the bulk of his career total of 650 lashes from 14 floggings. He was born in 1810/11; convict records are confused about whether he was a Catholic or a Protestant, and regarding his place of origin and his occupation. Physically he is described as being 5 feet 5 inches tall (165 cm), broad, with a fresh complexion, light brown hair, grey eyes, and with a scar on the outer side of his right eye. In 1832 he was sentenced

Hyde Park Barracks today, with the protests airbrushed from history (Robert Irving).

to transportation and seven years' imprisonment for breaking a shop window and stealing a piece of cloth, though the real reason may have been his participation in illegal political agitation.

Three months after arriving in the colony and being assigned as a servant, MacNamara was sentenced for an unspecified crime to six months' hard labour in a chain gang, toiling in leg-irons and chains. This was his first dose of a career total of three and a half years' hard labour in quarries and road building as part of an 'ironed gang'. Gradually MacNamara's period of servitude increased – he gained his Certificate of Freedom 15 and a half years after he was first sentenced.

Other punishments meted out to MacNamara included: a number of sentences in solitary confinement on a bread and water diet; two terms totalling three months on the treadmills located near the site of present-day Central Railway Station, where teams of between 10 and 18 convicts laboriously walked the endless stairway inside the barrelled contrivances that provided power for the commercial grinding of grain; a number of stints totalling some three years on the prison hulk *Phoenix*, moored and rotting in today's Darling Harbour. He completed his penal career incarcerated in Tasmania's notorious Port Arthur.

MacNamara challenged and defied the convict system. He petitioned the authorities on behalf of fellow inmates, destroyed government property, absconded into the bush five times for short periods of freedom, and refused to work in the deadly coal mines of Newcastle (this was probably the cause of one of his breaks for freedom).

As the result of an incident in 1842 MacNamara was elevated in official correspondence to the status of 'notorious bushranger', part of what the records describe as a 'formidable' gang. While engaged in road making in the Southern Highlands of New South Wales, he and four fellow prisoners overpowered their armed guards and took their weapons. The escapees were apprehended near Picton two days later. In the ensuing trial the five 'bushrangers' were found guilty of absconding and being in possession of weapons, and received life sentences. Which is what eventually took MacNamara to Port Arthur.

Some of Francis MacNamara's troubles were due to his poetic abilities, and the popularity of his compositions among the oppressed and dispossessed both within and outside the penal system. Hence the extraordinary lengths the brutal penal system went to in its determination to break his spirit. Within the penal system MacNamara gained a reputation as Frank the Poet, composer of cheeky and satiric ballads and reciter of verses he improvised at will. One of his poems was published in the *Sydney Gazette* in 1840; the rest, which had spread orally, were collected later by enthusiasts – the Australian oral tradition survived well into the 20th century.

There is some scholarly dispute as to which poems attributed to MacNamara were actually written by him, but his authorship of the 218-line satire 'A Convict's Tour to Hell', his *magnum opus*, is not in doubt. It was written in 1839 while he was assigned by the penal system to work as a shepherd in rural New South Wales. In this poem Frank dreams he is dead and makes his way to Hell, only to find it filled with a legion of well-known penal system administrators, scourgers, magistrates, hangmen, judges, informers and constables, all painfully standing

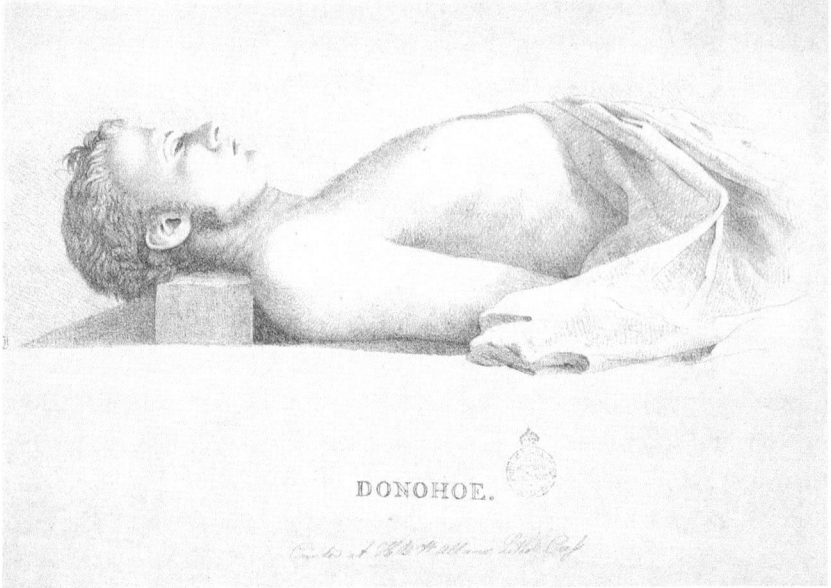

Bold Jack Donahue, sketched after his death. This bushranger was the subject of a very popular ballad attributed to Frank the Poet (sketch by Sir Thomas Mitchell; Mitchell Library, State Library of New South Wales, PX/361).

in lakes of molten lead, amidst the fiery paraphernalia of Hell, as worms and snakes enter their bodies and devour their entrails. Captain Cook is also there; after all, it was he who 'discovered New South Wales'.

Satan refuses Frank permanent residence, telling him that Hell is reserved for 'the grandees of the land', and directs him to Heaven, for that is where convicts go 'in droves and legions'. Admitted to Heaven by St Peter and Jesus, Frank is welcomed, and recognises familiar convict faces in the crowd, and 'many others whom floggers had mangled', as well as those who had died on the gallows. The poem ends as St Peter commands St Paul and other biblical heavyweights to prepare the table for 'a grand repast', and Frank joins hands with Moses, John the Baptist and others and rejoicingly sings 'hymns of praise to God'.

MacNamara was influenced by the poetry of Jonathan Swift and Robert Burns, and by the English 'street literature' broadside tradition.

His Hyde Park Barracks experiences with 'the cat' were possibly in his mind when he wrote:

> My back with flogging is lacerated,
> And oft-times painted with my crimson gore.

He also drew on the experiences of fellow convicts, and on stories that circulated orally within the penal system. MacNamara's poems celebrate rebellion and defiance, and reflect his hatred of authority. Two other popular compositions attributed to him mourn the death of the young, raffish, Irish bushranger Bold Jack Donahue, 'a young hero' killed by a squad of mounted police near Campbelltown in 1830, and celebrate the heroic seizure by convicts en route to Tasmania in 1829 of the brig *Cyprus* and their attempt to sail to freedom.

MacNamara received a full pardon in 1849, moved to Melbourne, and disappeared into the passing parade. Like Elvis, sightings of him are made from time to time by scholars excited by references here and there in contemporary newspapers and reports of anonymous 19th century wordsmiths who sound like him, but apart from one authenticated appearance in Mudgee (NSW) in 1861, that is it.

5

JOHANN LHOTSKY, REVOLUTIONARY

It is Dymock's Book Arcade today, but for almost 100 years it was the site of the Royal Hotel, a grand five-storey address for well-heeled visitors to town, fronted by three layers of deep verandahs held up by Doric columns. However, in its early years it was much more than a watering hole for country squatters and minor gentry from 'home'. Soon after it was built in the early 1830s professional actors began performing regularly in its saloon, and in 1833 the working men held their first large public meeting there. Because there was no town hall at this time, and very few large theatres, the Royal Hotel was central to public life for most of the middle decades of the 19th century. If you wanted your meeting to carry weight you booked one of its large saloons (200 reportedly attended the working men's meeting); if you formed a committee or organisation you hired office space in the Royal, as the Australian Patriotic Association (APA) did in 1835.

The APA was the culmination of the colonists' first push for self-government. But what was self-government meant to achieve? For the big pastoralists there was no question: it would mean cheap land and cheap labour (but no Irish, please). Meanwhile, Sydney was filling up with working men and their families, for whom land ownership was impossible, and whose wages were undercut by a flood of new immigrant and convict workers. And it was clear from the way the wealthy 'patriots' ran the APA that working men and shopkeepers would not be allowed to vote for a self-governing assembly, let alone stand for election. So they organised an opposition to the landowning elite of the APA: the 'trades union party'.

The public meeting became a regular part of Sydney's political life when workers and radical intellectuals began to meet in the Royal Hotel on George Street in the 1830s (W. Wilson, engraver: Royal Hotel and Commercial Exchange, Sydney; Mitchell Library, State Library of New South Wales, PXD 812/1).

It was at the Royal Hotel meeting of 1833 that the 'trades union party' took shape. After an earlier preliminary meeting, some leading men of the trades societies (which combined the functions of trade union, benefit society and pressure group) booked the hotel to lend seriousness to their strategy of petitioning the Governor. They wanted him to send 'home' (that is, to England) the information they had collected on the actual wages - not those touted by the immigration agents - earned by the colony's tradesmen and labourers. The meeting adopted the document, chose a deputation to go to the Governor, and the Chair was closing the meeting when a man who was unknown to most of them jumped onto the stage. In heavily accented English, he made a radical proposal: they should demand land grants for working-class families.

His name was Johann Lhotsky, and he had been in the colony only a few months. He was 37 years old, a scientist, and probably the best-educated man in the colony. He had studied at universities in Prague, Vienna, Berlin, Leipzig, Paris and Jena (in Germany). He had written a doctoral thesis (in Latin) on the metaphysical foundations of politics, and had also studied medicine and botany. Fluent in Czech, Polish, German, French and English, he was acquainted with some of the most distinguished scientists of the age.

If you look up Dr Lhotsky in the books about this period you won't find any reference to the fact that he was also a revolutionary. Instead, you will read about his exploration of the Australian Alps, and his unsuccessful claim for a reward from the government for discovering gold in the colony. You will not learn why the government refused to make him its official zoologist, nor why the colonial elite called him a 'madman' and 'impostor', whose views were 'absurd' and 'offensive'.

It was not until the 1960s, when Czech historian of science Vadislav Kruta looked at the police archives in Prague and Vienna, that the secret of Lhotsky's past in Europe was revealed. As a student in Vienna, Lhotsky had been a member of an underground revolutionary organisation, the Carbonari. This organisation was part of a movement in Europe which had attracted many young people, most notably Lord Byron in Italy, to fight for democracy and national liberation against the imperial regimes of the French Bourbons, the Austrian Hapsburgs and the Russian Romanoffs.

Lhotsky was much more than a fellow traveller. He had written pamphlets for the cause, and he had acted as a courier between revolutionaries in Vienna and northern Italy, which was then part of the Austrian Empire. His importance was confirmed when he was arrested by Chancellor Metternich's secret police in 1822, during a security crackdown before the Verona meeting of 'The Holy Alliance', the pact established in 1815 by autocrats from Austria, Russia and Prussia who believed that their right to tyrannise came from God. For the next five years, Lhotsky suffered for his principles in gaol. He used the time to keep up his scientific studies, and on his release he was able to find sponsorship for an expedition overseas to collect scientific samples. After spending 18 months in Brazil, he came to Australia to continue this work.

Knowing about his revolutionary past in Europe we can begin to see why the colonial elite might have detested him. But as he kept his imprisonment quiet, what did he do to upset them during his four years in Sydney? We have seen him associating with the emerging working-men's movement, but so did a handful of other radical intellectuals, none of whom attracted the kind of hatred Lhotsky generated.

One of his problems was that he showed no deference to officials and refused to ape the manners of the ruling class. Instead he embraced his foreignness, thus upsetting British complacency about the superiority of their culture and their system of representative government. He boasted that the Governor 'smelled the rat in me', and publicly referred to himself as 'a foreign dog'. Taking on the conservative Sydney press, he published three short-lived periodicals in which he expressed his disdain for their kind of journalism. He announced, with tongue in cheek, the formation of the 'Sydney Milk and Water Association'. It purported to offer a quarterly prize of 'fifty pounds sterling' to the newspaper or periodical which 'may have produced the greatest mass of nothingness and contemptible trash ... and which has tamely and cunningly shrunk from every deep and conscientious discussion of colonial matters'.

However, the crucial reason for the colony's rulers trashing his reputation was that he promulgated a revolutionary program for Australian democracy, the first such program in our history. He did this as part of the 'trades union party' in the last of his periodicals, the *New South Wales Literary, Political and Commercial Advertiser*.

Lhotsky proposed a popular uprising in New South Wales of the sort that had long been envisaged by Europe's revolutionary democrats. But how would this come about? He saw the APA as providing the opening. While the wealthy leaders of the APA concentrated on raising money to employ a lobbyist in London, Lhotsky emphasised agitation within the colony, with the aim of making the APA into 'an association rooted in and backed by the great mass of the people'. One way to do this, he thought, would be to mobilise the people through a mass petition, circulated throughout the colony by the activists of the association. It was an idea the Chartists would use a few years later in Britain. He understood that this agitation would bind more closely the members of 'the Political Association' (which was how he referred to

Prize of Fifty Pounds Sterling !!

SYDNEY MILK AND WATER ASSOCIATION.

A company of Gentlemen fond of pithy fun and frolic, have united themselves into a Society entitled as above, for the sake of awarding a QUARTERLY PRIZE to any of the Sydney Newspapers or Periodicals, which up to this time may have produced the greatest mass of nothingness and contemptible trash.— The Society held their first General Meeting on the 11th instant, when after the different papers had been again glanced over, the chairman put the following questions:—

"Gentlemen, which do you consider to be the meritorious publication ; that during the last quarter has excelled in seven line leaders, much ado about nothing, and a quantity of unconnected and undigested extracts—the meritorious paper I say, which has tamely and cunningly shrunk from every deep and conscientious discussion of colonial matters—the incomparable paper finally, the reading of which will send you first to sleep."

The contest, especially between some of the older established papers and other periodicals, was warm, severe, and protracted to such a late hour, that the meeting was of necessity adjourned until the next evening.*

☞ Gentlemen Editors are respectfully requested, to fill henceforth their publications with the most stale and worn out extracts from the home papers, tough tales and such like, to refuse peremptorily the insertion of any pithy, business-like, matter-of-fact correspondence, and they may rest assured, that their high merits in benefitting the colony, will be duly appreciated by the above MILK AND WATER ASSOCIATION.

* Since writing the above, we are very happy in being able to state, that at the adjourned meeting of yesterday, the merits of MR. TEGG'S MONTHLY MAGAZINE seemed to the association so paramount, that the prize for the last quarter was awarded to it by acclamation, and there is even some hope, that an especial letter of thanks will be addressed to him—into the bargain.

PRINTED BY A. COHEN, "AUSTRALIAN" PRINTING OFFICE.

Johann Lhotsky, European revolutionary, sardonically challenges the timid Sydney press to discuss colonial politics (*New South Wales Literary, Political and Commercial Advertiser*, 5, 1836).

the APA). They should also have a headquarters where members could rally, plan, and educate themselves by discussing the latest political journals from abroad.

But who were the masses? The second step in Lhotsky's program was to find the answer to this question. In Sydney, Lhotsky had no regular income. He bought a horse and cart and sold firewood, vegetables and mulberry cuttings on the streets, and supplemented Sydney's chancy water supply by bottling 'Dr Lhotsky's Mineral Water'. As he moved among the people he discovered that the division between emancipists (former convicts) and immigrants that the conservatives editorialised about was a fiction. Instead he found harmony, and common problems. The 'masses', whose leaders he had met (men of 'respectable standing'), needed land, secure employment, and cheap bread and flour. They had common problems because of their class position, which he identified. They were 'the class of tradesmen of limited circumstances', and in this class they could dissolve differences based on whether they were free, freed, or even unfree (for Lhotsky recognised convicts as working men). When he addressed the people, Lhotsky was talking to working men with identifiable needs, not a vague social force.

The people united had to have something to do. Lhotsky thought that the government was vulnerable to pressure on the issue of feeding the people. It was government policy to increase the labour supply, but the additional population was straining the colony's resources. Farming remained undeveloped and a flour-milling monopoly was pricing bread out of the reach of many families. Here was a need that could be met by government action and co-operative effort. Lhotsky proposed that the government should charter ships to bring in grain and flour when prices rose, and that the recently formed co-operative flour company should receive government assistance in the form of free use of the treadmill. Developing the pressure required to bring this about was an immediate task of 'the Political Association'. This was the third step in Lhotsky's program.

These three steps look like any other radical democratic program; things change when the fourth and fifth are considered. The APA had a small Directing Committee. Lhotsky said this should be enlarged to at least 100, with a quorum of 40. This was in line with his suggestion that the association should concentrate on agitation. Mass activity spearheaded by a numerous directorate would soon alter the balance of power between the people and the government, and the Directing Committee would in effect become a popular assembly. Was not this the way to get an assembly 'instanter, *de facto*'? And confronted by this *de facto* parliament, legitimised by popular organisation, 'could it be otherwise', he asked, 'than that the local government would be obliged to take notice of [the APA's] imperative, or rather dictatory, suggestions?' He repeated the point:

> All this [agitation], if accomplished would constitute – if not the whole
> at least the fundamental outlines of a real House of Assembly – in
> the beginning not chartered, but existing *de facto*, and supported and
> backed by the opinion of a spirited and unanimous population.

This model of revolution, as practised by Europe's democratic movement, was the fourth step in his program: the people would then be dictating to government. There was a final step. Like his European comrades, he encouraged a democratic imagination among the people. A 'free constitution', he said to the colonists, was useful not just because it could result in 'immediate' changes, but also because it could liberate the mind. A 'spirited and unanimous population' could reinterpret how everyday life should be lived. Although he never discussed this insight – because a democratic imagination would require more freedom than either he or his readers had at that moment – his message was clear: it was the *de facto* powers, the instantaneous and transforming powers, not the *de jure* constituted powers of 'the Political Association', that provided a revolutionary opportunity for the colony.

By the end of 1836 it was clear that the APA was not going to develop in the way Lhotsky desired, although the 'trades union party' was sufficiently strong to force the APA's wealthy leaders to withdraw to their big houses and country estates. There they remained as Lhotsky and others in its rank and file in Sydney struggled to keep the association alive. Disillusioned and broke he left for Hobart. By 1838 he was in London, where he lived as a pauper until his death in 1866. In London, he met the Italian revolutionary Giuseppe Mazzini, was arrested for throwing stones at the Brunswick Hotel where Prince Metternich was staying, and wrote pamphlets. One was titled *Hunger and Revolution*. He also warned his fellow political exiles of the operations of the secret police. Meanwhile, in the Australian colonies a new generation of working people and radical intellectuals took over the project of building a revolutionary 'political association'.

6

TUMULT IN PARADISE

THE WATCH HOUSES OF SYDNEY

In the 1840s, the Jolly Miller pub stood on the corner of Gloucester and Essex streets, in a notorious part of The Rocks known as Frog Hollow. Essex Street dropped sharply down to Harrington and George streets; Gloucester wound its crooked way along the escarpment, the refuse and sewage from the streets above falling into its backyards.

In The Rocks, working people hated the police. The constables, who were mostly poorly paid ex-convicts, were undisciplined and corrupt. Brutalised by their own past experience, their response to drunken sailors and obstructive crowds was to lash out with bludgeons and cutlasses. There were reports of prisoners being bashed in the cells. At the same time, the police were slow to come to the aid of members of the public and cowardly in the face of resistance. They felt safest inside their police watch houses, which were thick on the ground in the working-class areas of the city. There were at least three in The Rocks: on Harrington, Cumberland and Kent streets.

In January 1840, a few seamen from Her Majesty's ship *Druid* obtained leave on a Sunday for a spell on shore. What happened next was described by the *Australasian Chronicle*, a radical newspaper:

> they of course were a little merry, and some slight disturbance took
> place between them and the *habitans*; the constabulary interfered,
> at which both parties sided against them. When some strong
> reinforcements of constables arrived on the spot, under the orders of
> Captain Innes [they were opposed by a large crowd. The constables
> used their cutlasses, and several were severely hurt.] Captain Innes

stated in court that he would easily have cleared the street, and suppressed any disturbance, were it not for the ruffianly conduct of a large body of three or four hundred of the lowest *canaille* in Sydney, who opposed the police in every possible manner and excited to outrage the seamen, who allowed themselves to be made tools of by those ruffians.

Captain Innes was the head of the police force. A few days later, the *canaille* took their revenge. While riding along Grosvenor Street on 'his accustomed rounds', Captain Innes was thrown from his horse and almost killed by a clothes-line suspended across the street.

In 1841, a dozen or so visiting seamen from HMS *Favorite* were having some fun in the centre of the town, outside the Victoria Theatre in Pitt Street. As the respectable upper-class patrons entered the theatre the seamen were attempting to 'bonnet' them – that is, knock off their black hats. The police arrived as the theatre emptied and fighting broke out, the patrons siding with the police, the lower class siding with the seamen. A crowd of about 200 gathered, and the fighting spread. The rioters took possession of the streets, attacking police and destroying windows and lamps. There were many injuries. Before tempers cooled in the early hours of the morning, seven seamen, supposedly the ring-leaders, had been arrested.

What happened next surprised the authorities. The radical news-papers took the side of the seamen, responding to the popular view that the 'officious and violent' behaviour of the police started the riot. The seamen felt victimised. The magistrates, learning that the seamen were planning a combined attack on the police that evening, swore in 24 ticket-of-leave convicts as special constables.

That night the seamen again gathered outside the theatre. There was organised chanting, and when the leaders estimated that the crowd was sufficiently excited they led it back to the Harrington Street watch house in The Rocks. With four or five thousand cheering them on, the leaders used long poles and stones to overcome the three police at the watch house and free the prisoners from the cells. Then the crowd headed back to the centre of the city to break into more police stations.

Their first target was the St James watch house, which was next to the Supreme Court building on Elizabeth Street. Forewarned by the

SUPREME COURT & ST JAMES CHURCH FROM ELIZABETH ST. 1842.
BY J. RAE.

fate of Harrington Street, the police fled, leaving the cell doors open, and in quick time the watch house was wrecked. The crowd re-formed outside the theatre, where its leaders decided to attack the main police station and court, on the corner of George and Druitt streets. 'The suggestion was greeted with a shout', according to the *Omnibus and Sydney Spectator*, and five or six hundred set off for the imposing building, which had been designed by the convict architect, Francis Greenway. The building had Grecian pillars and a cupola that was visible across the city, and sat in a yard edged by a high fence of iron pickets. As one of the centres of ruling-class power, it was well defended by special constables, the police, and contingents of the military held in reserve a block away.

This was where the authorities got their own back. Finding the entrance well guarded, the crowd had to be content with lobbing rocks into the yard, where the 'specials' were gathered. As the rocks rained down, the police opened fire. At first they fired blanks, but when the crowd laughed they fired real bullets. The crowd panicked, the military began their charge with bayonets drawn, and the police and specials burst out of the yard, armed with cutlasses, bayonets and long poles. They attacked everybody who got in their way. There were 21 arrests that night. The papers reported that many bystanders had been injured.

Claude Burrows, a young shoemaker, lived in Pitt Street with his friend Thomas Phillips. Curious about the noise outside the theatre, they joined the crowd early in the evening, and Burrows followed it down to The Rocks and saw the Harrington Street watch house destroyed. He returned home, but unable to resist the excitement he rejoined the crowd outside the theatre. Later he reported to Phillips that he had seen the destruction of the St James watch house. Then

Watch house in Cumberland Street and the St James watch house below the Supreme Court. Watch houses were despised symbols of wealth and power in colonial Sydney, and were frequently destroyed by political mobs (Mitchell Library, State Library of New South Wales, GPO 1–06975; water colour by John Rae, Dixson Galleries, State Library of New South Wales, DG V*/Sp Coll/Rae/1).

they heard shots. Phillips begged his friend not to investigate, and Burrows agreed, saying, as he went out for the third time, that he was just going to Mr Peat's in George Street for some hemp. Then he made the fatal mistake of getting caught up in the crowd. Some hours later, after dodging the picquets of armed soldiers, he reached home. He had not been drinking and he carried no weapon, but a bullet had entered his thigh, deflected downwards by the iron fence at the police station. He was too frightened of being associated with the rioters to allow Phillips to call a doctor, but next day he was taken to the hospital. When the magistrates caught up with him there he was very ill. Some days later he died, of tetanus.

It was after this rioting that the *Sydney Free Press* wrote that the city had just seen 'an outrageous and dangerous attempt ... to overturn the social order'. However, there was also public concern about the undisciplined behaviour of the police. Their Superintendent issued an order that a constable 'is not, in case of affray or tumult, to rush indiscriminately upon the people, striking them with his staff, but he is to single out the ringleader or ringleaders ...'

In the early evening of 23 October 1843, the convicts in the Hyde Park Barracks, at the top of King Street, staged a rebellion, refusing to leave their clean dormitory for one infested with rats. Unable to enforce his orders, the Superintendent called for assistance from the Governor, George Gipps. He sent a military force: several companies of soldiers from the 80th regiment, eight mounted police, and 'a body of constabulary' - far more than was necessary to quell such a limited revolt, but Governor Gipps was anticipating something more. As the news of the rebellion spread, there was both anxiety and excitement in the town, and a large crowd followed the military and the mounted police up to the square. Hearing their arrival, the convicts responded with an ironic cheer that was audible three blocks away in Pitt Street. The situation had worsened. It was too dangerous to use force to clear the square and to suppress the convicts, so the Governor tried reason, warning the convicts that their punishment would be worse if they held out. When the convicts treated this with disdain, both sides waited. People were drifting away from the square.

Finally, at 4 am, the authorities decided to send in the troops to arrest the ringleaders. Armed force prevailed over defiant bodies. The ringleaders were convicted next day and sentenced to labour in irons at the city's notorious place of secondary punishment, Cockatoo Island.

Nine weeks later, on New Year's Day 1844, rioting broke out in the city, and once again the space outside the barracks now known as Queen's Square was the focus. The trouble began at a cricket match in Hyde Park, where drunken barrackers were so disruptive that play was interrupted twice. Perhaps the crowd resented the loyalist connotations of the gentlemen on the field, who were representing the Military and the Victoria clubs. However, what happened that afternoon went far beyond drunken larrikinism or class envy. It was a moment of sedition and incipient rebellion. The crowd formed, melted away when the mounted police arrived, and then re-formed. Its targets were the police and the buildings associated with their role. A number of arrested youths were freed by crowd action at the top of Bathurst Street. A posse of police and their prisoners were attacked near the watch house. The crowd then moved to Macquarie Street, forming a menacing presence outside the gates of the convict barracks. From inside, the convicts cheered back as the crowd called out to them.

Earlier that day the Governor had been surrounded by workers, men and women, demanding that he honour his promise to stop the convicts at the Female Factory taking in the washing of private customers. For over a year a quarter to a third of the working class had been unemployed. The delegates of the trades societies and radical intellectuals were working together to force the government to provide work for the unemployed, to end the competition between the unemployed and convicts in the city labour market, and to extend political rights to the working class. They had their own newspaper and campaigned vigorously, but the Governor was conceding as little as possible. So when in the late afternoon he had to intervene personally outside the barracks, in a situation that was becoming more dangerous every hour, the Governor was facing a political opposition, not a rabble. He addressed the crowd, and instructed them to return to their homes. Back from the crowd came the bitter response: 'What should we go to our homes for? We've got nothing to eat.' As the working-class newspaper, *The Dispatch*, explained the significance of this moment:

The feeling ... generally visible amongst the crowd, was that of disaffection with the Governor ... [The] coarse abuse bestowed on the Governor was purely of a political character, and arose out of his political measures ... We appeal to the Governor to be warned in time.

A more aggressive attitude was displayed in another reply to Gipps. Edward Phelan has left no other mark on the colony's history than these seditious words, for which he received 12 months in irons on Cockatoo Island: 'Although you cheered well and mustered in large numbers,' he told the crowd, 'you ought to go further and do as the Canadians did.' He was referring to the 1837 revolt in the Canadian colonies against Britain and its local agents.

Then the order was given to the soldiers and mounted police, with rifles and fixed bayonets, to clear the square. Phelan and some of the other leading agitators were arrested as one of Sydney's notorious brickfielders (southeasterly winds) sent the crowd scurrying for shelter. Having saved the social order on this occasion, the military marched off, but a section of the crowd caught up with them in King Street and pelted them with stones.

In the 1840s the function of the military machine was not to repel invaders but to maintain the authority of the colony's rulers by force, real or threatened. Three regiments were stationed in Sydney, and the main barracks was strategically placed on the York Street ridge looking over the town. In front of the barracks was a green, where Wynyard Park is today, which ran down to George Street. As it lay between the town's main street, the residences of the workers in Kent and Sussex streets, and those of the elite on the hill around St Phillip's church on York Street, it was a regular shortcut for many citizens. However, it was officially the parade ground. In 1844, Colonel Despard, the Commander of the 88th regiment, decreed that civilians would no longer be permitted to cross the green. For radical journalists this action was typical of the contemptuous attitude of the military towards civilians.

In September 1845 this paragraph, headed 'Despard's Own', appeared in *The Star and Workingman's Guardian*:

On Wednesday evening, a dreadful riot occurred on the Rocks, between the denizens of that locality, and a party of soldiers belonging to the 99th regiment. The first outbreak of the war was at the Jolly Miller public house, corner of Gloucester street, where in a few minutes windows, glass, and furniture were reduced to a state of immortal smash, and the landlord, his family, and some civilians were more or less injured. The Redcoated Marauders then formed into a body, and raising their Commander's cry of 'Stand off the grass!' rushed along Gloucester street, breaking windows in the course of their march, until they came to the corner of Frazer's lane, when they rushed into Wells' public house, and then went into Cumberland street, where there [sic] work of devastation was again commenced, and carried on with such a spirit that carpenters and glaziers will have work for a week to come. Here a picquet which had been sent for came up, but it was only adding fuel to the fire, as they were, if possible, greater scoundrels than the ones they were sent for to secure, as they called on the people to come on, as they wished no better sport than to 'skiver' a lot of them, and then employed themselves in taking several civilians to the watch house, instead of their own men to the barracks. A large number of persons were most seriously injured, many of them being wantonly attacked, as they were taking no part in the riot.

The tone of this report is similar to that on the 1840 riot: sympathetic to the people of The Rocks and hostile to the forces of law and order.

There were more tumultuous occasions in subsequent years, many of them involving attacks on police watch houses. On the Queen's Birthday holiday in 1848, the St James watch house was attacked, the prisoners liberated and the furniture and books destroyed. There was a similar attack a year later. On New Year's Day 1850 the rioting was on the scale of 1844. The houses damaged in The Rocks numbered 175. The St James watch house was again destroyed. The military came under attack in what was described as 'a planned outrage'. So alarmed were the respectable citizens that they formed a Society for the Protection of Life and Property. In his diary, solicitor and businessman George Allen wrote that he was fearful that 'scenes that lately disgraced Paris' would be repeated in Sydney, and Governor Charles FitzRoy warned the Secretary of State in London that 'the lower orders' were becoming 'discontented with the Government of the Mother Country'. A few months later the government was saved when the discovery of gold opened an escape valve that relieved the pressures of working-class life.

Between 1840 and the gold rushes there were 15 occasions in Sydney when force had to be used by the police, mounted police, or soldiers to restore order on the streets. Three of these occurred during the elections for the Legislative Council in 1843 and 1848. There were a further eight political demonstrations when contentious feeling was mobilised against opposing political forces or government policies. Finally, there were seven spontaneous eruptions of crowd feeling at public meetings, sometimes culminating in acts of violence. That makes a total of 30 moments when the face and muscle of popular power were revealed to the colony's rulers, 30 forgotten moments of tumult in paradise.

The Rocks was the breeding ground for the disaffection displayed in these riots. In the 1840s, mine host at the Jolly Miller was William McCurtayne. He was a member of Sydney's Irish community, which was well aware that the Anglo upper class detested it. McCurtayne was a public figure because he was one of the organisers of a series of meetings to protest the imprisonment in England of Daniel O'Connell, the man the Irish called 'The Liberator'. At that stage in the struggle against English supremacy, the Irish were fighting to repeal the Act of Union that had abolished the Irish Parliament. In language typical of secret policemen everywhere, McCurtayne was described in a report of 1849 as 'a wrong-headed litigious Irishman and a repealer'. However, McCurtayne was not only an Irish rebel; he was a prominent activist in Sydney's radical organisations. In 1849 he was encouraging the Irish workers of The Rocks to join the Constitutional Association, to ensure that political rights were extended to them.

The radical intellectuals knew that something important was happening in The Rocks. It was noted in 1844 by a journalist writing in a radical newspaper, *The Dispatch* – a paper that McCurtayne might have read, for it circulated among tradesmen and shopkeepers:

> The inhabitants [of The Rocks] are a separate and distinct people, peculiar in their habits and modes of life, and connected together by a feeling resembling clanship. The very style of dress is unique and characteristic ... [Their language] had more pithy emphasis, and bold figurative expression [than that of London's] Billingsgate markets.

Reaching for an explanation, the journalist pointed to the gender and ethnic aspects of life in The Rocks. The women, he said, were fond of a 'belligerent' stance, and it was 'contempt, not ignorance of the decorums of life' that fuelled their hostility to 'respectability'. Similarly, the young people were tumultuous because they were native-born Australians. They were 'not easily reconciled to the innovations of order and social discipline. They look with jealous eye upon the newcomers, and with contempt on the rules of decency of language and deportment which govern other classes.'

These radicals saw in The Rocks a plebeian working-class culture developing outside the control of church, state and landlord. They were amazed that 'the dwellers in the aristocratic terraces of Macquarie or Elizabeth streets, the lordly villas of the Surry Hills or Woolloomooloo' could not see what they saw. And they were ambivalent about their own relationship to it, for they themselves were mostly immigrants, products of a print-based popular politics. In a period of tumult, they could, however, see that this kind of disorder had the power to disturb the ordinary rules that made governing possible, rules that kept the people in their place.

What a force, they thought, might be released if immigrant tradesmen and native-born labourers acted together?

THE MUTUAL PROTECTION ASSOCIATION

THE CUSTOMS HOUSE

According to its website, the Customs House, one of Sydney's finest heritage buildings, caters for 'weddings, corporate gatherings, cocktail parties, seated dining, product launches and conferences/screenings'. Restored with the desires of Sydney's business elite in mind, the building sells itself on a promotional website that uses heritage as a vague abstraction, asking visitors to use their imagination to form 'mental pictures of things not present'. But will today's wealthy diners, sitting before their 'excellent quality food and wine', imagine the lives of the hungry families whose menfolk built the Customs House during the depression of the 1840s? Probably not. So, if our diners need something mentally substantial to chew on, they might start here.

The building we see today was mainly constructed in the 1880s, but it incorporated the original Customs House that was commenced in 1844 by the Colonial Architect's department, using workers who were either free immigrants or freed convicts. These tradesmen and labourers, about 150 of them, had been unemployed for many months, but pressure from the streets forced the government to initiate a public project – the Customs House – to provide work for them. It was the first time this had happened in Australia. It was also the first time that unemployed workers had stood up for their rights in a sustained way, in a campaign that ran from the beginning of 1843. Looking back on it we can see that it displayed three of the key elements often found when popular movements are successful: the workers had to demonstrate their anger on the streets; they had to show determination by improving their organisation and their capacity to put pressure on the government; and they had to find 'friends of the people' who could take their fight into the legislature and onto the pages of the liberal press.

In those days it was very difficult for workers to have a public voice. Before June 1843, when the Legislative Council met for the first time, there was no representative government in Australia at all, and after that date workers still had no representation. Most of them could not vote because they paid less than £20 a year in rent, and they could not stand for election because a member of Council had to own £2000 of freehold property. A lucky tradesman in the depression might earn £100 a year; a bush worker might earn £12 a year plus rations, say £50 a year – the rations (meat, flour, tea) were of the poorest quality and the pay was often in the form of an 'order' which had to be cashed at a city bank or merchant's office, and even then it might be dishonoured.

Even getting government to acknowledge that there was a problem was difficult. It was the workers' movement that had to provide government with information, because there was no official collection of unemployment statistics. It also meant altering the mind-set of government, which was ostensibly that what happened in the marketplace was none of its business. Of course, sheltering behind the economic dogma of *laissez-faire* had not prevented the government pricing and regulating the sale of land and financing the import of cheap labour. The workers who suffered from such policies saw them as the result of 'class legislation'. This was no more than the truth. When Governor Gipps arrived in 1838 he told a group of city employers that it was his aim to reduce wages by a third.

The workers of Sydney had a different approach to the responsibilities of government. Since the late 1830s about 40,000 government-assisted immigrants had arrived in the colony. Typically they were tradesmen, lured to the colony because the British government had spread tales of high wages and cheap land, and had promised to abolish convict transportation. However, what workers found was that land was expensive and tied up in the squatting system, and that a period of frantic over-speculation in wool production had created a crisis in which wages were falling and jobs disappearing. The workers said to

The original Customs House, built in the 1840s in response to government fears of organisation among Sydney's workers. This was the first example of public works being used to mop up unemployment and defuse political anger (Mitchell Library, State Library of New South Wales, GPO 1–48337).

the government: as you brought us here under false pretences, you have to attend to our plight. In particular, they argued that government had to provide employment and ensure that convicts were not taking jobs from free workers. If government could use convicts to create the foundations of this new society, why should it not employ free workers on that necessary, public task?

The workingmen had a network of 'delegates of the trades', and in January 1843 they called a public meeting, which was well attended. At this time the government was using convicts to build Circular Quay and the Darlinghurst Gaol, and assigning convicts to the *Sydney Morning Herald* and other employers in the city, so the main demand was that the government should remove all convicts from Sydney. But the Governor refused. Then the trades societies (as these early workingmen's bodies were called) received unexpected support from one of the candidates for the city in the inaugural election (in 1843) for the Legislative Council - the distiller Robert Cooper.

'Robert the Large' was one of the wealthiest men in the colony by the 1840s. Having left his convict past behind, he had built a fine villa on the top of the Paddington hill, from which he could see Botany Bay, the harbour and the city, including the head of Blackwattle Bay, where his distillery was. The villa survives on Oxford Street, enlarged into an imposing mansion, rejoicing in the name of Juniper Hall. The distillery is long gone, however. When it was built, Blackwattle Bay extended as swampy ground right up to Broadway, with a creek flowing in from the southern side of the road. Cooper dammed the creek, and built the Brisbane Distillery in Chippendale. 'The denizens of the Blackwattle swamp', as the *Herald* slightingly called them, were actually the workers of Ultimo, Glebe and Chippendale, employed in the local distilleries, breweries, tanneries and mills to produce the wealth of men like Cooper.

Among working people, Cooper was 'the old man', a kind-hearted rogue who had not lost the common touch. He seriously contended in the election that he had advanced the colony as much as the largest squatters had by fathering 28 children. Moreover, he had a knack of cutting through the power of entrenched interests with the knife of common sense, as witnessed in his proposal to deal with the avalanche of bankruptcies that was paralysing the economy. Because the courts of law were declaring people bankrupt, he said the courts should be closed down for the duration of the depression. Instead, in each district 'there should be a number of men appointed to take into consideration every man's circumstances that was sued for money; the man sued should bring his schedule before the persons appointed ... and show that if not sued in law how he would be able to extricate himself from difficulty'. Of course lawyers, officials and capitalist creditors thought that committees of local people regulating their own economic situation was an outrageous idea.

But the more Cooper was pilloried in the conservative press the more he was taken up by radicals and working-class leaders. Soon after the meeting against convict labour he organised a meeting to prevent the landowners substituting 'Coolies' (indentured labourers from India) for convicts, the supply of which had recently been cut off when Britain abolished transportation. This meeting, at which some of the trades delegates spoke, was held on the race course in Hyde Park, and drew a huge crowd. Workers were attracted too by his electoral addresses, in which he presented himself as a practical man, not a 'wordy theorist'. He was the only candidate to dedicate himself to 'the public good of the working classes', promising to advocate government policies to relieve the plight of the unemployed.

The election was marked by bloody rioting. There were injuries in Melbourne, Windsor, Campbelltown, Wollongong and Paterson (in the Hunter Valley), as well as in Sydney. Two people were killed in the fighting between rival groups of supporters, one on Brickfield Hill in Sydney, another on the main street of Paterson. Cooper's followers had adopted green as their colour, making a connection with the struggles of the Irish freedom movement, but also defying those members of the colonial ruling elite, such as James Macarthur, who publicly declared their hatred of the Irish.

In the French revolution of 1789, the revolutionary crowd bringing Louis XVI and Marie-Antoinette back to Paris from Versailles surrounded them with pikes topped by loaves of bread dipped in blood. It was a terrifying symbol of revolutionary vengeance for the starvation they faced under the old regime. In the 1840s, the British ruling class gave itself nightmares recalling this symbol, as the hunger of the Irish peasantry and the misery of industrialisation worsened. In Yorkshire, during the 'hungry forties', a poet recalled:

> I mind them times when lads marched down our street,
>   Wi' penny loaves on pikes all steeped i' blooid;
> "It's breead or blooid", they cried; "We've nowt to eat;
>   To Hell wi' all that taxes t' people's fooid".

In Sydney, Cooper's supporters terrified the propertied classes by marching through the town on the way to demolish the tents and banners of opposing candidates. They had speared loaves of bread on their banner poles. A journalist from the *Herald* knew the symbol: they were threatening revolution.

Cooper was soundly beaten in the election, and there was no revolution, but the trades delegates were emboldened by their experience of the election campaign to form the Mutual Protection Association

'Robert the Large' – portrait of distiller Robert Cooper, champion of the unemployed in the 1843 elections (from Robert S. Cameron, *Robert Cooper of Juniper Hall – A Family History* (1986), reproduced with the author's permission).

(MPA). It aimed to unite the working and middle classes in a political movement to press government into policies that would meet the people's need for work and desire for cheap land. It was Australia's first working-class political organisation.

The MPA grew to about 500 members, endorsed candidates in 1843 and 1844 for the City Council (they were elected), and published a weekly newspaper, *The Guardian*. A committee of four working men was in charge of the paper – Daniel Coughlan, a boot and shoe maker; William Crosbie, a carpenter; Robert Stewart, a cabinet maker; and Ben Sutherland, an upholsterer – and MPA members sold it on the streets. The organisation had a vigorous and democratic internal life. Its articulate and energetic leaders were soon organising public meetings and taking petitions to the Governor and the Legislative Council about working-class distress. When the officials and elected Councillors discounted the extent of the distress, and blamed the amount that did exist on the refusal of workers to accept lower wages in the city or shepherding jobs in the bush, the association carried out its own survey of employment in the city. This careful and systematic investigation showed that about 25 per cent of men in the city were unemployed at the end of 1843.

The 'delegates of the trades' who ran the MPA were tradesmen; they were not representative of the crowds of labourers who had supported Cooper and menaced the elite on the streets. But there was a connection between the two groups of workers. The larger the audience at MPA meetings – and at open-air meetings there were often 3000 people – the more likely it was that labourers and seamen would be in attendance, and the more likely it would be that there would be violence and calls for direct action. So, although the election riots were over, the turbulent activity of the working class continued. The two political traditions, of spontaneous mass activity and disciplined organising, went hand in hand, each looking to the other for openings for activity. This was particularly true in the second six months of 1843, when the government was finally persuaded to support an allocation in the budget for 1844 of £3500 to build the Customs House and thus relieve the plight of the unemployed.

The clincher in this success was the MPA's discovery of Reverend John Dunmore Lang, a 'friend of the people'. Lang was a member of the professional elite, an elected member of the Legislative Council, but at this time he was shifting his political ground, becoming more democratic, perhaps under the influence of these colonial events as much as of those of the democratic revival in the United States and Britain. Within two years he would be drafting his proclamation for the League of Liberators, whom he imagined arresting Governor Gipps and declaring the Republic of New South Wales. In the meantime, his newspaper, *The Colonial Observer*, publicised the issue of unemployment, he presented the MPA's petitions to the legislature, and he chaired a select committee into working-class distress in the city.

Meanwhile, the pressure for unemployment relief was increasing outside the legislature. At a huge MPA meeting the organisers only just managed to prevent a section of the crowd marching on Government House. The night before, the convicts at Hyde Park Barracks had rebelled against their conditions, and had been subdued with difficulty

| Customs House today (Robert Irving).

by the military. For two nights there were restless crowds on the streets. The Governor was rattled. This was the moment when he announced to yet another deputation from the MPA, with very bad grace, that he would finance the building of the Customs House.

Thus the Customs House came into existence. It was a triumph for street politics, working-class organisation, and an influential 'friend of the people'.

8

CABBAGE TREE AND TRICOLOUR

York Street in the 1850s was on the western edge of democratic Sydney, an area of six blocks that lay between King and Druitt streets, and extended eastwards to Castlereagh Street. Within this precinct the trades delegates and radical intellectuals debated, planned, published and socialised. Their audience was from Sydney's working class, and York Street was well placed for holding meetings to attract workers. Most of the city's working men and women lived in The Rocks to the north, around the Haymarket to the south, and in the crowded tenements of Sussex, Kent and Clarence streets, along the length of Darling Harbour to the west of York Street.

In 1850, John Malcolm opened the Royal Australian Equestrian Circus at the rear of his Adelphi Hotel in York Street, on the western side between King and Market Streets. With a pit, gallery and boxes, it could accommodate nearly 2000 people, making it one of the largest indoor spaces in the city. The circus performed on Tuesdays, Thursdays and Fridays, and on other days Sydney's radicals eagerly took advantage of the amphitheatre's location and size, hiring it for mass meetings to spread the idea that popular democracy was the form of self-government needed by working-class families.

There were 2000 inside and another 1000 outside the Circus one evening in February 1851. They were protesting the treatment in Van Diemen's Land of the 'Irish exiles', political prisoners arrested for participating in Daniel O'Connell's movement to repeal the act of union of Ireland with England. John McPhail, a carver, got straight to the class aspect of the matter. It was right, he said, to support the Irish patriots because they were protecting a poor and defenceless people. He concluded: 'It is high time we had free trade in Governors as well as all other commodities.' Among the other speakers were The Rocks publican William McCurtayne, boot-maker Daniel Coghlan, a Mutual Protection Association (MPA) activist who was one of the publishers of *The Guardian*, and Edward J. Hawksley, whose newspaper *The People's Advocate and New South Wales Vindicator* was commended at the meeting for having promoted the cause of democracy since 1848.

Hawksley was soon a regular speaker in meetings at the Circus. He was there to support John Dunmore Lang's candidacy for one of Sydney's three seats in the Legislative Council elections of 1851. Later that year, again at the Circus, he moved a resolution calling for responsible government, at a meeting where radicals endorsed the Chartist program of universal suffrage, vote by secret ballot, equal electoral districts (in terms of population), and no property qualifications for parliamentary representatives.

Hawksley had worked on the radical press in his native Nottingham before arriving in Sydney in 1838. For the next 20 years he was the indispensable organiser and publicist for every popular cause and radical election campaign in Sydney. His newspaper, which he published until 1856, was explicitly directed at a working-class readership. In each of the radical political organisations that sought to mobilise workers between 1848 and 1854 – the Constitutional Association, the Political Association, the Australian League, and the Democratic League – he was an official. In 1849, he promoted the idea of a co-operative to administer a 'People's Hall and Reading Room', and in June 1852 this came to pass, when the Political Association opened its office and reading room (seating 300) at 150 King Street, on the southern side and two doors down from Elizabeth Street. Soon it was known as 'the Red House'.

The most important of the radical campaigns that met at the Circus occurred in June 1852. The Political Association had placarded the town, urging the people to march with them to the Monster Meeting of the Anti-Transportation League that would commence at 7 pm at the Circus. They wanted to show the cautious middle-class men who ran the League that the time for physical resistance had come. After all, the

PEOPLE'S ADVOCATE

AND NEW SOUTH WALES. VINDICATOR.

VOL. I. No. 29.   SATURDAY, JUNE 16, 1849.   PRICE SIXPENCE.

TO THE
WORKING CLASSES OF NEW SOUTH WALES.
No. 2.

MY FRIENDS—Your conduct on Monday last shows that you are *thoughtful* men; there is now every hope for Australia. When we see men braving as you did, for hours together, one of the most inclement days we have in this country, we must be convinced that you are in earnest. Your conduct on Monday last will tell Earl them that you can *think*: awe them by your moral courage. When they see that you are capable of *thinking*, they will instinctively know that, if need be, you are equally qualified for *acting*. Indeed, what power can withstand the united force of a whole People! Despots crouch before it; factions fall beneath it; opposition cannot crush it. Peaceful, unanimous, and continuous, agitation is the lever with which the tabernacle of freedom shall be lifted to its place upon the altar of our country. Do not then, my friends, by riot, or by drunkenness, or they had any, were sent out with them, and an equal number of free immigrants were imported into the colony. Mr. Lowe, on the other hand, contends that no substantial alteration has been made in the resolution; that the words "on *any terms and conditions whatever*" were mere surplusage, and meant nothing. With all due deference to the opinion of Mr. Lowe, we must beg to dissent from him. We do think that a great deal was conveyed in those words, and that a great mistake has been committed in consenting to strike them

This radical weekly from the 1840s, aimed at Sydney's working classes, was edited by agitator EJ Hawksley. The mastheads of radical publications often became symbols of cultural and political dissent over the next 100 years (Mitchell Library, State Library of New South Wales).

campaign was nearly six years old. It had begun in 1846 when over 3000 workers attended a meeting called by the delegates of the trades and held at the race course in Hyde Park. Convicts, they said, were being used by the government and the squatters to depress wages and create industrial serfdom.

Then the cause was taken up by clergymen, lawyers, shopkeepers and landowners, for whom the issue was the moral pollution of convictism rather than the economic problems the system caused in the working classes. Their respectful petitions failed to persuade the British government, however. Meanwhile, in 1848, another wave of 'red' revolutions had occurred in Europe, and the tradesmen and shopkeepers of Sydney had defied their betters by electing a member of the Legislative Council. Moreover, since the gold discoveries there were thousands of workers in the colony from Britain, Europe and the United States who were accustomed to being listened to when they demanded 'rights of industry' (the freedom to engage in any kind of work, in any way you wanted – as employee, self-employed, or employer) and political liberty. The balance of politics was shifting again. So, in the words of the *People's Advocate*, it was time for the Anti-Transportation League to stop hoodwinking the people and state plainly to Britain that the colonists were ready to rebel if convict transportation continued.

At 6 pm on 29 June 1852, the leaders of the Political Association formed ranks at the top of King Street, outside their headquarters. As the leaders began to march down King Street, a crowd fell in behind their banner. On its front were representations of the red 'Cap of Liberty', a popular symbol in both the American and the French revolutions, and the 'Tree of Liberty' made famous by the poem of Robert Burns:

> Heard ye o' the Tree of France,
>> And wat ye what's the name o't
> Around it a' the patriots dance –
>> Weel Europe kens the fame o't!

And not only Europe. In Sydney, in 1849, the *People's Advocate* published Charles Harpur's poem about transplanting the Tree of Liberty to Australia:

> We'll plant the Tree of Liberty
>> In the centre of the Land,
> And round it ranged as guardians be
>> A vowed and trusty band;
>
> ...
>
> Then sing the Tree of Liberty
>> And the men who shall defend
> Its glorious future righteously,
>> For this all-righteous end:
>
> That happiness each man to bless
>> Out with its growth may grow –
> Our Southern Tree of Liberty
>> Should – *shall* ev'n flourish so!

The leaders were an interesting group, quite typical of the radical intelligentsia that was forming in the city. Richard Driver was licensee of the Three Tuns public house (almost opposite the People's Hall and Reading Room), another place where radical organisations often met. He had been elected to the Sydney City Council in 1843 through the efforts of the working men in the Mutual Protection Association. Edward Hawksley, the editor of the *People's Advocate*, walked arm in arm with James Dewhurst, a painter and glazier.

Both of them wore cabbage tree hats, from which a tricolour ribbon flashed. Red, white and blue, the colours of the French flag, which had been raised by a Scots carpenter in Windsor during the 1843 elections, were the colours of revolutionary democrats everywhere.

Arriving at the Circus, Councillor Driver was embraced by 'Slippery' Charlie Cowper, the wealthy Chair of the Anti-Transportation League. The presence of the radicals gave the resolutions about using physical force added significance. The fourth resolution suggested that the colonists might be forced to declare their independence; at least this was how its mover and seconder saw it. Henry Parkes (still a radical democrat at this stage) said that if transportation continued, 'resistance would be necessary to vindicate their character, at any price, at any sacrifice', and Daniel Deniehy declaimed, 'Up we the barricade, and invoke we the God of battle.'

There was no revolution. The British government understood what the squatters did not: that the dream of ruling Australia through a colonial pastoral elite (as Wentworth was proposing in his 'Bunyip Aristocracy' constitution) was endangering this part of the empire. Britain would gladly give up the sending of convicts to the colonies, and even accommodate itself to the influence of democracy in the Australian parliaments decades before the British constitution recognised Britain's working-class men and women as citizens, so long as Australia was saved for British investment, trade, and surplus population. So, late in 1854 Britain granted self-government and the right to determine their parliamentary system to the Australian colonies. Henceforth the power of British 'money, markets and men' would achieve what direct coercion from Downing Street was risking: the retention of Australia as a junior economic partner in the empire.

Because there were no barricades, the idea has got around that the radicals were a tiny minority and that democracy was desired by only a fractious few. This is a pretty obtuse conclusion, given that in 1858 the Parliament of New South Wales legislated for manhood suffrage, vote by secret ballot, and equal electoral districts – none of which was supported by the liberal businessmen who dominated parliamentary politics. Those democratic advances were the result of radical agitation as well as of liberal manoeuvring in Parliament. Organising at the grass-roots is what radicals do best, and Hawksley was a key player in that sphere, acting as secretary of the electoral committee for 'the bunch' of democrats elected to the first Parliament in 1856: three men who had been active in radical societies (Parkes, James Wilshire and Robert Campbell), and the liberal Cowper.

Historians who argue for the insignificance of the radicals have missed the meaning of the combination of the tricolour ribbons with the cabbage tree hats. In the Political Association procession down King Street, the ribbons represented European radical traditions, but the cabbage tree hat was an Indigenous symbol of resistance. It was associated with the tumultuous activity of the native-born youths, especially when they 'bonneted' the black hats worn by their rulers. Since the gold discoveries it was the favoured headwear of the diggers. In the *People's Advocate* the radicals argued that gold mining had decisively altered the balance of power between classes, in particular giving the working classes the capacity to control their labour. The cabbage tree hat now emerged as a symbol of working-class power. So when Hawksley and Dewhurst flaunted the ribbon of revolution on their cabbage tree hats, the message was clear: popular resistance by workers was an Australian tradition, too. The Tree of Liberty was putting down southern roots.

Premier Charlie Cowper rewarded Ted Hawksley, by then in his fifties, with a job in the Government Printing Office. Unable to keep away from politics, however, Hawksley became the first Chair of the Borough of Waterloo in 1860. For the next 10 years he was prominent in the municipal politics of this working-class suburb and its neighbour, Alexandria. There is a street named after him in Waterloo, but it would be a pity if he were remembered only as a kerbs-and-gutters politician.

Malcolm's Circus after it was rebranded as the Queen's Theatre. It was in the Circus that the middle-class anti-transportationists were pushed by radical working men and women to threaten to rebel against Britain (Mitchell Library, State Library of New South Wales, GPO 1–07042).

There is a final trace of Hawksley that shows him in a more typical role. He spent his last years in Fiji, where he had gone to be with his children in the 1870s. There we can imagine him, as an old man, still reading and talking about political ideas, in the bookshop he opened in Levuka.

The Circus on York Street did not long survive these turbulent years. It became the Queen's Theatre in 1856, and was demolished as unsafe in 1882.

9

THE 8-HOUR DAY AND THE HOLY SPIRIT

GARRISON AND MARINERS' CHURCHES, THE ROCKS

In Australia during the 1850s, skilled workers in Sydney and Melbourne generally worked a 58-hour week: 10 hours per day Monday to Friday and 8 hours on Saturday. For other workers it was longer: shop assistants, for example, worked 12-14 hours per day. Child labour was not uncommon - in 1876, the NSW Coal Mines Act was passed to limit the working week for boys aged 13-18 to 50.5 hours and to ban the employment of girls or boys under the age of 13 in mines.

The idea that working people should work fewer hours, enjoy and improve their lives, and have some control over their working conditions, was a radical proposition, as was the idea the working day should be based on 8 hours of work. Eight hours was problematical for employers and the state because it was an attack on untrammelled wealth production, and in that it left working people with unaccounted-for hours - if they were not producing wealth for employers and taxes for the state and getting tired and exhausted in the process, they might be out doing other things like thinking, improving themselves with reading, education and discussion, socialising, enjoying life, and maybe organising and challenging the status quo.

Robert Owen (1771-1858), a Welsh-born social reformer, factory owner and pioneer socialist, envisaged a world for working people that included more than the soul and body-destroying grind of work, work and more work. He formulated the goal of the 8-hour day as early as 1817, and coined the slogan 'Eight hours labour, Eight hours recreation,

Eight hours rest', which became part of the rich cauldron of protest and agitation known as Chartism, the great movement of popular political agitation and ferment in Britain during the late 1830s and 1840s that mobilised working people for social, economic and political reform, where socialist, trade union, democratic and co-operative ideas and impulses variously mixed, clashed, combined and inspired – and were called political crimes when the established political order was threatened.

But literature and ideas have currency and appeal that cannot be easily or totally monitored or suppressed, and they cross borders and seas in many ways ... unseen in the heads of believers, or secreted in luggage. Chartist sympathisers and movement personnel came to Australia in the 1850s, as immigrants, refugees escaping prosecution and persecution, some disappointed by the movement's apparent failures, others transported as convicts for political crimes. Chartist veterans were prominent in the early leadership of the struggle for the 8-hour day.

Inspiration also came from across the Tasman. The 8-hour idea took root in New Zealand in 1840, when a carpenter from London, Samuel Parnell, refused to work more than 8 hours a day, successfully negotiated that as a working condition and campaigned for its general application in the infant Wellington community. Another early and notable contribution was the campaign for the 8-hour day in Otago in 1849 by Samuel Shaw, a plumber, glazier and house decorator.

Traditionally, Melbourne claims parentage of the 8-hour day in Australia. Following agitation by Melbourne stonemasons in 1856, the 8-hour day (without loss of pay) was introduced in that city for workers employed on public works.

Masons were in the vanguard for a variety of reasons: they were skilled craftsmen, proud of their skills and trade, they were organised, doing a job that could not be done by the untrained and unskilled, and they were needed by employers and planners intent on erecting fine stone buildings. In the 1850s building boom that resulted from the discovery of gold in Australia, masons were in a strong position, with an essential role in the building industry that gave them considerable power should they decide to utilise it. The physical climate also contributed – working 10 hours a day exposed to the extremes of the

Australian climate, as masons did, sharpened the desire for a shorter working day.

Chartist veteran and mason James Stephens (1821–89), who came to Melbourne in 1855, was prominent in the event that made the breakthrough, a downing of tools by masons on 21 April 1856, at the construction site that was to become Melbourne University, and a march to Parliament House with other building trade workers. This demonstration came after meetings of Melbourne masons, led by former Chartist activists James Galloway and Stephens, had decided to seek the 8-hour day, and the matter had been taken up with employers. To some workers, it seemed there was more talk than action, and considerable prevarication on the part of employers.

The Melbourne success led to the decision to organise a movement, actively spread the 8-hour idea and secure the condition generally; as mason leader Galloway explained, he and others had come to the colony 'to better our condition, not to act as the mere part of machinery'. Subsequently and gradually the 8-hour idea – or 'short time', as it was also known – spread throughout Victoria, to other trades and industries, and to the other colonies. Gains were made, but not without struggle.

In 1903 the iconic Eight-Hour Day monument, funded by public subscription, was completed on the corner of Victoria and Russell streets, outside Melbourne Trades Hall. One thousand people gathered to hear veteran English socialist Tom Mann speak at the unveiling ceremony.

The achievement of the 8-hour day was one of the great successes of the Australian working class during the 19th century, demonstrating to Australian workers that it was possible to exercise significant control over working conditions and quality of life. The Australian trade union movement grew out of 8-hour campaigning and the movement that developed to promote the principle.

A less well known aspect of the 8-hour day struggle is that the Melbourne workers were actually pipped, and inspired, by brother colleagues in Sydney. Before the Melbourne stonemasons became active, stonemasons in Sydney had successfully organised, agitated for, and gained, the 8-hour day.

On 18 August 1855 the Stonemasons' Society in Sydney informed employers that in six months' time, masons would begin a campaign to only work an 8-hour day. However, men working on the Holy Trinity Church in the Argyle Cut, and on the Mariners' Church (an evangelical spiritual and welfare mission to seafarers, now an art gallery and café) in Lower George Street, The Rocks, decided not to wait. They went on strike, won the 8-hour day, and celebrated with a victory dinner on 1 October 1855.

In February 1856, in line with the notice of intent they had given six months earlier, Sydney stonemasons generally went after a reduction of hours on the 8-hour model, through negotiations, the offer to take a reduction in wages proportionate to the reduced hours, and strike action. Their main opposition came from the contractors engaged on the building of Tooths Brewery on Parramatta Road, but less than two weeks of strike action overcame that hindrance. By the end of March 1856 Sydney stonemasons had won their shorter working hours.

A popular argument against shorter working hours was that masons would use their free time to 'indulge to excess in intoxicating drink', but an anonymous mason responded to this in a letter to the *Sydney Morning Herald* (11 February 1856):

> masons are men of a different stamp, and if they had time, many,
> I doubt not, would have their names enrolled as members of that
> valuable Institution – the Mechanics' School of Arts; and their desire
> for mental improvement is another and a strong reason which urges
> them on to obtain a reduction in their present hours of labour.

By 1871, in New South Wales, workers in four trades, all of them part of the building industry, had won the 8-hour day. But it was not something everyone shared; adoption of the 8-hour day in New South Wales

The Garrison Church in Millers Point and the Mariners' Church in Lower George Street: during the construction of these in the 1850s stonemasons won their struggle for the 8-hour day, achievements that had Australian and international ramifications (Mitchell Library, State Library of New South Wales, SPF/434 and SPF/49).

was an ongoing and long industrial struggle, culminating in 1916 in the passing of the Eight Hours Act, which granted the 8-hour day to all workers in the state. Nationally, the movement seeded in 1855 by masons working on two Sydney churches and in 1856 in Melbourne by masons building Melbourne University resulted in the Commonwealth Arbitration Court's approval of the 40-hour five-day working week, beginning on I January 1948.

10

LUCIEN HENRY,
COMMUNARD

VICTORIA STREET, KINGS CROSS

During the 1880s, a rented apartment in Victoria Street, Kings Cross/ Potts Point was home to husband and wife intellectuals Lucien and Juliette Henry, who had links to the turbulent politics of the Paris Commune, and to France's offshore prison system in the Pacific …

In the stairwells flanking the Main Hall of the Sydney Town Hall are two dominating stained glass windows commissioned for the celebration of the Centenary of New South Wales in 1888. One depicts Captain Cook flanked by two of his commands, the *Endeavour* and the *Discovery*. He stands solidly and confidently on the deck of his ship, one hand resting on the bulwark rail. The viewer's eye is drawn upwards from the feet on the deck to the body, then the face of Cook looking outward, scrutinising, vulnerable. Across his body, Cook holds a large telescope. For a naval officer of his time this was an expensive and treasured instrument; here it is a symbol of observation, investigation, guidance, discovery. This is a weaponless Cook, a man of science and intellect, a symbol of the Enlightenment, not of imperialist expansion, grandeur and violence.

The other window depicts New South Wales as a young woman. She is self-assured, bold, confident. Her haloed head is crowned with the horns and wool of a ram, symbolic of the agricultural wealth of the colony. In her hands she holds a trident and a miner's lamp, symbols of the maritime and mining industries generating colonial wealth. She stands on a globe inscribed 'Oceania', a term coined by French explorer Dumont d'Urville in 1831. Surrounding her are Southern Cross stars, while the side panels of the triptych show mass displays of waratahs, flannel flowers and stenocarpus, a genus found in both Australia and New Caledonia. These panels bear the legend 'Advance Australia'. This dazzling, powerful triptych is more than a celebration of New South Wales: it is a representation of Australia, a political and cultural entity that did not exist at the time. More contentiously, it is also a geo-political statement about 'Australia' as a significant future presence in the Pacific region, one then carved up colonially by Britain, France and Germany.

Both windows are the creations of French artist Lucien Henry, who lived and worked in Sydney between 1879 and 1891. He is credited with the first serious efforts to create an Australian national art form, a radical intellectual and artistic project at that time. Yet these two windows are the only remaining work of his on permanent display, and he is still largely unknown. The windows are also a link with the turbulent radicalism of the Paris Commune.

The Franco-Prussian War (1870–71) ended with the crushing of the armies of Napoleon III. A humiliating peace treaty was imposed on France: it involved loss of territory, the payment of a huge indemnity, and the presence of a German occupation army until this was paid. Against a background of dissatisfaction with the way the French government had conducted the war, the bitter experience of a four-month Prussian siege of Paris, robust working-class political agitation and organisation, and radical republican and socialist political/intellectual ferment, the city of Paris repudiated the treaty.

A citizen army was formed to defend the city, and for 10 weeks (18 March to 28 May) Paris was run by an elected Commune. A general program of intent was announced. It involved the creation of a model republic based on social justice principles. The separation of church and state was decreed; religion became a matter of individual conscience. The general aim was to break down the foundations of state oppression: the army, the police, the bureaucracy, the church. On 6 April, the guillotine, the ultimate symbol of the power of the French state, was publicly and joyously burnt.

Social reform experiments were attempted, but the main work of the Commune was its own self-defence. The city's revolt placed it on a

Lucien Henry, photographed as he prepares to face the possibility of death for his political actions as a leader of the Paris Commune of 1871 (courtesy of Charles Deering McCormick Library of Special Collections, North Western University Library).

1788 NEW·SOUTH·WALES 1888

collision course with the national government. Hostilities commenced on 2 April. The citizen army successfully held the national army at bay until its defences were broken through on 21 May.

A week of slaughter followed. An estimated 25,000–30,000 people were massacred. Corpses piled up in the streets, which literally ran red with blood and stained the river Seine. Government troops sustained a death toll of 750. About 40,000 communards and suspected participants were arrested, of whom some 10,000 were eventually convicted. Courts ordered 110 death sentences; while accounts vary, of these, between 23 and 26 executions were carried out. Between 4000 and 5000 rebels regarded as most dangerous were deported to New Caledonia, a French penal colony in the South Pacific.

Among those transported was Lucien Henry, a 21-year-old art student. Henry had come to Paris at the age of 16 from southern provincial France, to gain the status of professional artist. He had supported himself – just – as an artist's model, while he worked at becoming a painter. He lived in the poor working-class areas of Paris and was part of the city's café-cabaret culture, where radical politics and art mixed.

In the heady days leading up to creation of the Commune, and in its early days, Henry flew the red flag of revolt and wore a Garibaldian plumed hat, international symbols of revolution and insurrection. He carried two pistols in his belt, co-edited a revolutionary journal, *La Resistance*, and was part of the rebel defence of Paris. Referred to as 'Le Colonel', he distributed food, arrested loyalist police, directed the building of barricades, positioned artillery, and generally organised defences.

Henry was eventually captured by nationalist forces, and was put on trial in 1872, facing the death penalty. He told the court he had been led astray by bad company. However, this failed to impress, as his account did not match the evidence, and he was condemned to death.

Stained-glass window in the Sydney Town Hall, designed by republican nationalist Lucien Henry. This is one of the few remaining examples of his art, showing his use of Australian motifs – and an absence of British imperial symbolism (Lucien Henry, Design for stained-glass window Centennial Hall, Sydney, National Library of Australia).

There was an appeal, and the death sentence was commuted to a life sentence of exile in New Caledonia.

For the communards, some of whom were deported with their spouses and children, New Caledonia did not necessarily involve prison cells and prison routines. The penal administration could be brutal and vindictive: for some there were forced labour, solitary confinement, and whippings, but for many, deportation meant confinement on prison islands, rudimentary housing and infrastructure, work for rations, but freedom of movement and association within a limited and policed area. All this against a harsh background of swamps, scurvy, dysentery, typhoid, tuberculosis, and the likelihood of drowning at sea for those who tried to escape.

For the French state, deportation solved the problem of what to do with a large number of political undesirables: it isolated them from their political and intellectual networks, and avoided national and international political fallout that may have accompanied an extensive program of executions.

When a general amnesty was granted to the communards in 1879, the majority returned to France. Henry headed for Sydney. The Australian colonies had been part of the world of the exiled communards. During the early 1870s, Port Phillip waterfront workers had protested against the appalling conditions the communards were subjected to on the French transports that used the port for supplies and refuelling en route to New Caledonia. Their protests and solidarity actions eventually forced French authorities to bypass Australian ports. Among radical Australian intellectuals, and within the growing labour movement, there were many who were sympathetic to – indeed inspired by – the ideals of radical French republicanism. In an internationally celebrated escape in 1874, political journalist and Commune supporter Henri Rochefort and five comrades successfully escaped from New Caledonia to New South Wales when they were on the way to Europe.

Between 1879 and 1891 Henry became part of Sydney's dynamic intellectual and artistic life, 'a citizen in the republic of the arts', as he put it. He brought with him perspectives and influences that were republican, utopian, socialist, and non-British, including admiration for Arabic culture and what he termed its 'magnificent art', an influence that found its way into his own art and design. In New Caledonia he probably had contact with some of the many Arab rebels who were inspired by the Paris Commune and deported from Algeria following their revolt against French imperialism.

Henry quickly established himself as an artist. In 1880 he married Frenchwoman Juliette Rastoul (1841-98), a teacher of French, and rented an apartment in Victoria Street. Rastoul had come to Sydney with her two children in 1874, having been deported from New Caledonia for assisting the escape of communards. Her de facto husband drowned in 1875 trying to escape the penal colony. During the 1890s

Backpackers now occupy the studio in Victoria Street, Kings Cross where Lucien and his wife Juliette lived – and influenced the radical nationalist culture of Sydney in the 1880s (Nick Irving).

Madame Juliette Henry became well known in Sydney intellectual circles.

Two related projects dominated Henry's Sydney years, both cultural in the broadest sense, and political. Henry articulated the need for, and sought to develop, art forms that reflected the intellectual debates then shaping the arts in Europe, but that were rooted geopolitically in the Australian environment and its emerging culture. He sought to create a 'national' art that both expressed and would help shape a unique Australian experience, one that was not dependent on an imperial past, and that was at once national and cosmopolitan.

Related to this was Henry's democratic vision of a system of technical education which aimed to empower working people in their appreciation and practice of the arts. This was not about art training as a pastime, but about the creation of skilled artisans who would apply their training to the general wellbeing of the community. In 1884 Henry was appointed as the first Instructor in Art at the newly created Sydney Technical College. There he left a teaching legacy that continued, through his students and those he employed as teachers, well into the 20th century.

Henry returned to France in 1891 with Frances Broadhurst, one of his former students. The following year they had a son. Frances died soon after, from birth complications. Back in Australia, Juliette later dissolved their marriage. In dire financial circumstances, depressed, and virtually unknown in the country of his birth, Henry died in 1896 from a form of tuberculosis contracted during his New Caledonian exile; he was 45 years old. In Australia his name and contributions to Australian culture and nationhood slipped into obscurity. Work by historians and curators associated with Sydney's Powerhouse Museum in 2001 helped draw him to public attention and to the interest of scholars.

JOHN NORTON AND THE DEMOCRATIC RIOTS OF 1887

The meeting on 3 June 1887 had been called by the city's leading businessmen and politicians – current and aspiring knights of the realm – to decide how to commemorate Queen Victoria's jubilee. Their favourite idea was to invite the working-class children of 'the metropolis and suburbs' to 'a grand fete' at the Exhibition Building in Prince Alfred Park. Facing Redfern, this building, with its four-storey towers and giant curved roof dominating the proletarian end of the city, was constructed in 1870 to mark the centenary of Captain Cook's landing. Prince Alfred Park, named after the Queen's second son, who was nearly assassinated at Clontarf in 1868, was a remnant of the Cleveland Paddocks, where the Indigenous people of the Sydney area who had survived the invasion used to gather a few decades earlier. The Exhibition Building, grandly designed in imitation of English exhibition buildings, would be demolished and replaced by a swimming pool in the prosaic 1950s.

For months *The Bulletin* had been scoffing at these toadying schemes to celebrate Victoria's accession to England's 'grand, glorious worm-eaten throne'. Still, no one imagined that celebrating loyalty to the Crown would become the catalyst for a vehement and prolonged expression of democratic opinion. At the 3 June public meeting, just a few hundred were in the Town Hall to hear the Mayor, Alban Joseph Riley, explain that the object of a proposed fete was to influence the parents through the children. If only he had realised what those subversive parents might do. No sooner was the motion on the table than a member of the audience, a leading member of the Secularist Society, jumped in with an amendment that:

> in the opinion of this meeting the proposal to impress upon the children of the colony the value of the jubilee year of a sovereign is unwise and calculated to injure the democratic spirit of the country.

Seconded by John Norton, it was carried by an overwhelming majority. It showed that democrats objected to the jubilee not because they were republican but because they hated the opportunity it provided to reinforce a class-divided society, in which gongs were handed out to the rulers while working-class children were taught to defer.

As ever, when its leadership is rejected the elite is unable to accept the result. In a peevish tone the Mayor chided the absent loyalists who preferred 'to sing themselves hoarse over a bun and a cup of tea' than

The Exhibition Building in Prince Alfred Park where the imperial loyalists tried to suppress Australian democracy in 1887 (City of Sydney Archives, SRC 663).

attend a vital meeting. He then announced a second meeting at the Town Hall in a week's time to give the loyalists a chance to redeem themselves, or, as *The Bulletin* saw it, another chance to 'teach the young the idea how to grovel'.

John Norton was then 29 years old. This is the same man who is remembered today as the drunken, wife-beating, brawling, scandal-mongering proprietor of *Truth*, but there is another side to Norton. Arriving as a journalist in the colony in 1884, he gave up a very success-ful and well-paid stint on a Sydney daily to freelance in 1885 so that he could assist the Trades and Labour Council as a publicist and agitator. He wrote the official report of the 1885 Inter-Colonial Trades Union Congress held in Sydney, and in the following year went as the official delegate of the Labour Council to the Trades Union Congress in Eng-land and to the International Trades Union Congress in Paris. Return-ing to Sydney he was welcomed at a huge meeting at the Town Hall, where he gave a fiery speech attacking the capitalist press for its hatred of the working man. He also edited and organised the Australian con-tributors to a 900-page book, *The History of Capital and Labour in All Lands and Ages*, which he introduced by writing:

> Labour from the first marked Australia for its own. It is the country
> upon which the old European systems have had the least influence; as
> it is the country where the institutions of the modern democracy have
> taken the firmest hold in the national character and life of the people.
> It is, moreover, a country, the foundations and structure of whose
> constitutions were laid and built up by labour ... In no other portion
> of the world are trade and labour organisations so numerous and
> effective.

The ethos of labour – not capital – was what democrats like Norton saw as the source of 'the democratic spirit of the country'. Naturally, when he looked for activists to organise people power against the wealth and connections of the loyalist elite, he turned to those he knew best, the activists of the trades union movement that he worked for.

The second Town Hall meeting was another fiasco for the estab-lishment. They had gone to the trouble of printing 350 tickets, which invited their holders to enter early via the Druitt Street entrance, but too late the organisers discovered that they were admitting scores of democrats with forged tickets. One of them was Norton, whom the police recognised and ejected more than once. In the lead-up to the meeting, Norton had written a widely circulated leaflet warning democrats that in order to protect 'the honour and independence of our country' they should turn up at the Town Hall and defeat the attempt by 'the toadies and office-seekers' to reverse 'the grand decision' of the previous meeting. The leaflet must have worked, for when the main doors were opened several thousand democrats rushed into the hall; an equal number were left outside – 'Standing room was unobtainable and the walls and niches were lined with men and youths', according to the *Sydney Morning Herald*. With the democrats sensing another chance to rout their rulers, fighting soon broke out in all directions, the press table was destroyed, and the leading loyalists were trapped on the platform, trying to keep their spirits up amidst this sea of turbulence by singing verses of the national anthem.

After an hour of uproar, in which leading secularists and trade unionists led the crowd in cheers for liberty, the meeting was abandoned, but not before 30 of the hapless loyalists (among them the Premier, former democrat Sir Henry Parkes) had retreated to a private room, there to console themselves with visions of soldiers from the British fleet, several warships being then in the harbour, putting the mob down by force. *The Bulletin* warned them to think instead of democratic reforms, such as popular election of the Mayor ... or else 'the people will take it upon themselves one of these days to settle the issues after a fashion peculiarly their own'. But the loyalists were thinking of a third meeting, at the Exhibition Building itself, on the following Wednesday, and this time their preparations were going to be thorough. Meanwhile, the police forcibly cleared the Town Hall by calling in reinforcements from the street patrols.

With their humiliation biting deeply, the elite were in the mood for a vindictive and immediate response. It was provided by Parkes. Revealing how far he had travelled from his radical past, on the following day, Saturday, Parkes proclaimed that all theatres would be closed on Sundays. His object was to deny audiences to the secularists and democrats, whose Sunday night meetings in these theatres were spreading

John Norton, usually portrayed as a muck-raking journalist and news-paper proprietor, began public life as a radical labour intellectual (from *The History of Capital and Labour*, Sydney and Melbourne, 1888).

republican and socialist ideas among the workers and their families. By the evening the rumour of the closure had spread through the city and the democrats were planning their response. Sure enough, on Sunday there were police stationed outside the theatres. According to plan, at the time when the lectures usually commenced, a crowd, said to be 6000 strong, assembled at the Queen's statue at the top of King Street, spilling over into Hyde Park. The organisers had a strategy: to bury the fear of disloyalty to the throne – potentially a divisive issue in working-class circles – beneath a common resistance to the more fundamental issue of an assault on the right to free speech.

Most of the speakers were trades unionists. William McNamara, who had recently founded the Australian Socialist League and would become a shearers' union organiser and then manager of a famous radical bookshop in Castlereagh Street, said that the struggle had gone far beyond a question of loyalty. Just how far, John Norton made explicit:

This [*diktat* by Parkes] was not so much an attempt to put down the quiet little meetings at the theatres as to get in the thin edge of the wedge of despotic rule; an attempt to feel the pulse of the people to see how they would put up with repressive measures.

A delegation from the meeting to the Premier on Monday got nowhere. The ban on Sunday meetings in halls and theatres stayed until 1915.

Meanwhile, the loyalists from the ruling class were organising the meeting at the Exhibition Building on Wednesday. This was one of those moments when the nature of rule in capitalist societies was revealed: having twice lost the battle for public opinion, the loyalists were determined to impose their will on the public, by force if necessary.

Loyalists with tickets filled the hall under police supervision. Inside they discovered how the organisers intended to deal with opposition. As the *Sydney Morning Herald* reported:

> A plan was drawn up of the building, and it was determined that certain sections of it should be reserved for particular military corps or other organisations ... The distribution of forces was such as to divide the audience into six squares ... Detachments of police were stationed on each side of the platform, whilst the front of it was committed to about 150 undergraduates of the University ... Extending down the body of the hall was a most determined body of Orangemen, and running at right angles to the right and left of this line, at certain points, were other lines formed of Lancers, the Newtown Reserves, footballers, the Primrose League and other bodies of loyalists.

Out of 10,000 in the building, about 3000 were there to demonstrate that coercion is the ultimate weapon of a ruling class when its values are rejected by those it rules. 'Gentlemen' spoiling for a fight arrived with overcoats buttoned up to the neck; others displayed the sticks with which they were armed. 'Loyalty enforced at the point of the bayonet' was how it was later described in Parliament by a conservative politician.

Although the capitalist press claimed that the meeting was a great triumph for loyalty, it was clear from their reports that many democrats had gained admission, and no doubt most of the overflow crowd of 10,000 outside the building were from the nearby working-class suburbs where there would not have been much sympathy for ruling-class

At the loyalist meeting in the Exhibition Building in 1887, police and martial reservists guarded the platform and ejected a would-be speaker for 'the democracy' (*Town and Country Journal*, 25 June 1887).

loyalists. Inside the hall it was pandemonium. As soon as disagreement was voiced, the interjector was pounced on and ejected. Fighting broke out, especially in front of the platform, where the trades union militants fought the undergraduates as John Norton tried in vain to mount the platform to move an amendment, of which the chairman had been informed. Though it was barely audible above the noise, the loyalists sang *Rule Britannia*. None of their speakers could be heard but the organisers had anticipated this by hanging placards from a pole on the platform (*The Bulletin* called it a gallows), and the resolutions were passed 'by dumbshow'. So, on this third attempt the Sydney elite managed to pass a declaration of loyalty, and wipe away the two earlier embarrassments.

As *The Bulletin* summed up the meeting:

More than 3000 soldiers, sailors, pugilists and bullies of all descriptions were collected to silence opposition and assail those whose 'loyalty' was suspected, and yet each successive speaker asked his audience to believe that the Australian party, against whom all these preparations were made, were only an insignificant handful of malcontents.

The spirit of democracy was not subdued; just the opposite. This mobilisation of democrats opened the way to the strikes of the early 1890s and the formation of the Labor Party. The young Henry Lawson was so uplifted by the explosion of popular energy in 1887 that he sent his first contribution to *The Bulletin* - 'A Song of the Republic':

Sons of the South, make choice between
(Sons of the South, choose true)
The Land of Morn and the Land of E'en
The Old Dead Tree and the Young Tree Green,
The Land that belongs to the lord and Queen,
And the Land that belongs to you.

THE HENRY LAWSON STATUE

ICONIC HENRY AND 'FADED' LOUISA

Not far from where Mrs Macquarie's Road crosses over the Cahill Expressway, on a grassy Domain knoll overlooking Woolloomooloo Bay, is a statue of short story writer and poet Henry Lawson (1867-1922). Unveiled in 1931 by the Governor of New South Wales, Sir Philip Game, the Lawson tribute depicts the writer accompanied by 'bush' symbols associated with his literary and real life: a swagman, a fence post, and a dog. As Governor Game (an Englishman) told the Lawson family members and Sydney notables who had gathered for the unveiling, Lawson was 'the voice of Australia' who proclaimed 'far and wide the ideal which, in the simple dialect of the bush, is called "Mate-iness"'.

The statue is in an area of Sydney that had been familiar to Lawson: the 'bleak Domain', as he once called it. During adolescence he had lived nearby with his mother. Up at five in the morning and walking through Sydney to Redfern station to catch a train to work, young Lawson became familiar with the homeless and unemployed, 'the wretched rag-covered forms on the benches, and under them', who dossed down in the Domain and Hyde Park.

Born in 1867 in a goldfields tent near Grenfell (NSW), Henry was the first of five children for Niels Larsen (anglicised to Peter Lawson), a former Norwegian sailor, and his Australian-born wife Louisa. Raised on a poor bush farm, Henry was trained as a carpenter and house-painter by his father. After his parents separated in 1883, Henry joined his mother in Sydney, and worked mainly as a coach-painter. In later

The Henry Lawson statue in Sydney's Domain, which tells the preferred Lawson story: Lawson without his radical mother (Mitchell
Library, State Library of New South Wales, GPO 1–23268).

life he earned his living in New South Wales, Queensland, Western
Australia, New Zealand and England from his trades, his literary work,
journalism, stints as a teacher and as a public servant. He ended his
days on a Commonwealth Literary Fund pension.

Alcoholism, depression and debt were long-time problems for
Henry, contributing to the breakdown of his seven-year marriage (to
Bertha, a nurse, stepdaughter of Sydney radical bookshop owner William McNamara) in 1903. During his last 20 years, he was no stranger
to prison (for drunkenness and debt), mental institutions and convales-
cent homes. Henry died aged 55, alone in the backyard of his Sydney

home, having partially recovered from a cerebral haemorrhage the previous year. The best of his literary work was produced between 1890 and 1902.

The Domain statue iconises Henry Lawson the storyteller – 'Australian literature's most famous son', according to the *Oxford Companion to Australian Literature*, and 'the first Australian writer granted a State funeral'. The preferred Lawson is the author who celebrates bush mateship, and the Australianness of stoically struggling to cope with/ survive the adversities thrown up by life and by the harsh Australian environment. In this account there is little room for the young Lawson, whose writings in the 1880s and 1890s were informed by politics that were radically republican and socialist; there is also little room for his mother, long absent from the public record and largely remembered simply because she was Henry's mother.

Yet it was she who encouraged his literary endeavours, who introduced him to the world of literature, who developed the intellectual milieu that shaped the emerging writer, who provided the forum for his first literary forays, in the pages of her radical monthly *The Republican* (1887–88), and in 1894 published his first book.

Born near Mudgee in 1848, Louisa (née Albury) married gold prospector Niels Larsen in 1866; she was younger than her husband, a man she hardly knew, and their marriage was strained and unsuccessful. Poetic, thoughtful, strong-willed and hardworking, Louisa helped provide for her family of five as a dressmaker, storekeeper and rural postmistress. After she separated from her husband, she moved to Sydney with their children, started a boarding house, and became part of the city's flourishing radical intellectual and social reform networks and culture. In 1888 she began publishing and editing *The Dawn*, an influential monthly journal for women. It was the first Australian journal solely edited, written, published, set and printed by women, and provided a voice for women – 'their journal and mouthpiece' as Louisa explained in the first issue. In *The Dawn* office, 10 women worked in full-time or part-time positions producing the journal.

The Dawn, which was published until July 1905, campaigned for the radical propositions that women should have legal, political and economic rights equal to those of men, and that women should be

Louisa Lawson, feminist, intellectual, inventor, poet, journalist, editor, publisher – and largely forgotten by history (Dixson, State Library of New South Wales, DL PX 158).

physically and psychologically healthy, educated, and self-reliant. High on *The Dawn* agenda were female suffrage, women's rights generally, female access to higher education, marriage and divorce reform, and equality of opportunity in the workforce.

'Women are what men make them,' Louisa told *The Bulletin* in October 1896:

> Why, a woman can't bear a child without it being received into the hands of a male doctor; it is baptized by a fat old male; a girl goes through life obeying laws made by men; and if she breaks them, a male magistrate sends her to gaol where a male warder handles her and looks in her cell at night to see if she's all right. If she gets so far as to be hanged, a male hangman puts the rope around her neck; she is buried by a male gravedigger; and she goes to a Heaven ruled over by a male God or a hell managed by a male devil. Isn't it a wonder men didn't make the devil a woman?

THE DAWN.

A Journal for Australian Women.

EDITED BY DORA FALCONER

Vol I. No. 1.   SYDNEY, MAY 15, 1888.   PRICE, 3D.

About Ourselves.

"WOMAN is not uncompleted man, but diverse." says Tennyson, and being diverse why should she not have her journal in which her divergent hopes, aims, and opinions may have representation. Every eccentricity of belief, and every variety of bias in mankind allies itself with a printing-machine, and gets its singularities bruited about in type, but where is the printing-ink champion of mankind's better half? There has hitherto been no trumpet through which the concentrated voices of womankind could publish their grievances and their opinions. Men legislate on divorce, on hours of labor, and many another question intimately affecting women, but neither ask nor know the wishes of those whose lives and happiness are most concerned. Many a tale might be told by women, and many a useful hint given, even to the omniscient male, which would materially strengthen and guide the hands of law-makers and benefactors aspiring to be just and generous to weak and unrepresented womankind.

Here then is DAWN, the Australian Woman's Journal and mouthpiece

The masthead of Louisa Lawson's influential monthly journal for women (*The Dawn*, no. 1, 15 May 1888).

Louisa wrote over 200 leading articles for her publication, and had subscribers in Fiji, New Zealand, America, Europe and Great Britain. In 1902, when women won the right to vote in New South Wales, Louisa was acknowledged by The Womanhood Suffrage League as 'The Mother of Womanhood Suffrage in New South Wales'.

At the same time as she produced *The Dawn*, Louisa was prominent in Sydney's radical republican and socialist intellectual circles. She also wrote and published a novel and a book of poems, and invented and patented a sealing device for mail-bags. This invention largely came about as a result of difficulties she encountered mailing *The Dawn*. It was adopted by postal authorities, but she went through years of expensive and exhausting litigation to protect her patent and gain adequate compensation. This litigation, together with years of writing, editing, publishing and other radical activities, led to health failure, the end of *The Dawn*, and retirement. Her application for a Commonwealth Literary Fund pension was rejected, apparently on the grounds that her son, Henry, was in receipt of one '[and] there are not sufficient funds available to enable an adequate pension to be granted to you'.

Louisa died in Gladesville Mental Hospital, Sydney in August 1920. A very short paragraph in *The Bulletin* noted her death, describing her as the mother of Henry Lawson, noting that she had once edited 'a paper called *The Dawn* and [taken] a prominent part in the demand for woman suffrage', and that she had since 'faded from the public eye'.

A 'DEMOCRATIC RENDEZVOUS'

THE BOOKSHOPS OF
RADICAL SYDNEY

Bruce Scates

George Black, founder of Sydney's Republican League and the first Labor member of Parliament in New South Wales, socialist, secularist, slanderer, boozer, Labor rat and sexual libertine, will no doubt be remembered for many things. But he should be praised by us all as an insatiable, inspired and extraordinarily eclectic reader.

When Black sat down to write the story of his all-too-eventful life, reading assumed a singular importance. The 1890s, he recalled, were a time of 'intellectual upheaval', when 'thoughtful youth ... studied night and day all the [books] which could be bought or preferably borrowed'. In Billy Hughes' extraordinary autobiography, with that really quite delicious title *Crusts and Crusades: Tales of Bygone Days*, he recalled the same 'great awakening' that had prompted him to politics. 'A bit highbrow and smelling of the lamp', Hughes and his 'hard reading crowd' devoured every text, challenged every orthodoxy. Many a historian has noted the role reading played in the shaping of Sydney's radicals. In a radical culture that looked out to the world, 'swags of socialist literature' from Britain, the United States and Continental Europe provided reformers of every political persuasion with rhetoric and inspiration. But a book's crossing from New York or London is only a small part of its story. A history of radical Sydney should be interested not just in *what* books where being read, but also *where* and *how* a reader might find them. Sydney's radical bookshops are the key to understanding the twilight world of 19th radicalism, its enthusiasms and ideals, failures and disappointments, dreams and frustrations.

The radical bookshop looms large in the memoirs of virtually every left-wing activist in this period. Entering its door is often depicted as a turning point in one's life, an initiation into an exhilarating new world of purpose and conviction. Jack Lang's career, he recalled, 'started in [William] McNamara's bookshop in Castlereagh Street in the early '90s'. Here this young man 'with a cause' found literature and inspiration: 'fresh shipments of cheap socialist pamphlets' conveyed the simple moral precepts of 19th century radicalism while socialist classics such as Gronlund's *Co-operative Commonwealth*, Schäffle's *Quintessence of Socialism*, even Marx' s *Capital*, demanded bouts of 'intensive reading'. The bookshop also catered for less scholarly diversions. Balzac's *Droll Stories* and *The Adventures of a Sydney Barmaid* tempted self-improving readers like Lang into the realms of pornographic fantasy. But ultimately it was the people, rather than the books, that figured first and foremost in Lang's autobiography:

> There flocked the poets and philosophers of Sydney town. The idealists and the materialists. The republicans and the anarchists ... They browsed and they argued. They planned and they plotted. To me, it was all very exciting.

The rise of the radical bookshop was synonymous with the rise of 19th century radicalism. When young George Black and Billy Hughes first took to reading, 'Sir' Robert Bear's Freethought Book Depot was the only commercial outlet for radical literature. Both the title and the capital for the venture were borrowed. By 1894, Sydney's radical *litterateur* could choose between McNamara's Book and News Depot and the Active Service Brigade's Reading Rooms a few doors down and opposite. Over in Pitt Street, the Australian Socialist League ran a bookshop of its own, while papers such as *The Democrat*, *The Dawn*, *The Workman* and *The Worker* were also depots for the dissemination of radical literature.

All these literary agencies were within walking distance of each other, on what James Tyrell called the 'book-selling streets' of Sydney's

McNamara's in Castlereagh Street, the most famous of the radical Sydney bookshops (City of Sydney Archives, NSCA CRS 51/1012).

busy inner city. They were situated between institutions which readers were already familiar with: the Public Library at one end of town and the School of Arts at the other. Within and around these boundaries stood the meeting places and landmarks of radical Sydney - the Queen's Statue and the Domain, the sixpenny restaurants, bars and boarding houses.

Radical literary networks were extensive, ranging across Sydney's centre and its suburbs; they were also extraordinarily mobile. Bookshops such as these changed premises several times, their fortunes linked to the rise and fall of radical societies. Nor was business always confined to business premises. Socialist, anarchist, feminist and single taxers set up stalls at almost every radical venue, peddling newspapers, books and pamphlets from parks, wharves and street corners. In this they were aided by the physical features of their literature. With the exception of a few weighty classics, radical works were generally fairly short, novels and political economy averaging between 100 and 200 pages. These pocket-sized editions, deceptively light considering their content, were easily stowed in overcoat pockets and shopping baskets and set out on stumps, platforms and sidewalks, to be whisked away with the arrival (as one peddler put it) of 'the inevitable detective'. To gauge the dissemination of radical literature, historians need to be more mindful of a book's physical character. What a book 'says' does not determine its popularity: in clandestine networks such as these, readership was also influenced by the book's weight, appearance, size and durability.

The high price of literature also necessitated a number of innovations. Books were borrowed rather than bought. McNamara's Lending Library, an adjunct to his bookshop, boasted 20,000 volumes. All could be hired out on a daily or weekly basis, 6d for the most popular titles, 3d for the others. But probably the cheapest way to obtain one's reading was to buy a colonial version of an expensive overseas import. In days when copyright laws were less than stringent, the most promising authors were re-released in pamphlet form, attractively bound and sometimes illustrated. Sydney's Single Tax League plagiarised Henry George under a number of appealing titles: *That We Might All Be Rich*, *The Music of the Spheres* and (with generous acknowledgment to the Bible) *What God Says About Land Monopoly*. This particular 'reworking' of literature was in the interests of both seller and purchaser; pamphlets were cheaper than books, easier to store and distribute, and placed fewer demands on the time and concentration of the reader.

The bookshops were not just about reading. They were also vibrant social centres, defying what historians have called the 'fragmentation' of public life and literature. In his early years Edwin Brady knew reading as a solitary pursuit, but later it was books (or rather his choice of books) that drew him away from the close circle of his family. In the Socialist League's Reading Rooms, Brady discovered friendship and romance as well as literature: to encounter radical papers from across the world was wondrous enough; even more exhilarating was to meet those, like himself, determined to read them. McNamara's book room styled itself 'the democratic rendezvous', a meeting place for ideas, individuals and cultures. For J.T. Lang, that working-class boy made good, it conjured up memories 40 years later. It wasn't just 'exciting' to 'plot' the overthrow of capitalism. Lang described McNamara's as the 'cure' for 'the political bug': it ended the isolation, loneliness and confusion that so often plagued the working-class reader. In the reading rooms, books and newspapers, light and warmth and companionship could all be had for a penny's admission. And a bed as well as a book was offered at many such establishments. The Headquarters of the Active Service Brigade (just down the road from McNamara's) offered accommodation, meals, a plunge bath and a library. Every night, its beds were taken by Sydney's unemployed; every day they gathered in the reading room to debate the cure of the social problem.

The women's movement, also very much a part of radical Sydney, developed its own distinctive literary circles. While reading may have been difficult for working-class autodidacts such as Billy Hughes, it was harder still to acquire books written for and by women. Louisa Lawson's life and bookstore illustrate both points admirably. A promising pupil teacher, Lawson was kept at home to care for younger siblings: her mother 'burnt her books'; her husband, a struggling selector, 'frowned upon' her reading. With their three children, Louisa escaped to the city. There she 'championed every cause that might improve [women's] condition'. The Dawn Club was one such endeavour. For a subscription of 6d a week, women could attend its reading room, borrow its books and join in the 'animated discussion' of literature. As a purely literary society, the Dawn Club had its limitations: time and time again Lawson complained of 'a poor stock of literature on the woman question'. The real function of the club was social and political. Women 'exchanged ideas' and experiences, debating the Divorce Act, temperance and suffrage, strengthening the friendships which sustained first-wave feminism. And here young women were encouraged 'to exercise whatever talents they may have in speaking or writing', gaining the apprenticeship male literary networks had long denied them.

The Dawn Club is the most celebrated of all the literary networks established by and for women, but it was hardly unique or unprecedented. By the mid-1890s Sydney was playing host to any number of such forums, creating, as feminist historians have noted, 'new political spaces' for women. Women gathered each Saturday afternoon in Rose Scott's drawing room in Edgecliff, enjoying tea, conversation and literature in what Miles Franklin would remember as Sydney's 'finest salon'. Of an evening they travelled to meetings of the Women's Literary Society, reclaiming the night and the city in a daring breach of social convention, reading, reciting, discovering the literature that 'electrified' Europe and America. In each case, these reading circles 'brought the world ... home' to women – 'history, poetry, fiction ... all things in heaven and earth' were suddenly within their reach. Here they claimed knowledge that men and women 'of the old school' had denied them, devouring 'BAD BOOKS' on sex and suffrage, drawing solace and inspiration from the depiction of 'advanced women' in recent literature.

The nexus between feminism, socialism, the single tax and anarchism is apparent when we consider the book lists of any of their societies. *The Woman's Voice* listed among the books 'that all women should read', *England's Ideal* by Edward Carpenter, *Politics for the People* by Morrison Davidson, Edward Bellamy's *Looking Backward*, and *Woman in the Past, Present and Future* by August Bebel. 'No thinking woman should neglect to read [these] books,' added Maybanke Anderson, the editor. Subsequent reading lists extended to Marx, Thoreau and Champion, the primers of 19th century socialism.

Socialist and feminist reading were interchangeable. Sydney's radical bookshops carried literature on 'the women's question', catering for a female as well as a male readership. And some, like 'Sir' Robert Bear's Free Thought Depot, challenged the stuffy morality of middle-class society. Pamphlets by Annie Besant advised readers in contraceptive technique: *The Illustrated Marriage Guide* and Dr Hollis's treatise on *Diseases of the Male Generative Organ* refined the pleasures and revealed the dangers of sexuality. Indeed, it could be argued that here Sydney's radical bookery performed its most radical function, promot-

Bear's popular Free Thought bookshop, 16 Park Street, one of Sydney's first outlets for radical literature during the late 19th century (Mitchell Library, State Library of New South Wales, SSV/1).

ing the discussion of sexuality in a highly repressive society, dispensing 'French preventatives' and vaginal syringes in the belief that women were entitled to control their own bodies.

I began this chapter with a brief reference to Billy Hughes' autobiography. I might as well end it in the same way. For many of us Billy Hughes is a rather sinister figure. He is the Labor rat par excellence, the one-time republican and one-time radical who broke the labour movement in his bid to introduce conscription in 1916 and 1917 and send Australia's youth to the killing fields of Flanders. Oddly enough, I remember Billy Hughes from a very different moment in history. In the early 1890s, a young man, 'adrift in a wide world' stumbled upon the company of Sydney's radicals. Amid what he called this 'hard reading crowd' he struggled to find a solution to 'the social problem'. Why, in an era of unprecedented human achievement, was there poverty and want? Why did the hovels of the poor border the mansions of the wealthy? Hughes' insatiable reading brought him to the work of Henry George, an American political economist who attributed all social evil to the private monopolisation of land – as long as a few could bar access to 'Nature's storehouse', others would be forced to pay a levy in the form of rent. In this way the producing classes were held to ransom by the landlord, a social parasite. George's solution was as simple as the analysis he set out. *Progress and Poverty* called for the socialisation of rent through the taxation of land value: the single tax.

It doesn't sound very exciting, and even the most diligent researcher can take many tiresome weeks to read *Progress and Poverty*. But that is not how the book was read by Hughes and his generation. Passages were read out loud, discussed and debated, and the book became a symbol all of its own, raised up before audiences on the Domain as if it had some talismanic significance. The excitement of reading Henry George is nowhere better captured than in *Crusts and Crusades*, the testimony of Billy Hughes, the reader, the radical, the visionary of the 1890s:

> It was a beautiful moonlit night; a soft cool breeze fanned our hair
> as we walked along [George Street]. It was night made for lovers and
> idealists . . . But there was a serpent in our Eden: for some weeks there
> had been an epidemic of measles ... I said they were a bit of a problem
> alright, but Christie, sensing in my words some lack of faith in the
> Single Tax, ... stopped short and tapping me solidly on the chest said
> 'Under the Single Tax, there will be no measles, no whooping cough, it
> will be a new and wonderful world.'

Such were the wonderful possibilities of radical Sydney.

14

A CONVICT LEGEND
OF THE 1890s

BULLETIN PLACE

Standing on Pitt Street today, across the road from the tiny lane known as Bulletin Place, and looking up the lane, past the charmless 1960s office tower on the northeast corner, we can see, on the Circular Quay side, the remains of a Victorian warehouse. It is situated on one of the most historic alignments in Sydney, created in Governor Macquarie's time, when the former convicts Andrew Thompson and Mary Reibey owned the land sloping from Macquarie Place to the Tank Stream. Downhill from the first Government House, adjacent to the government wharf and stores, their land was just a short distance from the bridge over the Tank Stream that gave access to George Street, the main thoroughfare of the settlement. To the east of the stream, in a jumble of buildings spread across the hill looking down on Sydney Cove, were the soldiers' barracks, the convicts' barracks, and two of the central institutions of a forced-labour economy, the hospital and the gaol. We are at the centre of convict Sydney.

This was the first part of the natural environment of Sydney to be completely transformed by the invasion of Europeans, and it was accomplished with convict labour. The stream of fresh water that had attracted Governor Phillip to the site was often reduced to a trickle, so Governor Phillip ordered the convicts to dig three tanks in the sandstone, each about the size of a backyard swimming pool, as an insurance against drought. With equal foresight, wishing to prevent pollution of the stream, he decreed a green belt along its banks, but 20 years later, under the rebel military officers who had usurped the government and thrown out Governor Bligh, businesses were allowed to ignore the decree – the lure of profitable development overwhelmed public needs.

Later Governors tried to reverse the situation, but because they needed the support of emancipist-businessmen like the Reibeys and the Thompsons, they had little success. So, for the next 20 years, the polluted Tank Stream endangered the health of the town, until a new source of fresh water began to flow through a tunnel built from the Centennial park swamps. This tunnel, almost 3.5 km long, is named after its engineer, John Busby, who was a hopeless supervisor of the work, rather than the convicts who dug through solid rock to make it.

In its natural shape, Sydney Cove extended as far as Bridge Street, but in the 1830s and 1840s convict labourers walled off the mud flats from the tide and 10 acres (4 ha) were added to the town behind the Semicircular Quay. Much of the rock they used was taken from another massive convict-built project, the Argyle Cut, which linked the east and west sides of Millers Point. Meanwhile, the Tank Stream had become an open sewer, and a drag on the commercial value of the land behind the wharves of Sydney Cove, so it was covered over and diverted under Pitt Street. This made it possible to connect Pitt Street and Macquarie Place with a lane, which was soon filled with warehouses.

The Bulletin Place warehouse whose remnant you can see today was built from Pitt Street along the northern side of this lane. The Pitt Street frontage was number 24, and it was here that *The Bulletin*, which had been founded a year earlier, relocated its editorial and printing departments in 1881. 'Banjo' Paterson recalled it as a 'shabby brick building hidden away among ship-chandleries, fish shops, and wool stores'. From this unpromising address, for the next 15 years, was published the most democratic, republican, nationalist, racist and misogynist journal in Australian history. By 1887 Sydney-siders called the lane 'Bulletin Place'.

The location of *The Bulletin*'s new offices on a site dating back to the convict years was a telling coincidence. Paterson's 'The Man from Snowy River' was published in *The Bulletin*, which encouraged the idea that the values in his romanticised picture of the outback were distinctively Australian. In turn, Paterson and other writers taken up by *The Bulletin* publicised a 'legend of the nineties', turning it into a glorious

One of the most famous sites in Australian literary history, the building from which *The Bulletin* was published, photographed in the 1960s (City of Sydney Archives, NSCA CRS 47/2288).

period of artistic and political ferment culminating in Federation and national self-consciousness. But 'the legend' neglected the darker side of the 1890s – the hardship of the depression, the violence of the great strikes – and the sinister picture of the country's past presented by *The Bulletin*.

Sydney's population in 1888 was mostly working class, and 63 per cent of the workforce were skilled or unskilled manual workers. Their overwhelming desire was to keep their hard-won dignity, self-respect and independence, but their vulnerability to disease and unemployment terrified them. Living in the slums of inner Sydney, where diseases were spread by inadequate drainage and sewerage, was like living with the pollution of the convict era. Working-class families died from tuberculosis and diphtheria, and there were almost yearly typhoid scares. Work was intermittent at the best of times, but when the property boom, which had contributed to Sydney's housing blight, ended in the late 1880s unemployment rose quickly. In 1888, when a government labour bureau was set up, one of its officials noted that the unemployed were 'at the point of revolution'.

In public, radical agitators – republican, socialist, feminist and anarchist – exploited resentment of the rich and powerful. Privately, working people regarded the Governor (Lord Carrington), the Premier (Sir Henry Parkes) and other leading politicians as frauds, questioned their morality, and mocked their talk of class harmony. Why should tradesmen make up 1 per cent of the Legislative Assembly when they were 36 per cent of the workforce? Was this a legitimate system of government? And if it wasn't, what had happened to the dream of a democratic Australia?

The founders of *The Bulletin*, especially J.F. Archibald and James Edmond, were obsessed by the convict period. They used it to construct an alternative history of Australia for a readership that wanted to understand why it felt so alienated from its rulers. Their answer to the question about Australia's lost democracy was that it had never escaped the legacy of the convict period. As J.F. Archibald explained the journal's origins:

> There was no health in the public spirit ... Sydney, socially, limped in
> apish imitation after London ideas, habits and manners. Politically and

industrially it was the same. And over all brooded in law courts, press, and Parliament, the desolating cruelty inherited from 'The System'. Sydney invited revolt from existing conditions, and *The Bulletin* was the organ of that revolt.

James Edmond expanded the idea to include the effect of the convict system on the people:

> the old slavish tint still clings to [Australia's] garments, and her chains of iron are merely exchanged for chains of gold ... English capital is 'imported' every day to 'develop the resources' of the new land ... and Australia is eaten up by the payment of eternal interest ... A century of grovel has almost abolished the virtue of self-reliance ...

In 1888 Archibald connected convictism to the unfinished march to self-government: 'New South Wales has never really been wholly emancipated. She drags a broken fetter at her heel ...'

The lesson of the convict period, according to *The Bulletin*, was that the cruel indifference of politicians and capitalists to the suffering of the people was systemic. Oppressive behaviour was not a failure of private morality alone but the result of a system that required it to survive.

Moreover, the oppressors were not free agents: they were minions of a British power structure, just as the Governors and the supervisors and recipients of assigned convicts had been. Their dependence on British money made the colony that they ruled dependent.

To maintain itself the system needed a language of deception. The system made the rulers corrupt, just as the convict system had, and they survived by shielding themselves with cant and hypocrisy.

The people living under this system, like the convicts, were passive or brutalised, but they also had a barely suppressed capacity for defiance of authority. The solution was to change the system by giving power back to a society made up of self-reliant individuals. Australia should be an independent republic, and *The Bulletin* began to promote that in aggressive, no-nonsense language.

This analysis was not 'scientific', nor even profound, but its strength lay in its appeal to feelings of oppression. Formulating the convict experience as 'The System' gave *The Bulletin*, in its early, radical years, a powerful historical framework from which to attack the status quo and respond to the public mood of alienation.

The Bulletin published historical articles about the convict period. Then in 1890 it discovered the man who would cement the journal's association with exposing 'The System' – radical journalist William Astley. As a young man Astley had become fascinated with convict history. He had interviewed ex-convicts, visited Port Arthur and other convict sites, and collected early colonial publications. After his first story based on this material was published by *The Bulletin*, he dominated its fiction pages for the next three years, his 'tales of the convict system' appearing almost weekly under the pen name of 'Price Warung'. In 1893 he became editor of the weekly *Australian Workman*, and a few years later he took part in a vigorous campaign in working-class suburbs to raise funds for Australia's first labour daily, the short-lived *Daily*

William Astley, author, journalist and labour agitator, who used the pen name 'Price Warung' for his stories of the convict system. A compelling orator, he influenced a generation of labour intellectuals (State Library of Queensland, 191928).

A façade of the building where *The Bulletin* was published still survives in Bulletin Place (Robert Irving).

Post. He also published a pamphlet, *Distrust the Politicians – A Letter to the Wage Earners of New South Wales*, and an incomplete novel, *The Strike of '95*, in which a revolutionary situation is created when it emerges that the wealth of the colony's capitalist clique is illegitimate, because it is based on the illegal appropriation of the colony's lands in the convict period.

Astley's 'convict tales' (there were over 80 of them published in *The Bulletin*) were not about convicts as romantic outlaws, or even as forced-labour participants in the taming of the natural world. His convicts were victims, often brutalised, who nonetheless resisted their oppression through cunning, violence, and their own culture. In his stories, conventional morality was inverted, and English institutions – the law, the church, the government – were despised. So scathing were they of ruling circles that a British publisher during World War II refused to republish them, and the Commonwealth Literary Fund refused to subsidise a selection of the stories lest the book give comfort to the enemy. As 'Price Warung' wrote in the Preface to his *Tales of the Convict System*:

> The Transportation System has knitted itself into the fibres of our national being ... No man can put his finger on the date when it ended, for the reason that it glided imperceptibly into the vigorous and splendid, if still imperfect, system [under which we live now].

In time, *The Bulletin* became less radical. Republicanism was dropped from its platform at the end of 1891, and socialism in 1896. What remained, alas, was its racism, first expressed in the notorious line from a leading article in 1888: 'No nigger, no Chinaman, no lascar, no kanaka, no purveyor of cheap coloured labour, is an Australian.' No longer a casual contempt for non-Europeans, *The Bulletin*'s racism became poisonous and persistent. As a narrative, this too was a product of *The Bulletin*'s obsession with the impact of the convict system on the country's struggle to rise from dependency to dignity.

Sylvia Lawson has explained the connection. The racist 'raving came out of terror: that they, who had plainly risen, might be dragged downward and back – into what pit of foreign barbarism they dared not imagine. It sufficed that they believed the pit was there.'

At 24 Pitt Street, the printers of *The Bulletin* were dangerously familiar with such a pit. Under the floor of the basement, the Tank Stream still flowed beneath the printing presses and the stores of paper. After a heavy storm, when the tide was full and the Tank Stream flushed the city, the polluted water backed up into the basement and the workers had to wade through mud and slush, spattered by the engine flywheel with filthy reminders of the convict past, as they laboured to produce the country's 'journalistic javelin'.

15

'GONE BUNG':
THE TERROR OF 1893

THE SAVINGS BANK IN
BARRACK STREET

The depression of the 1890s began to bite deeply in 1893, when unemployment rose steeply and the value of investments dived. A decade of frenzied speculation in pastoral properties, silver mining and urban building shuddered to a stop as foreign investment diminished, commodity prices fell, and farms baked in a prolonged drought. Half the building workers of Sydney were out of work. The private banks that had mightily benefited by lending recklessly during the boom now faced ruin. Capital fled the colony and panicking customers queued outside the banks to withdraw their savings. Thirteen banks closed their doors within a few weeks of each other as the financial structure of the country began to collapse.

Seeking an explanation for the depression, the public fastened onto the idea that the banks had deliberately created the boom as a debt trap for farmers and pastoralists so that their lands would pass to the banks. As *Hard Cash*, a clandestine anti-banking periodical, declared:

> [The Bank of New South Wales is] the largest land-gambling bank in Australia and it has in its possession more foreclosed stations than would make a decent-sized nation in Europe. It holds these lands illegally, and it MUST be forced to part with them somehow.

The depression was seen by the labour movement as an opportunity to reclaim the land for the people. Its agitators drew support from the deep xenophobia and racism that workers and their masters shared: as *Hard Cash* asserted, the banks were controlled by 'an avaricious ring of

The modest-looking Savings Bank in Barrack Street in 1870. Funds were allegedly carried from here by secret tunnel to keep the Commercial bank, opposite, afloat in the 1890s depression. The Savings Bank building survives but in a significantly extended form (Mitchell Library, State Library of New South Wales, SPF/15).

aliens [ie foreigners] and city Jews'. Among militants, the explanation for this was government complicity. They watched, bemused and then outraged, as bank directors illegally 'composed' their debts – paying a percentage of what they owed depositors – while colonial governments passed laws to ensure that the banking system survived. Clearly, representative government was at fault, and the remedy had to involve popular democracy: the inserting of people power into government to defeat the 'empire of finance'.

One morning in April 1893, in the midst of the banking crisis, a handwritten sign appeared on the front door of the Savings Bank in

Barrack Street. 'Gone Bung', it proclaimed. The police, having restored order among anxious depositors outside the bank, turned their attention to discovering the perpetrator, and arrested Arthur Desmond. He was a journalist and labour agitator recently arrived from New Zealand who wrote financial columns for *The Bulletin* and *Truth*. Surprisingly, the press averted its gaze from his arrest, the authorities having decided not to draw more attention than was unavoidable to the banking crisis. Desmond was fined and quietly released after a medical examination to determine whether or not he was insane (he was not).

A few days later, on the first of May, there was a gathering to celebrate May Day, the international holiday of the working-class movement. Only 100 or so socialists and the battered remnants of the trade union movement, recently defeated in the Great Strikes of 1891-93, turned up. The government took no notice.

The next day an unsigned handbill circulated in the city:

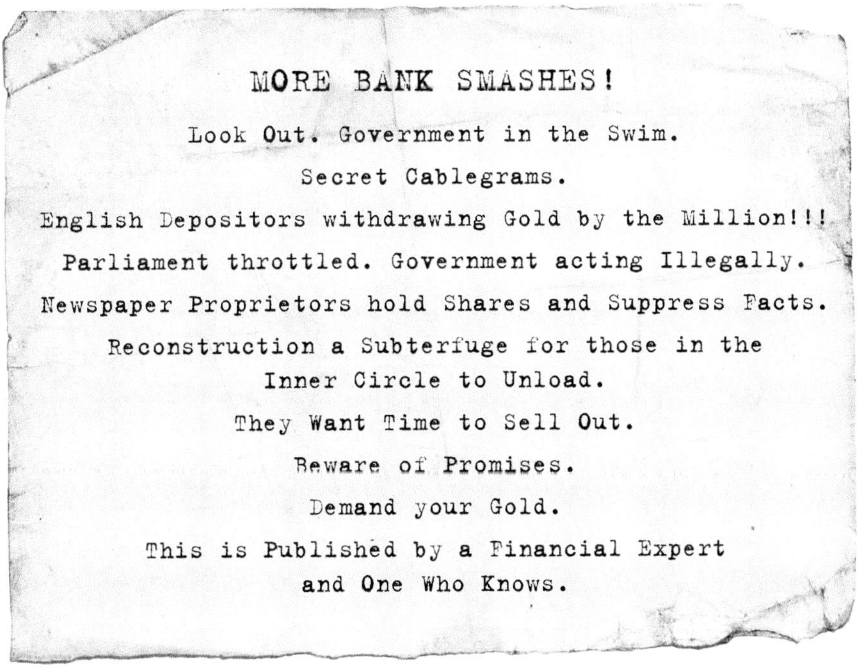

MORE BANK SMASHES!

Look Out. Government in the Swim.

Secret Cablegrams.

English Depositors withdrawing Gold by the Million!!!

Parliament throttled. Government acting Illegally.

Newspaper Proprietors hold Shares and Suppress Facts.

Reconstruction a Subterfuge for those in the
Inner Circle to Unload.

They Want Time to Sell Out.

Beware of Promises.

Demand your Gold.

This is Published by a Financial Expert
and One Who Knows.

Immediately, the Premier, Sir George Dibbs, signed a proclamation offering £100 reward for information leading to the apprehension and conviction of the author of this 'false, malicious and defamatory Handbill', whose intent was 'to excite alarm and distrust in the public mind, to defame the administration of the Government and to injure certain banking institutions'.

Why such a swift reaction? The idea of a conspiracy between the government, the press and big business to 'reconstruct' the banking system was such a routine radical charge that it could be ignored, but defamation of the ruling class was a much more serious matter. And Dibbs had personal reason to feel the danger. At the same time as he was saving the banking industry through his government's legislation, he himself, a bankrupt, was saved from ruin by a handsome cash gift subscribed by the grateful businessmen of Sydney. The legitimacy of the system was at risk when its leaders were accused of impropriety, especially when capital was fleeing the colony and militants were challenging Labor moderates for leadership of the workers. This was more than just a moment of financial crisis.

Hard Cash, which began to appear at this time, continued the handbill's attack, but with more facts and vitriol. To its writer-militants, it was time for the people to revolt. At the ceremony organised by the city's business leaders to hand over their gift to Dibbs, Dibbs waved a copy of *Hard Cash* in the air and blamed it for the flight of capital: 'This thing has cost us £3 million. What is the detective force of this city doing?' It was a call for ruling class action to eliminate 'distrust in the public mind', and to keep the Tank Stream of dirty deals flowing.

The detectives never arrested the people behind *Hard Cash*, and everything about its production is mysterious. How many copies were produced? Some later commentators say 200, but others suggest this is far too few, given its impact. How many issues were there? The greatest estimate is 40. Did they appear fortnightly or sporadically? Was it produced in Sydney's Sussex Street, or in Rose Street, Darlington, or in Underwood Street, Paddington, or 'in a cave near West's Bush in Paddington'? Claims are made for each of these sites, no doubt with some validity, for with the detectives on its tail, the journal could not afford to stay long in one place. The only way to contact its producers was through a box at McNamara's bookshop in Castlereagh Street. According to William McNamara, a boy would empty it and take away the proceeds of its sale from time to time. Those seeking to communicate with the editor were warned on the front page of *Hard Cash* that their letters would 'have to pass through three or four hands'. This was a seriously prepared underground operation.

A four-page squib on pink paper, *Hard Cash* was undoubtedly defamatory, defiantly incendiary and, in its understanding of ruling-class power at that time, right on the button. On its masthead was a quote from Walt Whitman: 'I am he who walks the state with a barbed tongue questioning everyone I meet.' A taunt to the state's insiders? Certainly the journal's writers were well informed. Below that warning appeared the caustic, driving motive: 'Money Rules the World.'

Hard Cash also understood the role of the capitalist press – its business was 'to hold a chloroform handkerchief over the people's nostrils while alien usurers pick their pockets'. *Hard Cash* detailed the banking interests of the Fairfax family, publishers of the *Sydney Morning Herald*, concluding by characterising them as 'a family of wealthy, avaricious, and insatiable usurers'.

Another recurring subject, under the heading of 'The Clergymen and the Banks', was the role of religion. The Christian priesthood, it said, had:

> sold the Great Redeemer for a money bribe ... While hired clergymen hold forth in sanctimonious tones to congregations of the well-to-do, Humanity is crushed and broken in the money-changers' horrible, blood-dripping accursed mills as of yore.

Then, in typical *Hard Cash* fashion, came the facts and figures: a list of 'reverends' and their share holdings.

Unable to find the people directly connected with the publication of *Hard Cash*, the police went after its distributors. In August, five book-sellers were charged. Among them were McNamara and Sam Rosa, also a socialist, who ran a bookshop on Parramatta Road in Petersham.

Hard Cash was a muck-rake, but it was also a weapon: 'the sacred right of revolt is an inherent right', it proclaimed. In Sydney at that time, as the misery of the working class increased, there were some young men and women who agreed. In July a seamen's strike began when masters cut wages to 3d an hour. When seamen refused to sign on at this rate they were arrested and sentenced to hard labour. Some of the militants began to consider the strategy of causing explosions with dynamite to spread fear and disarray in the ruling class. Rumour soon exaggerated the support for such a strategy, creating a moral panic whipped up by the daily press. Almost on cue there were a series of mysterious incidents on ships. On investigation of several fires and explosions it was found that they could *not* be linked to a supposed terror campaign by unionists. Of the remaining suspicious incidents – one minor explosion and several unexploded but ineffective devices – it seems highly likely that they were acts of provocation, for although one militant was arrested, the case against him was dropped for lack of evidence. It was known at the time that the police suborned witnesses in this case, so planting crude bombs may not have been beyond them either.

Most of the militants followed a different strategy. They looked at their movement and concluded that the trade unions and the Labor Party, by trying to reform the state, had lost their capacity to lead 'the democracy'. This argument supported *Hard Cash*'s description of the state as the home of 'hypocrites and brigands'. In a doss house near McNamara's they formed the Active Service Brigade. Like the Mutual Protection Association (MPA) of the 1840s, its organising principle was that 'every unemployed man should be an aggressive agitator'. Like the MPA, it insisted that every meeting of a democratic organisation should begin by electing its chair person, an idea that threatened the power of the perennial office-holders who ran the local Labor leagues. It stood for 'a commonwealth of free communities', a co-operative economy, decentralised government, and resumption and redistribution of 'the people's inheritance', the lands of the colony. But most importantly it aimed to create a popular tumult, through which the downtrodden would discover their power. To do this it organised itself along military lines. Its preferred actions included rallies of the unemployed at the Queen's statue at the top of King Street, disruption of church services, blasphemous processions on Sundays (behind a huge crucifix and bloody effigy identified as 'humanity ... murdered by the rich'), revo-

Arthur Desmond, looking like a city banker, and Sam Rosa, the radical bookshop owner who was gaoled in 1893 for distributing Desmond's scandalous anti-banking journal, *Hard Cash* (*Ross's Monthly*, March–April 1920; Mitchell Library, State Library of New South Wales, ML Q335.9/5 no. 16).

lutionary singing in the streets, and the capturing of conservative and Labor meetings: theirs was a politics of the spectacle.

The ruling class was terrified. Police surveillance of the unemployed movement was stepped up, the government shipping in extra detectives from Victoria and New Zealand to seek evidence against the leading agitators. Spies lurked in McNamara's. Undercover detectives, lacking shorthand skills, struggled to take down the speeches of Domain orators on Sundays. Several of the most militant of the radicals decided to go into hiding to avoid being arrested on trumped-up charges of planning terrorist activities.

It was in this situation of turbulence on the street and ruling-class determination to defend the system at all costs that the trial of the five newsagents who had been arrested for selling *Hard Cash* began in the Central Criminal Court. The charge was that the five had defamed the trustees of the Savings Bank of New South Wales. In an undated issue of *Hard Cash* a writer claimed that the bank was a 'trap to gather in the savings of the people for the profit of the joint-stock banks', and that there was a tunnel under Barrack Street from the government Savings Bank to the vaults of a private bank across the road.

Solemn testimony from bank managers and directors to quash the disturbing vision of portly capitalists scurrying through an underground tunnel with loads of cash was heard in court. But, ridiculous though this vision was, the idea that bankers were conniving to keep the banking system solvent for their own profit, at the expense of other capitalists and workers, was too close to the truth for comfort in ruling circles. Another militant, Joe Schellenberg, a refugee from Prussian militarism, hoped that popular derision aroused by the case would be increased if he volunteered that he too sold *Hard Cash*. He was promptly arrested and charged with that same offence.

Given that the case turned on the act of selling the paper, not much evidence was required for conviction, but the prosecution was determined to run a show trial against the socialists. Police testified about the kinds of literature the socialists sold and the speeches they made in the Domain. Questions from the defence barristers about the banking system were disallowed, and long speeches by the socialist booksellers were never printed in the daily press. Their convictions were never in doubt. Whereas the non-socialist booksellers were sentenced to prison terms of a few days, Rosa went to gaol for 3 months, McNamara for 6 months, and poor Schellenberg for 10 months.

Everyone knew that the person responsible for *Hard Cash* was Arthur Desmond. He became notorious after leaving Australia in 1895, as the author of *Might is Right, or Survival of the Fittest*, using the pen name 'Ragnar Redbeard'. It lauded the great conquerors of the past, denied that all men were created equal, scoffed at moral principles as 'slave logic', and told women that their 'grandest occupation' was bearing 'valorous sons'. It was titillating to some but irrelevant to most radicals.

When the revolt of the people failed to occur, the Active Service Brigade concentrated on the welfare of unemployed workers. It survived for almost a decade. Both bank buildings are still on Barrack

Street. The old Savings Bank is just a few doors up from George Street, looking much as it did in the 1890s, although an extra storey has been added. The Commercial Banking Company building is there too, on the corner of Barrack and George Streets, next to the former Head Office of the Bank of New South Wales, both of them imperiously facing Martin Place.

16

DEFENDING FREE SPEECH: ON THE STUMP IN 1915

SPEAKERS' CORNERS

By World War I, labour's open-air orators were a familiar sight in the city. After work, on Fridays and Saturdays, and sometimes during the week if politics was on the go – but never on Sundays, which the wowsers had excluded from the workers' week – they took to the streets with their 'stump' and their 'literature'. The stump was a simple wooden platform, often with a pair of wheels; when a large crowd was expected the speaker would stand on the back of a wagon or lorry. As the speaker delivered the message of social liberation, the literature-sellers moved through the crowd, for agitators believed that reading was as important as speaking in the education of the labour public. There were so many pamphlets and newspapers for sale by the Sydney branch of the Industrial Workers of the World (IWW) that its members needed a hand-cart to take their literature to meetings. With their usual cheek, and drawing attention to their opposition to the war, they called it the 'machine-gun carriage'.

The labour and socialist agitators did not have the street-speaking scene to themselves. Here is how *The People* described a Friday night meeting at Newtown Bridge in 1914:

> Three flaring beer joints (otherwise pubs) in full blast, a sky-pilot outfit
> with a cracked hurdy-gurdy harmonium, and a big three-horse drag
> with a load of fat exploiters, brother Hoskins of Lithgow [the anti-
> union owner of the ironworks] on the stump, among them, such was
> the field that two men of the Socialist Labor Party essayed to tackle on
> Friday night last. Verily, the path of the SLP man is beset with thorns,

but for two hours the principles of the coming social revolution was [sic] preached, nevertheless. From beginning to end the speakers were pestered by mugs, drunk and sober, in military uniform and in civil attire. A request came from the Jocook crowd [Joseph Cook was the Liberal Prime Minister] to the Socialist speakers to ring off, but the latter were not willing; they held on grimly ... The meeting was a fight from start to finish, and at its close hundreds remained in groups discussing the [war] situation. One cheering feature of the evening was the nods of approval made by erstwhile opponents in the crowd.

This meeting took place two weeks after Australia entered World War I, when jingoism was rampant. The pro-war hysteria could be comical, as when an alert citizen reported German submarines off the Victorian coast; they turned out to be a pod of whales. But as the war dragged on there was much that was sinister in the state's exploitation of jingoism.

Traditional public speaking space outside Hyde Park Barracks, now called Queen's Square: an orator addressing a crowd in 1903 (*Australasian*, 4 April 1903).

Almost 7000 people were interned, the press was censored, and thousands of suspected opponents of the war had their mail intercepted. Because it was leading the anti-war movement, the IWW was declared an unlawful association, and about 3500 prosecutions were launched under the regulations of the War Precautions Act. The presence of the capitalist Charles Hoskins in working-class Newtown, hoping to sap the strength of militancy by recruiting trade unionists into the army, indicated the reach and class character of this whipped-up patriotism.

Yet, as the SLP meeting shows, the case against the war also attracted support, even in the first flush of patriotic war-mongering. Six months later the situation was less favourable to the jingoes, and the crowds around the socialist and IWW stumps were growing. What had changed? Contrary to expectations, there had been no quick and glorious victory. In February 1915, enlistments began to fall, and by April they were negligible. Moreover, there was economic hardship among workers.

As soon as the war began, the Industrial Court (getting the nod from Labor Premier William Holman) froze wages, but there was no check on prices; they kept rapidly rising. So, as the public mood soured, the police decided to act. Taking advantage of the wartime acceptability of authoritarian action, they placed a ban on street meetings, and began arresting speakers for interfering with traffic.

Tom Barker, an IWW activist in Sydney, recalls how the Wobblies reacted:

> In Sydney for a while the police started to arrest men for speaking.
> We adopted all kinds of ways of counteracting this. We would start a
> meeting somewhere and then when the police were gathering around,
> we'd pack up and clear off to some other place that was already
> planned. By keeping the police running around, they never knew where
> we were going to be next. They got very tired of that. I remember on
> one occasion we had a wagon with a horse in it and a speaker sitting
> on a chair on the back of the wagon and everybody marching behind
> as we went along the street. That put the authorities in a spot because
> they couldn't say that the crowd was blocking the street or anything
> like that, which was their usual excuse for stopping these meetings.

Moreover, when the police were successful, the courts were unable to persuade the arrested speakers to pay their fines. Instead, they chose to serve their time in gaol (sentences were usually for one or two weeks), thus employing the tactic, pioneered by the IWW in the United States, of filling up the gaols. Within a few weeks, a campaign for the defence of free speech was in full swing. Labor leagues and socialist organisations passed resolutions asking that the ban on street meetings be lifted, and determined agitators continued to organise meetings.

Meanwhile, the internal struggles of the Labor Party were creating difficulties in caucus for Premier Holman. At the Labor state conference in April 1915 he expected trouble from a left faction in the trade unions, who would certainly use the free speech issue as ammunition. Holman's solution was to reshuffle Cabinet so that a former socialist agitator, George Black, became Chief Secretary. 'Baldy' Black was a likeable chancer who had made a career for himself as a labour journalist

Tom Barker, one of Australia's most famous radical orators, was often arrested for speaking 'on the stump' (State Library of Victoria, LT 10882/2).

and parliamentarian. He was once awarded a farthing in damages for winning a libel suit against John Norton, whose reputation as a drunkard and scandal-monger was notorious. However, Black had not forgotten what it was like to speak on street corners, and as a Minister he could now appreciate its value to the status quo.

On his first day as Chief Secretary, Black called the press corps to his office to announce his support for the agitators:

> These men who speak in the streets are men who have theories to expound, and should be permitted to do so there. I do not think there would be any interference with the public interests. There would be no interference with traffic, and I regard public speech as a great safety valve.

Two days later he repeated his support, softening the earlier statement's cynical close with a personal anecdote:

> Mr Black said that public speaking in the streets will now be permitted under certain conditions. He has a vivid recollection of being fined three pounds and six shillings for addressing a meeting from a lorry in Moore-street [now Martin Place] on the Federal referendum proposals. He told the constable who warned him not to harangue the assembled crowd that he was advertised to speak, and intended to do so if it cost him ten pounds. He got off lighter than he expected at the Police Court.

The police, however, continued to enforce the ban, causing further embarrassment to the government. When opponents at the Labor conference attacked the government's failure to protect free speech, Holman decided to make a further concession. His Minister announced that 30 sites in the city and surrounding suburbs had been agreed upon with the police as Speakers' Corners.

Of course this dispensation had limits. There would be no raucous crowds outside Parliament, or even in Queen's Square, where agitators had rallied the unemployed since the 1840s, because there were no sites listed between Circular Quay and Market Street. The deliberations of the powerful in the core precinct of business and government were not to be disturbed.

Government Minister George Black, who tried to limit and control the impact of public speaking by specifying official speaking sites in the city and surrounding working-class suburbs (Mitchell Library, State Library of New South Wales, P1/Black, George).

There were five sites around The Rocks, one at the bottom of Erskine Street, and a cluster of six sites at the southern end of the city between Goulburn Street and Central Railway. These were the areas in which the city's workers lived, in terrace houses jammed between warehouses and workshops. Here too were the halls from which the radicals organised their agitational campaigns. In 1915 the IWW hall was at 300 Castlereagh Street. When it was marked for demolition a few years later to make way for the entrance to the underground railway, the Wobblies found another headquarters (formerly a gospel hall, like their previous home) in Sussex Street, near Hay Street. The Socialist Labor Party had its headquarters on the edge of Railway Square; the Australian Socialist Party in 1915 had halls in Goulburn Street and the southern end of Pitt Street; and the International Socialist Club operated from Bathurst Street. This was the fringe precinct of the city's radicalised working class.

The official list also recognised the existence since the 1880s of open-air sites in the inner-city suburbs. These formed a narrow arc that stretched from Pyrmont and Balmain to the west, through Lilyfield, Leichhardt and Annandale, reaching into the southern suburbs of Newtown, Chippendale, Redfern and Surry Hills, before ending up to the east of the city in Darlinghurst and Woolloomooloo. There were 11 sites in this arc, no fewer than five of them in or on the boundary of Darlinghurst.

For the centre of the city, the 1915 list permitted speakers at some traditional sites. The most important of these were close to the markets in the Queen Victoria building and near the intersection of George and Bathurst streets.

These were the sites that were officially recognised, partly to appease the power of a radical tradition of open-air agitation that had existed for a generation, partly to provide a safety valve to relieve popular pressure on the state. Its promulgation was not a clear-cut victory for the defence of free speech, and what had been granted could be taken away.

This is exactly what happened when working-class agitation revived after the war. In 1919, the One Big Union had to fight to reclaim the right to hold meetings in Bathurst and George streets, and in 1923 the Communist Party deliberately held meetings there to defy a renewed state government ban on open-air agitation in the city.

17

THE BATTLE
OF CENTRAL

Central Station: Sydney's rail terminus, officially opened in 1906. It is a handsome landmark, intended by its political initiators to become one of the world's great railway stations. For one day in 1916 it was the site of an extraordinary act of protest and rebellion, a mutiny perhaps, that culminated in military gunfire, the use of bayonets, the shedding of blood, and death.

'Mutiny' is a contentious legal term and definitions vary according to nations' laws and cultures. The *Macquarie Dictionary* defines mutiny as 'a revolt or rebellion against constituted authority'. Depending on circumstances and definitions, a mutiny can involve one or more persons. Punishment for mutiny in a martial context can be death.

Since Federation in 1901, mutinies have not been uncommon in the Australian armed forces. The Royal Australian Navy has had at least 11 mutinies, possibly 19; mutinies have also been part of the Australian air force and the army, though not to the same extent. The army set an Australian record in 1942 with its conviction of 21 troops for mutiny in Palestine during World War II.

Australian defence authorities have successfully swept mutinies under the carpet; they also tend to be deleted from official histories. To minimise the number of actual mutinies, it seems the preferred Australian option has been, where possible, to treat alleged mutinous behaviour as something less legally controversial, thereby attracting less attention and scrutiny, and avoiding political fallout. Mutinies can be political and legal quagmires, and they are not conducive to recruitment.

Striking soldiers march through the city in 1916 behind battalion flags and the Union Jack, surmounted by the Red flag (*Daily Telegraph*, 15 February 1916, p. 7).

And so to an almost lost piece of Sydney, and military, history: what the Official War Historian Ernest Scott euphemistically described as 'serious trouble' at Casula in 1916. He glosses over it in 24 lines without mentioning bloodshed, but it is known elsewhere as the 'Liverpool Mutiny', the 'Battle of Central' and the 'Battle of Sydney'.

February 1916. The war is not going well: the Western Front is a foetid bog of mud and blood, and Australia is uneasily settling into its second full year of World War I. The nation is still trying to come to terms with the blood-soaked disaster of Gallipoli the previous year. Recruiting figures have plummeted and war weariness is creeping into the national soul. Initially, many people thought the war would be a short, thrilling adventure, but mounting casualty figures and the passage of time are shattering that illusion. The notion that the war reflects British imperial interests rather than Australian national interests is gaining ground, and before the end of the year an attempt by the government to introduce conscription will traumatise and divide the nation.

With this in mind, imagine breakfast time in the Light Horse training camp at Casula on the outskirts of Sydney. It is early morning, Monday, 14 February. Unrest is apparent as the men eat. There is a lot of anger and excited discussion. There is plenty of 'should' talk: 'we should do this' and 'we should do that'. The raw recruits have just been informed that the army has changed the training syllabus, increasing their training from 36 hours to 40.5 hours a week; the change and its sudden imposition are deeply resented.

There is a long list of grievances at the Casula camp already. A lot of the recruits, some only 17 years old, feel the food is not up to scratch. Others feel they have been worked too hard; some have recently been doing camp earthworks, working for 27 hours without a break. There have been problems with leave. Some of the officers are martinets. The syllabus change is the last straw.

Over a mug of tea, someone seriously suggests taking action: a walkout, maybe a strike, but certainly some sort of protest. There is a general feeling of being fed up with grumbling, and trying to go through the right channels. Among the breakfasters are men who have been involved in trade union activity in the past. Some may even have been influenced by the militant Industrial Workers of the World (IWW) organisation - this claim was made years later by IWW veteran Tom Barker.

So protest it is. Speeches are made, of varying degrees of sophistication; there is debate; delegates are elected; a quick plan of action is drawn up. Then at least 2000 men, possibly many more, all in army uniform, walk out of the Casula camp and head in an orderly fashion for the great training camp at nearby Liverpool. For the moment they intend to confront higher military authorities with their grievances and concerns, though some may have further plans in mind. Because of the numbers of men involved, Casula camp authorities are powerless to stem the tide.

Liverpool military authorities listen to the Casula men and agree to investigate grievances. But the 40.5-hour matter, they point out, is Commonwealth business, not a local issue. Basically, it is in the realm of the non-negotiable. Some of the men are satisfied, and decide to return to Casula.

But the audacious example set by the Casula walk-out has a flow-on effect in the Liverpool camp. There are undercurrents among the Liverpool men. Apart from the news about the training changes, the camp has had problems with leave, and there is the conviction, possibly unfounded but part of 'camp culture', that the camp is unhealthy and has an abnormally high mortality rate. During the year ending 30 June 1916, cerebro-spinal meningitis killed 256 recruits in Australia's crowded training camps. So thousands of the Liverpool men join the protest and quit the camp. For the protesters, the issue of the 40.5 hours rankles; if nothing can be done locally, then why not take their concerns to the wider world? They are on a roll. And with this in mind the men head for the town of Liverpool, and the railway station.

Figures relating to the number of troops involved in the Casula event, and subsequently, are shrouded in confusion; they have been consistently, and understandably, downplayed by military and political authorities, and most historians have simply echoed the official line. According to the *Sydney Morning Herald*'s account of the day, and a few political memoirs, some 15,000 men were involved; official sources claim it was only 'a small number' – figures in the hundreds are cited. Contemporary photographs of the protesters in Sydney, however, indicate that large numbers were involved, and this is supported by the logistical extent of the operation eventually mounted to end the protest.

Reaching Liverpool, some of the protesters decided to call it a day and broke off to commandeer the town's extensive alcohol supplies from various hotels. Liverpool was a camp town, and had a lot of grog. Because of the amount of alcohol liberated from bars and cellars, and the number of available drinkers, shops were relieved of cups, glasses, pots, pans and buckets for use as drinking utensils. Bread, pies and fruit were also appropriated. When retailers demanded payment for goods, the reply was 'Put it down to Kitchener', a reference to Lord Kitchener, Britain's War Secretary. Any opposition encountered by the sol-

Striking soldiers loot a pavement stall, Sydney 1916 (*Daily Telegraph*, 15 February 1916, p. 7).

diers was met with vandalism, and there was extensive property damage during the day.

Overwhelmed by the invasion, Liverpool police kept a low profile until the arrival of reinforcements from Cabramatta and Parramatta later that afternoon, by which time the majority of soldiers who had stayed in town were exhausted, or drunk, and order was restored with only a few fist fights between the opposing forces; 'several arrests' were made.

The bulk of the protesters had pushed on to Sydney before midday. They established a cordon around Liverpool station, blocked the tracks, and commandeered trains until railway authorities cottoned on and stopped the supply. The last train out of Liverpool was jam-packed with troops, the carriage roofs precariously crowded with men.

A large number of troops who made it to Sydney simply went home for the afternoon, but the last trainload had a political agenda. Disembarking at Central they lined up on the platform in fours, and began to march in a very long column towards the city. They were led by two buglers, a placard plainly announcing that they were on STRIKE and would not train for 40.5 hours per week, battalion flags, and the Union Jack surmounted by the Red Flag.

As the column moved through the city, down Pitt Street, into Hay Street, then George Street, soldiers snatched time to explain why they were on strike to ever-increasing crowds of onlookers, while keeping formation; they 'made a really fine picture, and, keeping good time, the fours properly dressed, the men marched as if on parade'. So wrote a *Sydney Morning Herald* journalist, noting also that the organisation on display indicated they were 'evidently under someone's leadership'.

The column wended its way down to the Quay, and then on to the Domain, where a 'smoko' was called. After that the column broke up. Troops spent the rest of the day drifting about the city in small groups, some sightseeing, others apparently bemused, wondering what was going to happen to them when they returned to camp. Many got into trouble. Food, tobacco, alcohol and lollies were appropriated in large quantities; some hotel windows were smashed, as were the windows of shops apparently owned by people of German origin – the windows of the German Club in Phillip Street were smashed. Foot police were taunted, squirted with soda siphons and assaulted with projectiles, including beer bottles, but mainly fruit and vegetables; there were reports of police being punched and kicked. A ground-floor window of the *Evening News* was smashed following evening headlines critical of the protesters; a verbal apology was extracted from newspaper staff. Civilians also got into the act and tried their hand at stealing and vandalism.

As night fell, sightseers crowded into the city. The *Daily Telegraph* was 'astonished' by the number of women who joined the crowds, 'some of them shamelessly arm in arm with drunken soldiers'. There was a knife-edge air of expectancy as crowds followed protesters around, waiting for anything to happen and for something to give, and hampering police in the process. When shots were heard near Town Hall at about 9 pm, a large crowd of nearby protesters and camp followers scattered into the grounds of St Andrews Cathedral.

A number of protesters engaged in a form of standover. Selecting wealthy-looking men they inquired, 'Are you the sort of person we are going to fight for?' When the answer was 'Yes', the men demanded, 'Well dig into your pockets and pay us.'

The strategy for ending the protest developed during the afternoon. An over-extended police force confined protesting troops to the city centre as much as possible, away from the waterfront and the Quay and possible further dispersal and mayhem. Hotels were ordered to close. Most city shops closed their doors; so did many eateries. An official army notice was posted around the city, ordering the troops back to their camps and advising that there would be an 11 am muster the next day (Tuesday); they were also informed that failure to comply would be a breach of military law.

All available metropolitan police were brought into the city, then despatched to the city police stations and onto the streets. Posses of mounted police went into action early in the afternoon and were targeted by protesters with blue metal, and lemonade and beer bottles; police and horses were injured. Motorcycle police acted as scouts, and all police and state motor vehicles were pressed into service ferrying squads of police to trouble spots as needed. On standby was a reserve of 250 civilian volunteers, including ex-servicemen. By the end of the day 32 soldiers had been arrested by civilian authorities.

A large contingent of armed loyalist troops was brought into the city and Central Station was virtually placed under martial law. From about 7 pm onwards the threat of fixed bayonets quelled any disturbances once the protesters had reached the station environs. Back on the streets, police used their batons. The despatch of protesters to camp began around 8.30 pm; the *Daily Telegraph* noted that many 'decent fellows who had been menaced into accompanying the rioters' went peacefully. The rounding-up process continued well into the early hours of Tuesday, 15 February. Loyalist troops remained on duty at key railway stations between Central and Liverpool throughout Tuesday and Tuesday night.

Some time after 10 pm (Monday), possibly closer to 11 pm, violence erupted at Central. As the entraining process continued, an iron gate was closed on 30 protesters. Apparently fearing that a decision had been made to trap them in the area near the station's toilets and the lost property depot, the men grabbed a fire hose and turned it full bore on the military picket, calling its members 'scabs' and 'blacklegs', and knocking a few over 'like ninepins'.

Despite being ordered to desist, the men maintained the water flow. A revolver was then discharged into the air, allegedly by a protester; this was the only suggestion all day that any of the protesters might have been armed. In response, the picket was ordered to 'fire low', and shots were loosed off into the protesters. Men fell. The firing was followed by a bayonet and baton charge. Press reports claimed the picket fired 20 disciplined rounds; bullet marks in the station's roof and a wall, evident for many years afterwards, indicated a less restrained response.

In the melee six protesters were wounded: there were bullet wounds to heads, a variety of baton and rifle-butt wounds, severe enough in one case to result in a coma, and a bullet-shattered kneecap. A police constable involved in the charge sustained a facial wound requiring an X-ray. Two civilians trying to get home were wounded: one was clubbed, the other shot in the leg. The station's refreshment rooms served as a makeshift hospital, and an army medical team tended the wounded.

A protester from the 6th Light Horse was killed by a bullet through his left eye and bayonet wounds to his neck and shoulder; he was 19 years old, and he died in the arms of a police constable who risked personal injury to comfort him. The corpse was spirited away to the city morgue, and official attempts were made next day to depict the soldier as the man with the revolver, and one of the protest's ringleaders.

At the 11 am muster next day, most men turned out. An official warning was given that the new training syllabus would go ahead, and that any refusal to train would be regarded as 'assisting the enemy'. It was a clear indication that any future protest would feel the full weight of military law.

The rest of the day went ahead normally. It was pay day, so the men were paid; those normally entitled to leave were granted their leave. The army took the pragmatic approach: no direct order had been disobeyed by protesting troops, and there had been no intention to subvert military authority, therefore no mutiny had taken place. No strike had taken place because in the lexicon of military law the word 'strike' does not exist.

However, soldiers identified as protest leaders were arrested upon their return to camp, and later summarily discharged. The grievances the protesters had raised were investigated, and enough changes were made to restore calm.

Despite claims that the invasion of Sydney by rebellious troops had been instigated by German agents and saboteurs, a view supported by Sir George Pearce, Minister for Defence, most people were happy to settle for something less dramatic; the *Daily Telegraph* preferred a less inflammatory explanation, and confidently put it down to the work of 'a few malcontents'. The behaviour of troops in the camp town of Liverpool suggested alcohol was to blame. This interpretation appealed especially to the strong Prohibition lobby in New South Wales, headed by Brigadier Albert Bruntnell of the Salvation Army, who was also the State member for Parramatta.

Following a referendum in June, all hotels in New South Wales closed at 6 pm, ending late-night trading. This was intended to be only a war precaution, but continued until the restoration of late-night closing in 1955. The long 'six o'clock closing' interregnum was a shot in the arm for the Sydney underworld, as the illegal supply of alcohol and venues generated criminal fortunes and careers, created networks of corruption, and laid the foundations of organised crime in New South Wales.

18

VERE GORDON CHILDE
AND THE PACIFISTS

THE FRIENDS' MEETING HOUSE,
DEVONSHIRE STREET

The Religious Society of Friends, or Quakers, built their new Meeting House in 1903 in the working-class suburb of Surry Hills. Its design reflected Quaker values: simple, accessible to the community, and democratic in its approach to worship. The Quakers practise social responsibility and non-violent resistance. For over a century, in these quiet rooms they have counselled conscientious objectors, encouraged adult education, and provided a space for activists to reflect on their efforts for peace, community-based child care, and Aboriginal rights.

Not surprisingly, our suspicious rulers have kept an eye on the activities at the Quaker Meeting House. During Easter 1918, words spoken there elicited a patriotic panic that threatened a clergyman with gaol and began a process that drove one of Australia's greatest scholars into exile.

The occasion was the Third Inter-State Peace Conference, which brought together over 100 delegates from 54 organisations, including pacifist groups, Labor Party branches, trade unions and socialist bodies. The clergyman was Frederick Sinclaire, the President of the conference, who was prosecuted and fined for remarks deemed 'prejudicial to recruiting'. The scholar was Vere Gordon Childe, who was hounded out of Australian academic and public life by a campaign whose vindictiveness and persistence has rarely been equalled.

The conference occurred at a time when the jingoes were getting desperate. Twice the voters had rejected Prime Minister Billy Hughes's

Society of Friends' hall in Surry Hills, venue of the Australian Peace Conference where Gordon Childe delivered a speech that resulted in his being blacklisted for employment at Sydney University in 1918 (Robert Irving).

referenda to introduce conscription. A Royal Commission had confirmed the brutal truth that death and injury in the trenches and indifference among young men at home had created a huge deficit in recruitment that threatened the capacity of Australia to contribute to the imperial war machine. Labor councils and branches of the Labor Party were calling for a negotiated peace. The government responded by increasing its repression of the anti-war movement, through arrests and prosecutions, raids on printers, censorship of mail, and the gaoling of activists.

In self-defence, radicals from otherwise disparate groups sought each other out, and began to make connections. The peace conference allowed them to build a program for common action. Since the beginning of the 20th century the peace movement had stood for international arbitration of disputes, curbs on the armaments industry, opposition to conscription, and democratic control of foreign policy. At this conference, these aims were confirmed, but in a new context: as part of a radical analysis in which 'the abolition of the Capitalistic system' was asserted as the only way 'the fundamental causes' of war could be 'permanently removed'. Other resolutions called for 'understanding and agreements between the peoples of Asia and Australia', for the mobilisation of women against war, for freedom from censorship, and for trade union action for peace. An alliance of pacifists, socialists and feminists was taking shape.

When Vere Gordon Childe rose 'in ungainly fashion' to deliver his paper, no repercussions were expected. He was not a good speaker. According to an observer, 'his speech, when on his feet, was slow, measured, scholastic - no vigour, no fire, but insistent, relentless, hammer-like'. His topic was 'Peace, Imperialism, and Internationalism', and, as he admitted, it was an academic discussion of J.A. Hobson's views, plus

Young Sydney radical intellectual Vere Gordon Childe, on the eve of his departure in 1921 for London as NSW Labor government adviser on the progress of social democracy in the world (Flinders University of South Australia Library, Evatt Collection).

a few throwaway lines warning against Australia's retention of Germany's colonies in the Pacific.

Not long after his return from Oxford, where he had been secretary of the university branch of the anti-war Union of Democratic Control and the Socialist Society, Childe became Senior Resident Tutor at St Andrew's College in the University of Sydney. The college was autonomous, so Childe was not employed by the university. The university would never employ him: senior members of staff were heard to refer to him 'with shuddering dismay and horror' as 'that swine'. It is worth remembering that many professors worked for military intelligence as censors. They could not move against him, however, until he associated himself with the Sydney radicals by delivering a paper at the peace conference.

The business and professional elite now opened up two fronts against the college, threatening to withdraw financial support and to create difficulties between the college and the university. The principal of the college, in distress, appealed to Childe to resign – for the good of the college – and Childe agreed. There were other positions that a brilliant graduate of Sydney and Oxford could hope to fill, or so Childe mistakenly believed.

A few weeks later a university selection committee recommended him for a post in Ancient History with the Department of Tutorial Classes. Up to this point, the role of military intelligence may only be inferred, but now there is evidence of their intervention. In an earlier letter to the Australian High Commissioner in England, where he was studying, Childe asked whether it was true that to obtain a passport in Australia one had to agree to join the army. If so, he could not return because he 'could under no circumstances give any pledge which might involve my helping, however indirectly, in a war which I believe to be destructive to civilisation and true liberty'. This letter now began to circulate among the university higher-ups.

Next, the Secretary of the Department of Defence contacted the Chancellor about Childe. And the Chief Censor in New South Wales (who was, coincidentally, the Professor of French) proposed the bland but insinuating form of words that was used by the University Senate to explain its refusal to accept the selection committee's recommendation: it was 'not desirable at this time' to appoint Childe.

In private, Childe reacted with despondent irony – 'I now recognise that ideals are an expensive luxury that should be left strictly to poets and visionaries' – but publicly he increased his activity. He organised lectures on peace issues, wrote for a British labour paper on the Australian labour movement, and tried to set up a Labor College. He took pleasure in altering his will so that a bequest that would have gone to the university was diverted to the Labor Council of New South Wales. And his friends rallied round. Bill McKell (the future Governor-General) twice raised his case in the Legislative Assembly (since it was clear that the University Senate had applied a 'political test' that the University Act expressly forbids). The Australian Peace Alliance issued a press statement listing Childe's case as the third since 1900 in which the university had restricted the freedom of the teacher. But he was unable to find regular employment. Eventually, letters from Percy Brookfield, McKell and others extracted a promise from the Queensland Labor government that it would find a post for Childe.

So Childe went to Brisbane, and then to Maryborough to teach in the Grammar School. He lasted one week before the press campaign, fed by military intelligence, incited the boys to refuse his tuition. Back in Brisbane he continued to write for the labour press and to lecture for the Workers' Educational Association, waiting for another opportunity. He had exactly the right qualifications, it seemed, for a temporary lectureship at the University of Queensland. He applied, but was passed over. In the archives of the university, the minutes of the Senate show that what radicals suspected at the time was correct: Childe's Oxford academic achievements were ruled inadmissible because he had not enlisted. Moreover, by some curious logic the successful candidate's war service was deemed to make him a suitable university teacher. Without evidence, it is asserted that 'Mr Childe's fitness in this respect is open to grave doubt.' This is how these supposedly apolitical scholars reacted when the foundations of their world-view were crumbling.

On the other side of politics, however, another door opened for Childe. NSW Labor was preparing for an election, and Childe was called upon to become the Labor leader's private secretary. The main campaign speech, written by Childe, included commitments to industrial democracy and further state enterprises. When Labor won the election, Premier John Storey arranged for Childe to be accepted into the Public Service. Although Childe was a lonely radical voice in government, Storey valued his advice precisely because it linked the party with social democratic thinking in the rest of the world. For that reason he was happy to accede to Childe's request to continue his assessments of progressive European and North American state policies as a member of the Agent-General's staff in London. And then the last blow fell. Storey died in office, Labor lost the 1922 election, and the new conservative government removed Childe from his position in London.

Stranded in England because of his native land's rejection of him, Childe also had to contend with English academic disdain for colonials, especially for one who was known as a socialist and pacifist. But his powerful intellect could not be denied. In Britain, where liberal academic ideals were stronger, Childe had an academic career of great distinction, becoming one of the world's foremost prehistorians and archaeologists. His books included the phenomenally popular *What Happened in History* and *Man Makes Himself*, books that introduced a generation of readers in the 1940s and 1950s to a materialist understanding of history.

Childe returned to Australia in 1957. He accepted an honorary degree from Sydney University, the university that had scorned him in the past, and delivered mordant talks on the failure of Australian socialism. However, concluding that he was no longer capable of contributing to scholarship, and wishing to avoid becoming a burden on the state (he had never married), Childe decided to commit suicide. A few weeks later, he placed his spectacles on the edge of a cliff in the Blue Mountains, and the next day his remains were found below Govett's Leap. His friend Bert Evatt, leader of the Parliamentary Labor Party in Canberra, spoke at a service for him at the church in North Sydney where Childe's father had been the rector.

MERV FLANAGAN, LABOUR MARTYR

THE MORTUARY STATION, REGENT STREET

Lucy Taksa

Built in 1869, the Mortuary Station was the city's major landmark for public displays of grief. Mourners would gather here to wait for the funeral train that would take them and the cortege to Rookwood cemetery.

In 1917, the Mortuary Station witnessed a massive outpouring of collective grief by Sydney's working people. On Saturday, 1 September, thousands of bare-headed trade unionists marched from the Sydney Trades Hall to the Mortuary Station as part of a funeral cortege for Mervyn Ambrose Leslie Flanagan, a striking carter who was killed the day before during an altercation with a scab in Camperdown.

A month before, 5780 railway and tramway workers had launched the greatest industrial upheaval in Australian history by refusing to work with a new system of recording work times and output that had been implemented in their workshops in late July by the Department of Railways and Tramways. They regarded it as the thin end of the wedge which would lead to the adoption of a modified version of the Taylor system of management. They opposed not only the time and motion studies that were the system's most prominent feature, but also its implementation by a public authority.

Workers saw this system as a direct attack on collective work practices and trade union principles. From early August, the dispute quickly spread to other workers, other industries and other parts of the state.

Hundreds of thousands of women, men and children marched in processions alongside the strikers on a daily basis. Mass meetings were held in Sydney and in towns throughout New South Wales. This huge mobilisation of working people became known as the NSW General Strike of 1917.

The government's response was coercive. In mid-August it amended The Coal Mines Regulation Act to enable the introduction of 'volunteer' labour, arrested strike leaders and dismissed striking railway and tramway employees for misconduct. From 20 August the deregistration of unions involved in the strike became a daily affair, and on 24 August the Acting Premier announced that the government would no longer negotiate with individuals or unions acting on behalf of the strikers.

During the General Strike of 1917, thousands of unionists and their supporters marched from the Trades Hall to the Mortuary Station on Regent Street accompanying the corpse of labour martyr Merv Flanagan (Charles Pickering, Mortuary Station, Redfern, 1871, Mitchell Library, State Library of New South Wales, SPF/35).

Such actions led to more protests and demonstrations, and the ranks of the strikers swelled. When the government instructed Benevolent Societies to refuse assistance to the families of strikers, the atmosphere in the working-class suburbs was bitter.

By the beginning of September 77,350 workers in New South Wales had joined the strike. They represented 33 per cent of the state's registered trade union membership. Only 15,000 of the NSW Railways and Tramways Department's 48,000 employees did not strike.

Flanagan's funeral procession on 1 September stretched for over a mile (1.6 km), accompanied by the deep boom from a muffled drum, the weird notes of funeral music, the rhythmic tread of feet on the whitened roadway and the measured tolls from a nearby convent bell, marking the passing of the dead. The mourners, accompanying the corpse of their comrade, marched in solemn array before a funeral hearse led by four horses. They held up traffic for one hour. Seeing 'those weeping folk, that sorrowing wife', the dead man's four sons, aged between 2 and 11, 'clothed in deepest black, their eyes reddened with tears of grief' and the 'broken men' alongside them, moved one eyewitness to remark on 'the tragedy of despotism now sweeping over our fair land gathering its victims one by one'.

The man in the polished wooden casket had been carried out of a little cottage at 4 Marsden Street, Camperdown before being lowered into the hearse. His wife's cries of grief as she leaned on the arms of other mourners stabbed the hearts of observers like daggers.

Merv Flanagan was born on 27 November 1884 at George Street, Waterloo, eldest child of John Flanagan, a horse-driver, and his wife Susan Laura McMahon. He was one of seven children, two others having died. He grew up in Sydney's inner-city suburbs of Chippendale, Camperdown and Darlington, surrounded by industrial waste, disease and poverty. When Merv was two years old a typhoid epidemic swept through the inner city and four years later his childhood was marred by a great economic depression.

In 1905, soon after he married Beatrice, the illiterate 19-year-old daughter of a sawyer from Newtown, Merv was described as a groom. By 1909 he had become a general carrier's carter and two years later a carrier's clerk. In 1917 he was a horse-driver.

The funeral procession of Merv Flanagan wends its way through Sydney. It was a massive public display of grief and solidarity (*Daily Telegraph*, 3 September 1917).

Merv had been a bit of a larrikin. Between 1901 and 1912 he had many brushes with the law for 'throwing stones', being drunk and disorderly and assaulting a police constable. Although kept in check for the next five years, in 1917 during the general strike his fiery temperament re-emerged.

At 4.45 pm on 31 August, opposite Camperdown Children's Hospital in Bridge Road, Merv became involved in the altercation that cost him his life. In response to the abuse that he and some fellow striking carters hurled at two passing strike-breaking carters, one of them – the driver, Reginald James Wearne from Bingara – raised his revolver against the group. Merv was shot through the heart. His comrade, Henry Williams, was hit in the leg.

Reginald Wearne, brother of the conservative NSW Member of Parliament for the rural seat of Namoi, W.E. Wearne, was part of the army of 'volunteers' brought to Sydney during the strike's second week by the Fuller government, with help from the Farmers' and Settlers' Association and the Primary Producers' Union. The strike breakers were given temporary accommodation at camps established at the Sydney Cricket

Ground, Taronga Park Zoo and the Eveleigh railway workshops.

Strike breakers had to be enlisted from rural districts because of the pressure on those in working-class communities to maintain solidarity. Moral and physical abuse of scabs was widespread. On 8 August, Robert William Forster, aged 44, pleaded guilty at Newtown Police Court to a charge of attempting to prevent a tramway officer from working at the Enmore Terminus, and Bernard Gleeson was convicted of breaking a window of a tram and of assaulting its conductor at Marrickville. Horace Hoyle, 18, was charged with behaving in a riotous manner in Liverpool Street on 7 August. He had been part of a crowd of about 400 that had followed Sergeant McBride and the prisoner he escorted from Goulburn Street, near Trades Hall. Edward Webb, a mail assistant with the Postmaster General, aged 31, pleaded guilty to having used obscene language while loading mail into a wagon at Sydney Railway Station. Shortly after he had completed the job at 8 pm, Webb was heard saying to a crowd of strike-breaking workers: 'If I had my way I would bomb every man who assisted the Commissioners against the strikers.' Similarly, Phillip Hogan, aged 33, was charged with having threatened violence to Arthur John Hubert with the intent of preventing him from following his lawful occupation. Hubert was working in the mail rooms at Central station when Hogan allegedly approached him saying: 'You mongrel! Talk about scabs! We'll find out now who the scabs are.' Hubert put his docket in, and did not appear at work again.

Such action was not limited to locals. On 18 August, several thousand people gathered outside the strike breakers' camp at the Sydney Cricket Ground, where they 'boo-hooed', hooted, and threw blue metal at the 'volunteers' inside until being dispersed by mounted police. In the city, strike-breaking tram drivers were called scabs and 'mongrels' on different occasions by John Lucy, Mary Francis and Amie Calderwood (wife of a Wharf Labourers' Union official). Roy Darcy and John Martin Collins did the same in Glebe, while George William Albert Moody used offensive language against 'free' labourers working near Pyrmont Bridge.

The government's policy of enlisting strike breakers and distributing revolvers to some of them only increased working-class hostility. The killing of Merv Flanagan did little to dampen tempers. Violence continued during the first week of September. In facing a charge of using insulting words against Constable Dobie in Glebe, it was alleged that Jane Taylor, an elderly local resident, was the leader of a gang of women who went to the stables to harass 'volunteers'. A few days later, a number of women threw acid at a 'loyalist' on Glebe Island bridge as he was driving strike breakers back to the Cricket Ground.

How did Merv Flanagan die, and how was his killer dealt with by the authorities?

As one might expect, there are differing versions of how Merv Flanagan lost his life. The *Sydney Morning Herald* reported that the incident began at 4.45 pm in Bridge Road, when a group of striking carters began yelling abuse at two 'volunteer' carters.

'You — scab and —,' called one, as another jumped on one of the lorries being driven by a 'volunteer' and yelled, 'You —, I'll get you' before hitting the driver, Reginald James Wearne, and knocking him off his seat. Similarly, the driver of another lorry was attacked and knocked off his cart. He was then seized by the strikers and taken to a nearby vacant lot, where he was beaten. Wearne, drawing a revolver, approached the group of strikers. They responded by throwing rocks and stones at him. Wearne aimed at the group, and shot Henry Williams in the leg and Merv Flanagan through the heart.

Merv's brother, James Everard Flanagan, commonly known as 'Darkie', subsequently saw events rather differently. On the day of the shooting he had been with his brother throughout the afternoon, leaving him only for a few minutes to go to the blacksmith's shop. On his return he saw his brother on the ground. He stressed that neither he nor any one else had assaulted Wearne on that afternoon. He did, however, admit telling Wearne what he thought of him in forcible language after his brother had been shot.

In 1952, Wearne offered his own interpretation. As he put it:

He [Flanagan] got shot by jumping on my back from behind while I had the gun pointed at his mate in front of me. He jumped too high, or I jerked him over my shoulder, but the first I knew I shot Flanagan was when I saw him stagger around in front of me and fall down. We did not know he had been shot or that he was dead until I forced his brother to come with me on a horse sulky to Hospital.

THE SEQUEL

The judicial system responded to Mervyn Flanagan's death in a bizarre fashion, seemingly confusing assassin and victim. James Flanagan and Henry Williams, the striker who was wounded, were arrested on a charge of having used violence to prevent Wearne from following his lawful occupation.

Wearne was charged with both 'felonious slaying' and manslaughter and was released on bail to his brother, Wearne MLA, who apparently assured the defendant, 'You have played the game in [a] manner which makes your family feel proud.'

Mr Love SM evidently agreed with Wearne's sentiments. He dismissed the 'felonious slaying' charge, following in the footsteps of the City Coroner, who had drawn a similar conclusion. Intriguingly, there seems to be no record of Wearne ever being tried on the manslaughter charge. As *The Worker* noted on 6 September 1917, the circumstances of Wearne being granted bail with such ease and speed were also highly irregular.

By contrast, James Flanagan and Henry Williams were convicted of their charges. At Newtown Court in mid-September 1917, Mr Clarke SM concluded that the case had been proved 'beyond any doubt' and that the evidence brought forward by the defence had not been conclusive. He stressed that the offence was a serious one, punishable by a fine of £29 or 6 months' imprisonment, but he decided instead to send both men to gaol for 3 months, because he recognised 'that a certain amount of punishment has already been inflicted. Williams has been wounded and Flanagan has lost his brother as one of the results of this most unfortunate strike.'

For the many who assembled at the Mortuary Station and travelled to the Roman Catholic section of Rookwood Cemetery, where Merv was buried, Merv's action's stood out as a beacon – going to the aid of a mate who was being harassed by an armed man made him a martyr of the class war of 1917.

In stark contrast, Reginald Wearne assumed the mantle of a coward, and the kid gloves treatment he received from the authorities confirmed the views and actions of those thousands of workers who joined the general strike and protested against government coercion.

A deputation of strikers' wives (some of whom appear to be Aborigines) to the Premier in 1917. Determination and anger are etched on their faces. Many had husbands working at the Eveleigh Railway Workshops; some Aborigines were employed there (*Sydney Mail*, 15 August 1917, p. 10).

20

A NERVE CENTRE
OF REVOLUTION

RAWSON PLACE

The history of political surveillance as a continuing but publicly unac-
knowledged function of the Australian state begins during World War
I, when the British government insisted that Australia co-ordinate its
military and police intelligence operations in a Counter Espionage
Bureau, under the ultimate authority of MI5 in London. As there were
no secret agents of the Central Powers in Australia, the bureau was free
to develop a predilection for sniffing out possible seditionists. These
might even be found among Labor parliamentarians, or so Prime Minister W.M. Hughes believed after he was expelled from the Labor Party.
Pacifists, militant trade unionists, Irish republicans and revolutionary
socialists also came under suspicion by this Labor 'rat' and his government. Right from the start, Australia's security service, egged on by
Hughes, had a clandestine political role: the surveillance and intimidation of radicals.

Its task was made easier by the concentration of offices of radical
organisations in Rawson Place. Named after the current Governor of
New South Wales, this short street was pushed through from George
Street in the early 20th century to link up with the new railway station
at Central. Within a few years its single block was itself central – to a
revolutionary politics that despised the imperial connection. In 1914
it contained three imposing, multi-storeyed buildings, each containing hundreds of little offices. Rawson Chambers occupied almost the
entire northern side, from Pitt Street to the Prince of Wales hotel on

George Street. Today the characterless McKell Building has erased all traces of it. But we can still see what Rawson Chambers looked like, for facing it, on the southern side, were two similar hives of radical activity: Station House, on the corner with George Street, and Daking House, on the Pitt Street corner – both of which have survived.

The trio of buildings on Rawson Place was soon integral to the labour movement in this proletarian part of the city. In 1917, Daking House was 'one of the nerve centres' of the General Strike, according to the *Daily Telegraph*. By 1920, the headquarters of two of the largest unions of industrial workers – the railway workers and the coal miners – were in Rawson Chambers. Smaller and less militant unions followed, among them those for telephone operators, undertakers, bank officers, tramway officers, and water and sewerage workers. Rawson Place was its own labour community, and at the end of each day its activists and officials, militant as well as moderate, gathered in the basement cafés and the Prince of Wales pub.

In the feverish political atmosphere at the end of World War I, it was the presence of the militant industrial unionists that mattered in the politics of Rawson Place. In 1919, after a failed effort to get the NSW Labor Party to support the One Big Union, the socialists and industrial militants, led by A.C. Willis of the coal miners' union, walked out of the party conference, and many of them joined the Socialist Labor Party, which had an office in Rawson Chambers. Not long after, Will Andrade, the country's leading publisher of socialist pamphlets, sent a trusted colleague up from Melbourne to open a branch book-shop in Rawson Chambers.

It is no surprise, then, to find that in 1920, looking for a sympathetic environment, the first Consul-General of the Soviet government of Russia set up his office across the road in Station House. From room 28 in that building, Peter Simonoff spent the next two years directing revolutionary politics in Australia into channels approved by the Communist International in Moscow. He introduced a new source of intrigue and conspiracy to Rawson Place.

Born in Russia in 1883, Peter Simonoff was part of the exodus of Russian radicals fleeing the repression that followed the failed revolution of 1905. By 1917, many of them had arrived in Australia via China

An early picture of Rawson Place in Sydney, when it was the centre of revolutionary activity in Australia. On the southern corner with George Street is Station House, next to Daking House. The Prince of Wales Hotel is on the northern corner, with the west side of Rawson Chambers just visible (City of Sydney Archives, SRC 994.441 PH1).

and Japan, setting up active socialist groups in Sydney, Melbourne and Brisbane. In that year, Simonoff, who was already a supporter of the Bolshevik faction of the Russian socialists, became secretary of the Union of Russian Emigrants in Brisbane and the editor of its paper, *Workers' Life*. So when the Bolsheviks seized power in November, he was able to persuade the new regime that he should represent it in Australia, and in February 1918 he received a cable from Trotsky appointing him Consul-General.

The Australian government, which did not recognise the new regime in Moscow, had no intention of dealing with Simonoff, who was already under suspicion because of his membership of the Industrial Workers of the World – which had been banned by the government in 1917. For his part, Simonoff made no attempt to work with the government or have the ban lifted, instead lecturing to Labor councils and writing articles for the labour press on the Soviet system. The Sydney *Worker* published his pamphlet, *What is Russia*, with an introduction by Arthur Rae, one of the rebels who left the NSW Labor Party in 1919.

Simonoff quickly became notorious, especially in xenophobic circles of the ruling class, where Russians were replacing Germans as 'the enemy within'. In a letter to the Prime Minister's private secretary, a conservative journalist wrote, 'I recognise in Simonoff the superior-criminal type, the suavity, the "Jew-eye", the delicate "thief-hands", the modulated voice of persuasion, and the look with which he regards one as a possible dupe.' Such letters of denunciation were the product of a 'red scare' that was being manufactured by the capitalist press and secret conservative paramilitary organisations in order to justify the military intervention of the Allied powers in Russia to assist the counter-revolutionaries. The government played its part by banning Simonoff from lecturing and publishing, and when he defied the ban, arresting, fining and gaoling him for 6 months for refusing to pay. It also tried to deport him.

Government persecution did not deter Simonoff. He was dedicated to his mission by conviction as well as self-interest, although jealous comrades liked to remark that he preferred to eat in good restaurants and drink in the saloon bar after he became Consul-General. As soon as he was released from gaol he set up his office in Station House. From here he published a monthly periodical, *Soviet Russia – Official Organ of the Russian Soviet Government Bureau*. He also initiated a move to form a Communist Party, an action designed to bypass the existing socialist organisations, and, no doubt, his comradely critics.

Filled with zeal for the cause of proletarian revolution, the conspirators, all in their early thirties, were alienated from the previous socialist generation by its failure to stop World War I. Bill Earsman was a Scots-born engineering tradesman who had been active in the industrial militancy of 1917-19. In Melbourne he had joined Frederick Sinclaire's Free Religious Fellowship. Chris Jollie Smith, the daughter of a Presbyterian minister, left Melbourne as Earsman's partner in 1919. She was a socialist and a solicitor. Together they set up a Labor College in Sydney; it quite possibly held some classes in Rawson Place. Jock Garden, who

Exiled from Tsarist Russia, revolutionary socialist Peter Simonoff came to Australia, and after 1917 became Consul-General for the newly formed Russian Soviet government. He helped form the Australian Communist Party (frontispiece of P. Simonoff, *What is Russia?* Sydney, 1919).

had been a clergyman in Victoria, was a union official. In 1918, as leader of the industrial militants, the 'Trades Hall Reds', he became secretary of the Labor Council of New South Wales. Meeting secretly in Simonoff's office, these four conspirators drew up a manifesto, and in October 1920 they organised a small gathering of socialist delegates for a 'unity conference'. This meeting culminated in the announcement of the formation of the Communist Party of Australia. The first meeting of its Provisional Executive was held the next day in Simonoff's office.

His mission completed, Simonoff returned to Russia in 1921, where he was rewarded with a series of Comintern tasks. He disappeared in 1938, presumably executed during Stalin's purges. Earsman, after spending the mid-1920s in Russia and Britain, was refused re-entry to Australia. He left the British Communist Party in 1927. Like Garden, who had resigned from the Australian party the previous year, Earsman subsequently made a successful career for himself in the mainstream labour movement. Chris Jollie Smith, alone of these conspirators, remained loyal to Communism. After being admitted as a solicitor in New South Wales, only the second woman to be admitted, she built up a practice based on political and industrial cases. In the Depression she did much unpaid work defending evicted tenants and victimised workers. She briefed counsel for the 700 miners charged during the 1930 lockout in the Hunter Valley coal mines, and in 1934 secured a writ of *habeas corpus* that led to the release of Egon Kisch, the Czech Communist journalist who had dramatically defied a federal government ban on entering Australia by jumping from the ship onto the wharf at Port Melbourne. In 1951 she briefed H.V. Evatt in the High Court case that successfully challenged the validity of the Act introduced by Menzies to ban the Communist Party.

Jock Garden, one of the founders of the Australian Communist Party. In later years he became a labour movement numbers man and fixer (City of Sydney Archives, NSCA CRS 54/79).

Apart from creating the party, Simonoff's other legacy to Communism was his room in Station House, but when the party took it over, apart from a few correspondence files, there was just a pile of half-smoked cigarettes. Before long the party was also operating from Rawson Chambers, where it ran a Communist children's Sunday School. Even when the party moved into separate premises (in Sussex Street in the 1920s and 1930s, George Street in the 1930s and 1940s, and Market Street in the 1940s and 1950s) there was always a strong Communist presence in Rawson Place. *The Workers Weekly* and its successor, *The Tribune*, were published from Rawson Chambers, and for some years the Pioneer Bookshop traded from Station House.

In 1923, Rawson Chambers was the venue for a conference of Plebs Leagues devoted to developing independent working-class education, and the Militant Women's Movement held its first conference there in 1929. An organisation of radical teachers, the Educational Workers' League, had its office in room 32 of Station House in 1933. The Movement Against War and Fascism also had its office in that building in 1937. The party's publishing arm, Modern Publishers, operating in the late 1930s, was in room 312 in Rawson Chambers. Room 438 was the office of the Left Book Club in 1939. The Australian Labor League of Youth was in room 814 of Daking House in 1939–40, and when the Commonwealth government closed down the Friends of the Soviet Union, it was operating from room 432-3 in Rawson Chambers. The Communist Party's fight to regain its status as a legal party was directed by the NSW Legal Rights Committee from Daking House, and after the fight was won, the Sydney District Committee of the party met in Station House in 1943.

For over 30 years Rawson Place was indeed a 'nerve centre' of revolution. One can imagine how busy the government spy assigned to it must have been.

21

THE TRADES HALL REDS VERSUS THE DOMAIN FASCISTS

One morning in 1921 several hundred unemployed men set out to present their demands to the state's Treasurer, Jack Lang. Arriving at the Treasury Building on Bridge Street, they found it well guarded by police. However, they had a plan. As they surged towards the entrance, and were beaten back by police batons, a drayload of stones pulled up on the edge of the crowd just at the right moment, and three demonstrators jumped up on the dray. Police reinforcements arrived just in time to see a volley of stones smash a window on the ground floor. Blocked by the police, the demonstrators switched targets. Running down Elizabeth Street, they broke a window at the Labour and Industry Department before dispersing quickly to avoid arrest. That night their grasp of strategy was again displayed. Gathering at the Trades Hall, they sent a deputation to the Labor Council, then holding its weekly meeting, which passed a resolution demanding that the Labor government comply with its promise to dismiss policemen who used their batons on the unemployed.

A few days earlier there had been an uneasy commemoration of Anzac Day, for there were many ex-servicemen among the 15,000 unemployed in Sydney. Two hundred and fifty were sleeping under canvas in Hyde Park, and there were others huddling beneath newspapers and tarpaulins in the Domain. The war-induced boost to the economy was over.

This was the fourth year of agitation on the streets, and in the big end of town, among those who ruled the state, there was a sense that the enemy was now within the gates. Political life had polarised, and the leaders of the unemployed were part of a strong left wing in the labour movement. The Labor Party had expelled the supporters of military conscription, thereby also ridding its ranks of many who opposed industrial militancy. After scabs broke the General Strike of 1917, the militants embraced the idea of One Big Union to avoid future defeats. Meanwhile, the socialists were turning to Communism, following the Bolshevik revolution in Russia. By 1918, control of the Labor Council in Sydney had passed into the hands of the industrial militants and the Communists. The street demonstrators could now look to 'the Trades Hall Reds' for resources and co-ordination.

This was not the intended role of Trades Hall. An imposing, Italianate, four-storeyed building on the corner of Goulburn and Dixon Streets, its octagonal tower peering south and west over the city's railway yards, wharves, markets and factories, it was a monument to the idea that the mission of the labour movement was to discipline the working class. Built on a gift of land from the state government, it took shape slowly, in five stages, from 1893 to 1916, financed by the savings of the unions and the proceeds of the annual Eight Hour Day festivities. By the early 1920s over 50 unions had offices in the building, and it was where the Labor Council met on Thursday nights. Mostly the Council delegates adjudicated disputes between unions and discussed their relationship with the Labor Party, but in these radical years they also talked about working-class power. Responding to similar pressures, the building itself took on new functions, as it became a centre for labour's alternative public. Its two halls, numerous meeting rooms and library were always busy. Among the intellectual and cultural bodies that used the facilities in the 1920s were the Labor Choir, the Eight Hour Day Committee, the Labor Research and Information Bureau, the Labor College, the Militant Women's Committee, and union-owned Radio 2KY, which broadcast from the Tower Room. The executive of the Labor Party moved to room 32 in 1923, and there was a separate Trades Hall branch of the Communist Party. The Trades Hall Reds and their allies in the political wing of the movement protected and encouraged these activities.

At the same time, their enemies were mobilising the business and officer classes behind the banner of imperial patriotism, gaining control of the main ex-servicemen's organisations, and creating a fascist

Trades Hall in the early 20th century: the labour movement made an architectural statement about its significant place in the politics of the state (courtesy of UnionsNSW).

movement along Italian lines in the middle-class suburbs and country-side. Major General Sir Charles Rosenthal, the model for the sinister character 'Kangaroo' in D.H. Lawrence's 1923 novel of that name, was

Colonel Rosenthal, who organised the proto-fascist demonstrations in 1921, is the model for the Australian fascist leader 'Kangaroo' in D.H. Lawrence's novel of the same name (Mitchell Library, State Library of New South Wales, PXA 1011/23).

the organising secretary of The King and Empire Alliance, which had a secret paramilitary capability: stored in disused railway tunnels under Sydney were the arms and ammunition (sent by the federal government) that it would use against the Bolsheviks and Sinn Feiners if they embarked on revolution.

The Sunday following the demonstration by the unemployed was May Day, the international celebration of working-class solidarity, and this year, for the first time, the march was organised by the Labor Council. At two in the afternoon, after song sheets had been handed out and the red flag raised, 4000 men and women set off from Eddy Avenue to march to the Domain, singing 'Solidarity Forever', the 'Marseillaise' and the 'Red Flag'. According to the *Daily Telegraph* there was 'an immense assemblage' in the Domain, where the Acting President of the Labor Council took the chair. A young girl brought greetings from the Socialist Sunday School, and other speakers demanded the release of the last two of the 12 Industrial Workers of the World (IWW) prisoners who had been framed by police, as a Royal Commission in 1920 showed, for conspiring to burn down Sydney in 1916.

Suddenly there was a melee. A wedge of 20 or so men waving Union Jacks pushed towards the platform to capture the red flag. The *Telegraph* described a 'scene of wild tumult':

> The leaders of the demonstration gathered around the red flag, and with the light of combat in their eyes, excitedly called on those in front to form a last line of defence, a rampart of human bodies against the point of assault. A few lines of the 'Red Flag' were sung, and the flag itself waved defiantly. Meanwhile, the Union Jack was faring badly. It was torn ... and shreds of it strewed the grass.

Foiled, the attackers withdrew. As they did so, unobserved by most in the crowd, part of a Union Jack was set alight. From the platform, Tom Glynn, one of the released IWW prisoners, broadcast the incident, saying that:

> as an Irishman he had no love for the Union Jack, or any other flag save the red flag that waved over the meeting that day. (Cheers) He hoped they would stand solidly behind that flag and their movement ... to break up the capitalistic class and demand that the boss should give the workers back all that he had stolen. (Cheers)

The organisers, not foreseeing that the incident would be used against them, closed the meeting on a high note, declaring that henceforth May Day would take the place of the annual Eight Hour Day celebrations.

By the time the Labor Council distanced itself from the burning of the Union Jack it was too late. At the office of the *Sydney Morning Herald* a 'trio of popular [military] officers' announced that 'the Diggers about town' had authorised them to organise a counter-demonstration at which the May Day disloyalists 'must be prepared to take the consequences'. Calls for 'drastic action' were made by suburban branches of the ex-servicemen's organisations and reported by the daily press. According to the British Services Association, the supporters of May Day were 'outlaws, and as such they should be hunted down'. The Waverley sub-branch urged 'stern, direct action ... to force the authorities to remove the traitors from our midst otherwise we recommend to all comrades to act themselves in the matter'. The *Herald* salivated at the idea that the Reds would soon meet their 'Nemesis, with the whip of retribution in one hand and the scales of judgment in the other'. At the very least, the Reds should be banned from parading and meeting in the Domain.

Meanwhile, Sir Charles Rosenthal and his 'Diggers about town' were mobilising their forces for the following Sunday in the Domain. Because they blamed the state Labor government for not suppressing 'the Reds', there was no pretence that they were acting on the same side as the lawful forces of order. Their 'patriotic demonstration', in fact, was also a challenge to constituted authority: it was a cover for fascist violence.

This was understood both by the government, which ordered 800 police to the Domain on Sunday, 8 May, and by the Labor Party, whose *Labor News* warned that under the guise of 'loyalty leagues' a 'military caste' was plotting to take over the state. Among the huge crowd in the Domain – estimated to be over 100,000 – were bands of 'Digger Vigilantes', to whom alcohol was dispensed during the afternoon from two lorries on the edge of the crowd. Because the crowd was so large, the loyalists had arranged to set up four different speaking 'stumps'.

In addition to those four 'loyal' meetings, there were three separate labour platforms. The Socialist Labor Party's was the first to be menaced. Each time Ernest Judd tried to speak he was counted out, and the vigilantes gathered more tightly around his supporters.

Judd knew what was in store for him and finally drew a pistol out of his pocket:

> What followed was chaos. In the wink of an eye Mr Judd had disappeared. Groans rent the air. Flags were waved. Crowds surged around the platform ... Superintendent Drew at once grabbed Mr Judd, and a large number of police ran to the superintendent's assistance. All was confusion. The police found it difficult to make any headway out of the yelling mob ... In the midst of the uproar was the crash of wood. The table and chair were dashed to pieces by the irate crowd. One man was knocked out (*Sydney Morning Herald*, 9 May 1921).

Both Judd and the superintendent were among a dozen people later treated at Sydney Hospital. The platform of the Communist Party was next. Jock Garden, the secretary of the Labor Council, was speaking. The vigilantes rushed the platform, crying out for Garden's blood. As the mob destroyed the platform, the police protected the speakers, hoisting a woman above their heads and using a police van to rescue those most in danger. Then it was the turn of the meeting organised by the Labor Party's Ex-Servicemen's section, where the speakers were on the back of a lorry. Their attempt to dissociate themselves from the militants did not save them. Putting their shoulders under the tray of the lorry, a group of vigilantes tipped the speakers into the crowd, where they were kicked until rescued by the police. One of those injured was the Minister of Agriculture, Captain W.F. Dunn. As the police drove the lorry away 'Rosenthal's hoodlums' (as the *Labor News* called them) burned a red flag. At the end of the afternoon five men (including Judd) had been arrested.

But the violence was not over. That night a mob of about 2000 loyalists raced through the southern parts of the city, labour's precinct, intent on besieging the halls where the militants were used to meeting on Sunday nights. The mob gathered first in Elizabeth Street outside the Concordia Hall (which survives today as the Australian Hall). Here a Communist Party meeting had been advertised, but when the caretaker saw the mob he refused to open the hall.

Next to be targeted was the Southern Cross Hall in Castlereagh Street, in the building that today houses the Catholic Club. Here the Labor Party's Propaganda Committee was in session. As inflammatory speeches were not to be expected from the parliamentarians and aldermen who were running this meeting, the mob moved on to the Australian Socialist Party hall, above Fay's boot shop on the corner of Liverpool and Pitt streets (it also still survives). Soon the blocks between Castlereagh and George streets were filled with Rosenthal's men, and there was a solid line of police from Pitt Street to the Central Police Court. Inside the Socialist Party hall, about 300 supporters of the party were holding their regular Sunday night meeting. Although outnumbered, they refused to close their meeting. The police then proceeded to break up the crowd, helped by a decoy (probably a policeman) waving a Union Jack and drawing the crowd to other parts of the city. All was dark at the

Crowd of North Shore and country loyalists, fired up by proto-fascist organisers, angrily demonstrate their loyalty to Britain and its empire in the Sydney Domain in 1921 (*Sydney Mail*, 11 May 1921).

Trades Hall, so they moved on, finally dispersing around midnight. 'On Monday morning the trains were full of young lightweights, with badges on and portmanteaux packed, going back to the country – a dreadful put-away,' the *Labor News* reported.

Meanwhile, the Communists at Liverpool Street had decided to defy the fascists by organising a self-defence force and holding further 'red flag' meetings. The King and Empire Alliance was not so resilient – there was little organised opposition to the labour militants on the following Sunday when 50,000 gathered in the Domain. On this occasion the militants all spoke from the same platform, specially constructed to be high and sturdy, and their main resolution proclaimed the right to free speech. After the meeting, *The Communist* reported:

> The body-guard lifted up on their shoulders the big box which had been the platform and marched along from the Domain ... As the Reds marched, the crowd followed behind until practically everybody in the

Socialist orator Ernie Judd, surrounded by police, defies the loyalists in the Sydney Domain (*The Sun*, 16 May 1921).

Domain was walking in procession behind the big box – the symbol of the Right to Free Speech ... The procession was about 1000 yards in length [almost a kilometre] ... There were more Reds in Sydney than it was thought, and the crowd was overjoyed at finding the fact out. So the procession did not stop at the gates of the Domain. On went the Reds and their sympathisers along the Woolloomooloo roads, singing revolutionary songs. It was growing dark as the crowd, now numbering thousands, broke up in College Street.

That evening the Concordia Hall was opened, and Mrs Adela Pankhurst Walsh addressed a large meeting on 'The Flag'. A member of the famous suffragette family in England, she was married to the Seamen's Union leader, Tom Walsh, whom the federal government would try to deport in 1925. She said that 'the Union Jack was not the flag of the workers, but the flag of the master class. The Red Flag, which was the workers' flag, was red-dyed with the blood of thousands of martyrs of

Concordia Hall, Elizabeth Street, early 20th century: this was a favoured meeting place for the left of the labour movement (City of Sydney Archives, NSCA CRS 51/2655).

the working class.' Outside, a few hundred 'press-inflamed patriots' demonstrated with Union Jacks, before moving off to repeat the performance at the Liverpool Street hall. There were no arrests.

The culture and politics of the left grew despite these dangerous conditions, surviving subsequent fascist attacks by the New Guard and its successor 'secret armies' in the 1930s, 1940s and 1950s. The labour precinct survived too, at least for a time. The halls and meeting rooms of labour's alternative public in the southern part of the city continued to be used for another 40 years, before the property boom swept most of them away in the 1960s and 1970s. The most emblematic of them all, Trades Hall, still stands, now owned and refurbished by Unions NSW. With its banner room and labour museum, its spaces for alternative culture and ideas, Trades Hall continues to nurture the radicalism of the city.

22

AUSTRALIA FOR AUSTRALIANS: FRED MAYNARD MAKES PROGRESS

St David's Hall, Surry Hills

Malcolm X, the charismatic spokesperson of the Black Muslims in the United States, treasured a memory of going as a very young child with his father to meetings of the Universal Negro Improvement Association in rural Michigan. Twenty years earlier in New York, Marcus Aurelius Garvey, a West Indian, had founded the Association, for which Malcolm's father was a dedicated organiser. At its peak it had four million members, making it the largest black liberation movement in the history of the United States. Government repression, culminating in Garvey's deportation on a trumped-up charge, and white hatred, had forced it more or less underground by the time Malcolm wrote about these meetings, where a few earnest supporters gathered in private homes:

> I remember seeing the big shiny photographs of Marcus Garvey that were passed from hand to hand. My father had a big envelope of them that he always took to these meetings. The pictures showed what seemed to me millions of Negroes thronged in parade behind Garvey riding in a fine car, a big black man dressed in a dazzling uniform with gold braid on it, and he was wearing a thrilling hat with tall plumes. I remember hearing that he had black followers not only in the United States but all around the world, and I remember that the meetings always closed with my father saying several times, and the people

chanting after him, 'Up, you mighty race, you can accomplish what you will!'

Did Malcolm X know then that in faraway Australia there were black followers of Marcus Garvey? In Sydney, on land that had been stolen from Indigenous people by invading Europeans, there was a branch of the Universal Negro Improvement Association (UNIA) in 1920. In fact, Black Nationalist ideas had arrived earlier, brought to Australia by West Indian and African seamen, and by the famous black boxer Jack Johnson. Articulate and politically aware, Johnson, who had suffered only one defeat in the ring, and that one hotly disputed, was prevented for some time, by racism, from challenging for the world heavyweight crown. But he was a hero to black people everywhere. His fights in Australia in 1907, and again in 1908, when he established his claim to be the greatest fighter in the world by knocking out the Canadian, Tommy Burns, at Sydney Stadium, emboldened Australia's Indigenous people to believe that they could accomplish what *they* willed; it was a new stage in their struggle to win self-determination.

One of the leaders in this new stage had a photograph taken of himself with Jack Johnson. In 1907, the Coloured Progressive Association organised a farewell dance for their champion. It was held at Leigh House in Castlereagh Street, a centre for Sydney's cultural and political radicals from the 1880s to the 1930s. In the photograph, Johnson is surrounded by black admirers, and among them is a man who would become one of the leaders of the first united Aboriginal political organisation, Fred Maynard.

Fred Maynard identified with his mother's people, the Worimi, from the Port Stephens area north of Newcastle. Born in 1879, he spent several years as a bullocky, drover and photographer, before coming to Sydney, where he found work on the wharves. Here he came into contact with black seamen from around the world, many of whom spread Garvey's message by distributing the UNIA paper, *The Negro World*. Maynard read voraciously, frequented the Domain, and went to meetings in the halls where city workers gathered on Sunday nights to discuss their emancipation. By World War I he was an activist in the Waterside Workers' Federation.

But for Maynard, working-class politics was not enough, particularly as the labour movement ignored Aboriginal rights and workers used their whiteness to claim privileges at work and in national life. Moreover (and this is not properly understood), the subjugation of the Aboriginal people was not completed by the invasion and the early decades of land theft by Europeans, and nor did it proceed thereafter in an orderly fashion; it proceeded (and proceeds still) in fits and starts, picking up and slowing down according to the needs of the institutions of white society, especially the markets and state organisations of capitalism. In the early decades of the 20th century, white oppression was intensifying. In response to market pressures, the NSW government evicted Aboriginal families from their farms (many of which were on the north coast), herded them into reserves, and ramped up the kidnapping of children from their families so that they could be placed in institutions and prepared for servile labour.

The rhythm of subjugation also depended on the degree of resistance the oppressors met, and in New South Wales the Aborigines Protection Board, the chief instrument of white rule, had an unexpected confrontation with this truth. Hit by the new round of dispossession and family destruction, Aborigines fought back. Young people absconded from their 'employers'; others, too 'incorrigible' for the servility required by the system, were sent back to the reserves. Fred Maynard contacted a white woman who set up a refuge in Homebush for these 'recalcitrants', to get them out of the way of the police and officers of the Board. He also toured the Hunter region, mobilising his people to resist white depredations, and using the white media to publicise the cause of Aboriginal rights. Episodes of more overt defiance also occurred. In a daring raid early in 1925, he helped black families from Nambucca Heads rescue their children from the Board's custody on Stuart Island.

A few months later, Maynard launched the Australian Aboriginal Progressive Association (AAPA) in Sydney. Its strength depended on the network of activists that had developed in the fightback on the mid-north coast, and the power of the ideology of black pride and self-determination that had reached Australia via the followers of Marcus Garvey. Among the office bearers of the new organisation were

Maynard, Tom Lacey and other men who had been members of the Sydney branch of UNIA in 1920.

Garvey, who often expressed himself poetically, summed up his philosophy:

Europe cries to Europeans. Ho!
Asiatics claim Asia, so
Australia for Australians
And Africa for Africans

'Australia for Australians' – it was an electrifying phrase for Maynard and his fellow workers, and it became the slogan of the AAPA, inscribed in a circle around their logo, in the centre of which was an Aboriginal man. There was no argument about who was Australian in this context.

In May 1925 the first conference was held in Surry Hills, at St David's Hall, where Labor leagues (party branches) met. Over 200 delegates from Indigenous communities all over the state attended. There were women as well as men, young people and elders among the delegates. The president, Fred Maynard, opened the conference: 'Brothers and Sisters, we have much business to transact, so we will get right down to it.' He went on: 'We want to work out our own destiny', and then he specified the four areas of self-determination that Garvey's movement had identified: 'spiritual, political, industrial and social'. Like many other self-taught adults, Maynard was a powerful thinker and orator, and could call on a wide knowledge of history and current politics. He said that the legislation enforced by the Aboriginal Protection Board 'stinks of the Belgian Congo', a reference to the horrific exploitation and slaughter of the Congolese under the Belgian colonialists at the turn of the century.

Soon the Association grew to 500 members, in 11 branches. An office was set up in Crown Street. Its Manifesto, which was sent to federal politicians and the press, went right to the heart of successful black politics, then, now, and in the future: land rights and protection of cultural identity. It called for a land grant for every Aboriginal family, an end to the removal of children from their families, full citizenship rights, the scrapping of the Aboriginal Protection Board and its system of reserves, a Royal Commission into the condition of Aborigi-

Sydney 1907: Coloured Progressive Association dinner for visiting world champion American boxer Jack Johnson, who was denied the world heavyweight crown on the basis of race. This dinner was attended by Aboriginal activists including Fred Maynard (courtesy of John Maynard, from his book *Fight for Liberty and Freedom: The Origins of Australian Aboriginal Activism*, 2007).

nes, and the setting up of a federal body, composed of Aborigines, to take charge of the affairs of Indigenous Australians.

Although there were three further successful annual conferences, in Kempsey, Grafton and Lismore, the AAPA could not withstand the relentless hostility of the Board's officers and the police. The leaders were refused entry to the reserves, and their letters were intercepted, so they were unable to sustain the contacts necessary to turn initially

St David's Hall, Arthur Street, Surry Hills, where 200 Aboriginal delegates met for the first conference of the Australian Aboriginal Progressive Association in 1925 (Robert Irving).

successful agitation into a viable movement. Board officers undermined the AAPA's representations to politicians by telling lies about the organisation and its leaders. And it failed to elicit support from white progressive organisations. Apart from one or two white sympathisers, not a single white politician, clergyman, union leader or revolutionary showed any interest in the AAPA. After four years the leaders were burnt out, and the organisation faded away.

Fred Maynard married and returned to the wharves. In the 1930s, in what might not have been an accident, he was injured so badly at work that he could no longer support his family. But the legacy of his political work remained. Families held onto memories of the hope and excitement and pride that the AAPA's crusade had generated; this was true of the families of Pearl Gibbs, Bill Onus and Gary Foley. A tradition of black political thinking and campaigning had been established. In 1937, the Aborigines Progressive Association was set up in Sydney by Jack Patten and William Ferguson, who drew upon the name and the lessons of the AAPA in 1938 as they organised 'The Day of Mourning Conference and Protest' to counter the white celebrations of the sesquicentenary of the invasion.

Waterside worker Fred Maynard, founder of the Australian Aboriginal Progressive Association, and his sister, in The Rocks in 1927 (courtesy of John Maynard, from his book *Fight for Liberty and Freedom: The Origins of Australian Aboriginal Activism*, 2007).

23

JOY AND ROUGH MUSIC ON THE PICKET LINE

According to the headlines in the *Labor Daily*, in July 1929 Sydney was a battlefield:

TIMBER WAR

EXCITEMENT AT GLEBE

FIVE THOUSAND PEOPLE ROUND HUDSON'S
UGLY POSITION NARROWLY AVERTED

DEMONSTRATION TO-DAY

But more than timber workers were involved in this war. As unemployment grew at the end of the 1920s, employers had gone on the offensive. Notorious decisions by Arbitration judges had cut wages and worsened working conditions, particularly on the wharves and in the coal mines, places that provided a livelihood for tens of thousands of working-class families. The 8000 timber workers in New South Wales learnt their fate in January 1929, when Judge Lukin decreed that employers could make changes, including extending the working week by four hours, cutting wage rates, doubling the ratio of juniors to adults in the yards, and reclassifying jobs as unskilled. And so a war between labour and capital began; it was ended only by the mass unemployment of 1930. In 1929 more than a million work days were lost through workers being on strike or locked out by their employers.

Hudson's in Glebe, on Pyrmont Bridge Road, where the Blackwattle Campus of Sydney Secondary College stands today, was one of the epicentres of class conflict in 1929. For a period of six months before the events described by the *Labor Daily*, the timber workers had been locked out for refusing to work under Lukin's award. Their resistance developed into a struggle that involved the arc of working-class communities around the centre of the city.

The Disputes Committee of the Labor Council set out a plan for the fight. Workers at each of the 70 or so yards or mills, if they elected a picket captain and picketed their workplace, would be entitled to strike pay. Meanwhile, the leaders at the centre would try to persuade the most vulnerable employers to re-hire their workers under the old award, thus breaking 'the Timber Combine'.

With growing unemployment, raising money for strike pay was difficult. Bert Evatt, a barrister who would become a future leader of the federal Labor Party, and his wife Mary Alice Evatt, who championed

Timberland: Blackwattle Bay, Hudson's timber yard, the Kauri Hotel and Wentworth Park (in the distance). During the timber workers' strike in 1929, this area was the scene of running battles between pickets and scabs protected by police (Mitchell Library, State Library of New South Wales, ON2/37).

May 1929: the Enmore Timber Workers' Relief Depot distributes provisions collected locally for the strikers (*The Sun*, 25 May 1929).

contemporary art and formed a co-operative with Balmain women to make clothes, could afford to give £20 to the fund, but most working-class families, making do on less than £3 a week, could only give a few pence. It was obvious that organising in the community would be crucial to the success of the strike, so attention turned to collecting groceries for the strikers. This meant that the distribution of relief had to be localised. Labor Party and Communist activists swung into action, collecting groceries and setting up relief depots. Within a few weeks there were 20 depots, mostly in the inner ring of working-class suburbs: Pyrmont, Glebe, Balmain, Annandale, South Annandale, Leichhardt, North Leichhardt, Five Dock, Bankstown, Newtown-Erskineville, Enmore, Botany, Rosebery, Mascot, Redfern, Paddington, Belmore, North Sydney, Ryde and Oatley.

Women were active in the campaign from the start. In February, Edna Ryan, whose leadership in the 1960s and 1970s of the campaign for equal pay for women would make her famous, led a march of women from the Trades Hall to an Industrial Peace Conference in the Town Hall, where a few of them managed to get into the gallery to heckle the speakers. This protest was small, but it was symbolic, giving more support to the Labor Council secretary, Jock Garden, as he argued that industrial peace on the bosses' terms was not what his constituents wanted. He then walked out of the conference. Equally theatrical was the raid by wives of timber workers on the offices of the Timber Combine in May. Led by Edna Ryan and Joy Barrington (whose partner was Esmonde Higgins, the editor of the *Workers' Weekly*), they caught a tram to the Quay, refused to pay ('Send the bill to the government'), burst into the office of the Combine and shouted at a trembling Combine official: 'How would you like to work an extra four hours in the timber yard?' Thrusting into his hands a resolution from a meeting of the wives, they dashed downstairs before the police arrived.

As the struggle became more community-focused, the tactics changed. Women in Glebe picketed a grocer who hired out his car so that the employers could transport scabs to the timber yards on Blackwattle Bay. The grocer looked at his diminishing receipts and decided to put his car in the garage. Other shops in these working-class suburbs were boycotted when it became known that their owners sided with the Timber Combine. Meanwhile, collecting food for the strikers and their families was a never-ending task. Some grocery chains made regular donations, but it was persistent door-knocking by committed supporters that was most significant, politically and in terms of results.

In Bankstown, Betsy Matthias, a former Wobbly (member of the IWW), became the picket captain, a natural progression from her role as organiser and collector of strike relief. In Glebe, where a women's committee met fortnightly, the depot was at the house of Mary Lamm. She recalled that the collection of food went on all year, with the wives of the locked-out workers taking part. Mary's husband was a wharfie who often earned less than £3 a week. 'It was a bit of joke in our family,' she said:

> Sometimes there wasn't much for dinner, but that store couldn't be touched. I kept the door locked and I kept a list of the donations and had someone else check them into the cupboard and out again. I didn't want anyone thinking we ate them.

By May, the dedicated activity of women like Edna, Joy, Betsy and Mary was a major reason for the struggle being able to enter a new stage: mass picketing.

Mary Lamm remembered the first mass picketing outside Hudson's clearly:

> I'd got up early, put Polly in the pram - I don't know where she thought she was going but into the pram she went - and down we went to join the pickets. There were a lot of other women came down and they formed this beautiful line of pickets from Glebe Point Road down to Wentworth Park. I enjoyed myself immensely.

These demonstrations occurred at other timber yards too, and continued for four months. Sometimes hundreds attended, sometimes thousands, and always they were confronted by a large contingent of police, whose job was to shepherd the scabs into the yards in the morning and out again at knock-off time. It was -2°C when the picketers got out of

Mary Lamm, photographed in her Glebe backyard in 1927. During the timber workers' strike the Glebe strike relief depot operated from her house, and she helped organise pickets (from Audrey Johnson, *Bread and Roses*, 1990).

bed on Thursday, 18 July 1929, the coldest morning since 1895. Jock
Garden addressed several hundred of them in Johnston Street, Annandale, before leading them through the streets to Hudson's. At knock-off
time, the workers and their supporters gathered there again in a huge
crowd. They did the same on the following day. As the scabs emerged
from the yard the crowd threw stones at them, assaulted them with pal-
ings and spat on them, and as they trudged up the road a woman at an
upstairs window emptied her washing-up water on them. There were
many arrests, including of the future federal Labor politician Eddie
Ward. The next Saturday morning there was a huge protest meeting in
Wentworth Park.

For the pickets, these mass occasions were moments of angry
release, but also of playful resistance. The *Labor Daily* reported one of
these moments, under the heading, 'Lighter Side – Timber Picketing –
Early Morning Session – Records Broken'. Suddenly 300 pickets raced
away from Hudson's with the police in pursuit, After a mile and half
(about 2.4 km) running through the streets of Glebe, the 'marathon'
came to a halt and mock placings were announced: first, John Burns,
wire-rope splicer; second, J.S. Garden; third, Inspector Farley. Garden
addressed the panting crowd:

> I'm sorry if we have made the pace too hot. The police are only doing
> their duty. It's a cold morning, and I hope everybody, including the
> police, is feeling a little warmer.

Back at Hudson's, where there were fewer police to protect them, the
scabs coming to work were also having a warm time.

On another occasion, Joy Barrington –'dazzling', 'golden beauty',
'athletic' were the words her friends used to describe her – charmed the
constables with her smile and then behind their backs pinned handwritten notices on their navy uniforms: 'I'm a scab's nursemaid – kick me!'

The Blackwattle Campus of Sydney Secondary College, built on
the Hudson's site, is today justly proud of its prize-winning band. In
1929, the kids of Glebe also had a band that played in Pyrmont Bridge
Road. In those days, small kerosene heaters were the cheapest way to
heat a room, so kerosene tins were readily found in the local grocer's
backyard. During the mass picketing the kids of Glebe paraded up and

down the police lines banging their kerosene tins. The pickets cheered them on. The police, goaded at last into taking the names of band members and confiscating their instruments, seemed not to appreciate this rough music.

No wonder Mary Lamm enjoyed herself on the picket line. It allowed working-class families in the direst of positions a rare opportunity to express their deepest feelings, a rare moment of self-government.

24

THE DEATH OF
THE WORLD

This is the story of how the labour movement lost a daily newspaper and was deceived into giving a leg-up to the Packers, the super-wealthy family that is now one of Australia's main centres of business and political power.

With these words the Australian Workers' Union (AWU) appealed to unionists in 1921 to subscribe to a fund for a new paper, *The World*:

> Come with us to Macdonnell House ... a Trade Union House entirely owned by Australian Trade Unionists, and built to provide a permanent home, free of rack-renting and landlordism, for a *Labor Daily Paper*, owned and controlled by Trade Unionists – and nobody else.

While a daily labour newspaper seems fantastic today, in the early 20th century there were many trade union-owned papers, mostly weeklies, but also some ambitious attempts to combat on a daily basis the anti-labour bias of the commercial press. Brisbane's labour paper was the *Daily Standard*, in Hobart there was the *Daily Post*, in Adelaide the *Daily Herald*, and in Sydney the *Labor Daily* and *The World*. It was *The World* that the AWU was getting ready to launch from Macdonell House in 1921 as the flagship of a chain of labour dailies.

The AWU's own Sydney-based weekly, *The Australian Worker*, had a large circulation and a strong reputation among thinkers. Founded in the 1890s, it was at different times published from a large building in St Andrew's Place (now swallowed up by Town Hall House behind the cathedral) and a purpose-built building in Bathurst Street. But neither of these establishments was on the scale needed for the headquarters

Macdonnell House, Pitt Street, Sydney, home of *The World*. Financed by trade unionists, it was intended to be the national labour newspaper. The building still survives behind a modern façade (from *A Little Journey to Macdonnell House*, Sydney, no date).

of a chain of labour dailies – and this was the labour dream in 1910 as the Labor Party swept into office in the federal elections and formed the first majority Labor government in the world. Clearly, the flagship paper had to be called *The World*. Its masthead proclaimed 'A Continent to Win – A Newspaper to Win It With', with a map of Australia at the centre of the globe.

So Macdonell House was built in 1910 by Labor Papers Limited, a company whose largest shareholder was the AWU. Other trade unions were invited to invest, but the biggest burden was carried by the individual members of the AWU, who were levied for the building and newspaper machinery in 1910, 1911, 1914 and again in 1921.

It was one of the most imposing buildings in Sydney in 1910. It was eight storeys high, and its sign – 'The World' – on the top floor dominated the skyline in the centre of the city. Four lifts serviced the building, whose lower floors were rented to commercial tenants. The editorial, printing, and photo/art departments occupied the top three floors, and were connected to the rear entrance despatch bay by a separate lift. The 'commodious' roof, according to the AWU publicity for the building, 'we have dreams of some day utilising for assemblages of working-class import ... with all the accompanying artistry, culture and beauty rightly to be ours ... Our dictum verily is – the best for the wealth producers.' Unhappily for the union, it would be conned into doing 'the best' for a couple of wealth-producing entrepreneurs.

Trouble marked the project from the start. The directors dithered until the outbreak of World War I, when newsprint was impossible to buy. During the war, the split between left and right within the labour movement weakened support for the idea of a chain of labour papers controlled by the powerful AWU, a right-wing union. The left-wing Miners' Federation opted out, putting its funds into the *Labor Daily*, which first appeared in Sydney in 1922. Also, with the commercial renting of the lower floors actually making a small profit, Labor Papers Limited were under no financial pressure to publish *The World*.

But finally, in 1931, *The World* hit the streets as an afternoon daily. The decision to begin publishing at the worst moment of the Great Depression, a foolish one, was made in response to the bad publicity the AWU leadership was receiving for its failure to honour its undertaking to publish a daily newspaper. Also, the AWU needed a voice to counter the *Labor Daily*, which remained in the hands of the AWU's opponents in the factional wars of the labour movement. More bad decisions followed. Because the directors refused to determine whether *The World* was to be a popular or a labour paper, joint editors were appointed, one a Labor loyalist, the other an experienced newspaperman with no Labor sympathies. This confusion about its identity fell to its nadir on the eve of the 1932 election, when *The World* carried full-

A Little Journey to Macdonell House

Office of "The World"

AND

Headquarters of the Chain of Labor Dailies

"Feed me on facts."—Carlyle.

UPTON SINCLAIR ASKS:

WHO owns the Press, and why?

WHEN you read your daily paper, are you reading facts or propaganda? And whose propaganda?

WHO furnishes the raw material for your thoughts about life? Is it honest material?

No man can ask more important questions than these.

☞ Speaking for 700,000 Trade Unionists, the All-Australian Trade Union Congress (June, 1921) asked for a Chain of Labor Dailies in Australia, starting in Sydney, and pledged Unionists to raise the capital by a Levy of 10/- per man and 5/- per woman.

Worker Print, St. Andrew's Place, Sydney

Subscription appeal for the start-up of *The World* (from *A Little Journey to Macdonell House*, Sydney, no date).

page advertisements for Labor's conservative opponents. Soon after, citing political interference, the non-Labor editor and the most experienced journalists resigned.

After a year, faced with competition from *The Sun*, an already well-established commercial afternoon paper, *The World* was still struggling to gain a profitable circulation. The directors, now desperate, started looked for private investors and even considered a scheme to force a takeover bid from the owners of the competing afternoon paper by undercutting its price. The managing editor of *The Sun* was R.C. Packer, and his son Frank was also on its board. Unbeknownst to the AWU, one of *The World*'s journalists secretly informed Frank Packer of the plan to provoke the takeover bid.

What happened next may have been serendipity for the Packers, or it might have been a conspiracy. The man approached by Frank Packer to be his go-between with the AWU was the man also being consulted by the union for advice about how to rescue its investment in *The World*. The double-agent was E.G. ('Red Ted') Theodore, former Labor Premier of Queensland and president of the union, who was now on the lookout for a career in business – the defeat of the federal Labor government, in which he had been Treasurer, a few weeks earlier had left him jobless. Over a few whiskies in a Melbourne hotel, Theodore persuaded the union's negotiators to sell the Labor paper to his new friend, Frank Packer, who would pay £34,000 a year for three years, and employ its staff on a cheap non-political afternoon paper using the existing presses in Macdonnell House. A pound note was signed among the whisky stains, and within days there was a formal agreement and the union had received £5000 from the new owners.

Of course Packer and Theodore had no intention of publishing the paper. They had a lever now to extract money from Sir Hugh Denison, the owner of the *Sun* – which they did, negotiating a deal with Frank's dad *not* to publish for three years! The amount needed to buy them off was said to be more than 100 times what they had actually paid to the union. *The World* was dead, but its assets were put to good use by the two buccaneers. Now contractually precluded from publishing a daily newspaper, Frank Packer and Theodore hit upon the idea of a weekly paper directed at women. And so began the *The Australian Women's*

High Water: 10.10 a.m.,
10.39 p.m.

FINAL
EXTRA

The World

FORECAST: Cloudy with showers

TO-DAY

Athletics and
Turf .... 2 & 3
Talkies and Stage 4
Ships and Radio 5
What's Moving
On Change 9
Women's Feature
Section 11

Sunrise To-morrow: 4.57 a.m.

Moonrise: 10.5 p.m.

Vol. I. No. 5.

SYDNEY, FRIDAY, OCTOBER 30, 1931

PRICE 1½d.

'Phones: M2081 (10 lines)

Part of the foundation of the future Packer media empire: the presses of *The World*, a failed labour movement daily (*The World*, 30 October 1931).

Weekly. It was printed with machinery acquired by Theodore's cunning, and originally dedicated to working-class interests, and it was an important part of the foundation of the Packer media empire.

The union had been betrayed. It had to pay the workers on *The World* their severance pay, and it had to continue to service the massive debt left by its ill-timed foray into daily newspaper publishing. Meanwhile, the *Labor Daily* carried on until the end of the 1930s, when it too succumbed to commercial pressures and internal warfare. The dream of a national labour media project was over.

25

THE VENERABLE BOOTE

The Worker Building, Castlereagh Street

Peter Kirkpatrick

The Worker building at 238-40 Castlereagh Street began life as the Protestant Hall in 1878, owned by the Loyal Orange Institution. Seating 2000, the Protestant Hall was one of the largest auditoriums in Sydney, and from the 1890s to the 1920s it was often used by unions, socialists and other radical or reforming groups for meetings and conventions.

William McNamara opened his radical bookshop in the shopfront at number 236 in 1892. According to Colin Roderick, this was also the address of a Labour Bureau run by the anarchist Larry Petrie, and police harassment soon caused McNamara to shift his business across the road to 221 Castlereagh Street, where the bookshop became a centre for left-wing thought until its demolition in 1922.

One early highlight in the history of the hall was an inter-colonial conference of union delegates on 12 September 1890 that formed the Labour Defence Committee to manage the great Maritime Strike. On 4 November 1894 the *Australian Workman* advertised a meeting here to agitate for female voting rights, urging 'every woman suffragist within the metropolitan area' to attend: 'Undoubtedly if woman wakes up and shows the first sign of her waking on Monday next she will not have to mourn long her political inclusion among "children, lunatics and criminals".' In 1895, according to the *Woman's Voice*, the hall was being used for the monthly meetings of the Womanhood Suffrage League. Earlier that same year the Labor Leagues organised 'one of the largest

Formerly the Protestant Hall, the Australian Workers' Union Building, Castlereagh Street – site of many notorious and legendary labour movement stoushes (Robert Irving).

public meetings ever held in Sydney' to call upon the state government to take practical steps to solve unemployment.

The American writer and humorist Mark Twain began his Australian tour here in September 1895, giving four public lectures, or 'At Homes', which attracted huge crowds. Twain avoided political comment, but he increased the publicity for his performances when, shortly after arriving in the colony, he made an unguarded remark in favour of free trade that was taken by some in the press as a direct attack on Sir Henry Parkes, then a protectionist. Another offhand remark raising doubts about Henry George's proposal to nationalise land ownership provoked the *Australian Star* to fume: 'having cursed Parkes and protection and flattened the single-taxers Mr Clemens should go a step farther and boom Mr Reid [the Premier], and his general policy'.

In the first year of Federation the hall was the site for the formation of the Amalgamated Railways and Tramways Service Association (ARTSA). Its deregistration and the gaoling of its executive during the General Strike of 1917 highlighted the vulnerability of state-based labour organisations. A meeting to discuss the amalgamation of rail industry unions with the Australian Workers' Union (AWU) was held in the hall in September that year, but it would take three years, and the rise of the One Big Union movement, to build the national ARU.

Jack Lang recalled, in *I Remember*, a conference of Labor Party branches – or Political Labor Leagues as they were then known – at the Protestant Hall in 1913, 'a real Parliament of Labor', which severely criticised the McGowen government. Lang, at least, also had the rising William Holman in his sights: 'For a fortnight we were the master of the Government, and Holman never forgot the experience. It made him very cynical about the use of Political Labor Leagues except at election time, when they were needed for canvassing.'

In 1916 the most recent incarceration in a mental asylum of the sex reformer W.J. Chidley led to a large protest meeting in the hall. Chidley was well known on the streets of Sydney for wearing a short tunic while selling copies of his book *The Answer*, which advised 'natural coition' as a solution to the problems of human existence. As Sally McInerney has written:

> By now, people had become fond of him; he was a kind of institution, like most harmless eccentrics in cities, who, seeming to represent the dark side of the moon, make passers-by appreciate the homes they have to go to.

At the meeting a Miss Lambrick declared 'The insanity ... was not on the side of Mr Chidley, but on the side of those who had put him where he is.' A motion asking the Premier to release Chidley was passed unanimously. In June, a judge of the Lunacy Court released him, but by September he was back in custody; he died suddenly at Callan Park in late December.

In the early 1920s the building was the venue for the annual 'demonstration' or general meeting of the Workers' Educational Association, the WEA's *Australian Highway* noting 'The Protestant Hall takes some filling, but if every reader ... resident in or about Sydney makes himself responsible for bringing two friends, we will have an overflow meeting outside.' The building was renovated in 1924, renamed Empire Hall, and for a time lost some of its radical associations.

In 1937, when the AWU bought the building, it became the seventh home of *The Worker*. At the time Henry E. Boote was in the last years of his long editorship (1914-43). Boote was a legendary figure in the labour movement because of his leading role in the campaign against conscription – 'The Lottery of Death', as he called it – during World War I. His fiery journalism also assisted in the eventual release of 10 of the 12 IWW (Industrial Workers of the World, or Wobblies) members gaoled for conspiracy to commit arson and sedition in 1916. A socialist but no revolutionary, Boote was also a trustee of the Public Library of New South Wales.

He was also a fiction writer, allegorist, essayist and poet; poetry became, in Ian Syson's words, 'his dominant mode of literary expression' after 1930. Boote's poetry embraces the Shelleyan Romantic idiom of much late 19th and early 20th century socialist verse, but also shows the influence of his friend Henry Lawson, as in 'This Paper', written to celebrate *The Worker*'s 50th anniversary in 1942:

> Midst tempests of passion, midst whirlwinds of hate,
> It has stood with the masses, as mate stands with mate,
> At Democracy's gate,
> Repelling the onslaughts of treacherous foes,
> For always the one sacred duty it knows
> Is the tyrant to dare and the traitor expose ...

The young Clyde Cameron first met the venerable Boote at the 1941 AWU Annual Convention in Sydney, and described the then 76-year-old as: 'this thin, quietly spoken man with deep-set eyes, who appeared to be suffering from paralysis of one side of his body. He seemed lonely. He certainly seemed sad!' Boote had every reason to be sad. Over recent years his views had increasingly been in conflict with those of

Activist and dreamer Henry Boote, the influential Labour movement journalist who edited *The Worker* newspaper from 1914 to 1943 (National Library of Australia, PIC/9454).

the AWU hierarchy, and in March 1940 they censored his editorial 'Should We Fight Russia?', endorsing the 'Hands Off Russia' resolution of the NSW ALP conference. Only the intervention of H.V. Evatt prevented Boote's resignation from *The Worker*. The old man stayed on and, in an echo of his glory days, in 1942–43 vigorously agitated against Prime Minister Curtin's proposal to introduce conscription. Though the AWU supported him, ALP and public opinion were against him. In March 1943, seriously ill, he finally left the editor's chair.

The Worker building has been protected by a conservation order since 1984, and is listed on the Register of the National Estate. It was damaged by fire in 1994. Above the top floor of its historic façade, the faded words, 'The Worker', may still be read by the passers-by who lift their eyes from the pavement.

26

DEFENDING DARLINGHURST FROM THE REDS

ANGEL PLACE

Wingello House was once where the City Recital Hall in Angel Place stands today. In its quiet corridors the intellectuals, administrators and activists of the far right rubbed shoulders. Here were the headquarters of the Returned Soldiers and Sailors' Imperial League, the Racial Hygiene Association and the Constitutional Association, all of which had close connections to the anti-Labor parties of the day. It was in this citadel of conservatism that the most dangerous of all the organisations contemptuous of democratic values, the New Guard, set up an office – in room 5 on the second floor – in 1931.

By this time the suffering and disorder created by the Great Depression was sapping the legitimacy of liberal political institutions. Parliamentary government had proven unable to protect the economy or succour the millions who were losing their jobs, their homes and their savings. The Communists in Australia were calling for revolution, but outside their minuscule ranks were thousands of unemployed workers, embittered by the failures of 'the system' and emboldened by earlier episodes of resistance.

The New Guard was a right-wing response to these ominous developments. Their role in ruling-class politics was to prepare for a military-style takeover of government and defence of property if social revolution broke out, and in the meantime to rough up the Reds on the streets. The New Guard divided Sydney into zones, and each zone into divisions. Soon the New Guard's typist in Wingello House was making copies of a sinister document for the Divisional Commander of Darling-hurst, instructing him on how to resist the inevitable uprising of the vengeful poor:

> Sudden risings may be expected from Surrey [sic] Hills, Paddington, and Woolloomolloo [sic] and all three are the ways of access to the residential and rich districts of Darling Pt, Elizabeth Bay and Pott's Point. One must also take into consideration the possibility of rioters being driven out of the city into the Domain and Hyde Park, and from thence attempting to raid the residential quarters mentioned above.
>
> Taking the line from the extreme harbour end of Pott's Point – Victoria Street – King's Cross – Taylor Square – Flinders Street – Cleveland Street: this line ... is a stretch of high ground commanding the whole of Woolloomolloo and in some places the Domain. The maintenance of this will be safe-guarded by the patrolling in force of the whole Woolloomolloo District. The two sets of steps will be barricaded, and the system of patrolling in the low ground should ensure that no hostile forces can approach the cover of the high ground mentioned, and so collect with a view to advancing through Victoria Street on to the Residential District.

Another page was headed 'Street Fighting Tactics'. Here the instructions concentrated on preparing the defenders, in the absence of orders from higher command, to rely on their own resources:

(a) Obtain good positions for field of vision to guard against any chance of surprise.
(b) Assault parties of one section should proceed in advance taking as much cover as possible; the remaining troops keeping in readiness to move forward at a given signal.
(c) To ascertain what buildings are being held it is sometimes necessary to draw fire (discreetly); and not return the fire indiscriminately, but rather confer and arrive at a definite plan of attack.
(d) It can be anticipated that the right-hand side of a street is almost invariably the most strongly held – the reason being that the body is less exposed to fire when using a rifle.

The New Guard was not just another anti-Labor fundraiser or pressure group. As its name suggests, it was a paramilitary organisation, and as the instructions for the defenders of property quoted above confirm, it was ready to take up arms. At its peak, the New Guard in Sydney was a force of 40,000 disciplined men, with a core of 10,000 'shock troops'. Although this hard core alone was several times larger than the state's police force, the New Guard is often laughed off as amateurish and bombastic. Of course some of its members were cranks who delighted in spying on their neighbours, like the man who reported to Headquarters that:

Hughes of Hughes Fish Shop (near Tempe Depot) distributes propaganda and is Red Hot Red

and that:

73 Crown St. St Peters. Meetings are held practically every night of 12 to 15 men. Occupants are an aged couple and usually converse in a foreign language. Woman keeps guard on Verandah during meetings. Investigate please.

It is true, also, that the New Guard promoted the naïve belief that it could rise above politics, summed up in its aim of 'uniting all loyal citizens' in the 'suppression of disloyal and immoral elements in Governmental, industrial and social circles'. This has affected how it is remembered. Every Sydneysider knows about the comical action of Francis De Groot, who at the official opening of the Sydney Harbour Bridge rode his horse up to the ribbon, cutting it the instant before the Labor Premier, Jack Lang, could perform the ceremony. That De Groot was not a lone eccentric is underlined by the New Guard's instructions on defending Darlinghurst, which have survived in his private papers.

De Groot was in fact a Zone Commander, and thus part of the 'council of action' that ran the New Guard. Most members of this inner circle were ex-AIF officers, and many had links with the big end of town. The first moves to form the New Guard took place in the Imperial Service Club in O'Connell Street, then the heart of the business district, and the first headquarters were a block away in Castlereagh Street, in Twyford House, where the New Guard shared a floor with the Japanese Consulate. The money to run the outfit came from the men who

The urbane Francis de Groot in military uniform. He was one of the leaders of the fascist New Guard organisation. It planned to bring down the Labor government of Jack Lang, by force if necessary (Mitchell Library, State Library of New South Wales, PXA 708).

owned and managed Sydney's biggest companies, especially its retail stores and insurance companies. Finances were under the control of 'Commander James R. Patrick, a self-made owner of a shipping line'. Most of the rank and file was drawn from the middle and upper-class suburbs around the harbour and along the North Shore line.

After the election of Jack Lang's Labor government in New South Wales in 1930, Sydney's ruling circles were gripped by fear. 'The Big Fella' to his followers, Jack Lang was 'that mad dog' to the well-heeled residents of Killara and Double Bay. No fantasy about Lang was too far-fetched to be believed. In October 1931 the New Guard's Director of Intelligence received from GHQ a report that:

Lang is supposed to converse with Russia each Monday morning about 7 a.m. on the short wave (20–22 metres). Please investigate. Hill of St Peters reports the above. Hill's two sons have listened in.

Lang was a populist. His speeches blamed the Depression on 'the money power', controlled by Jews and British bankers, and encouraged false hope among ordinary people. He made vague references to 'socialising credit' and constructing public works. However, it was his intention to suspend interest payments from the state treasury to British bondholders that upset 'right-thinking' people. This was repudiation of Britain, still the mother country – only one step away, in their view, from socialisation. In fact, Lang had no coherent economic policy, and the federal Labor government rejected his ideas. Nor was Lang the general of an army of labour militants. The trade unions, after a series of big defeats, were retreating, and the revolutionaries in the Communist Party numbered only a few hundred. If the poor were to revolt, they would have no one to organise them.

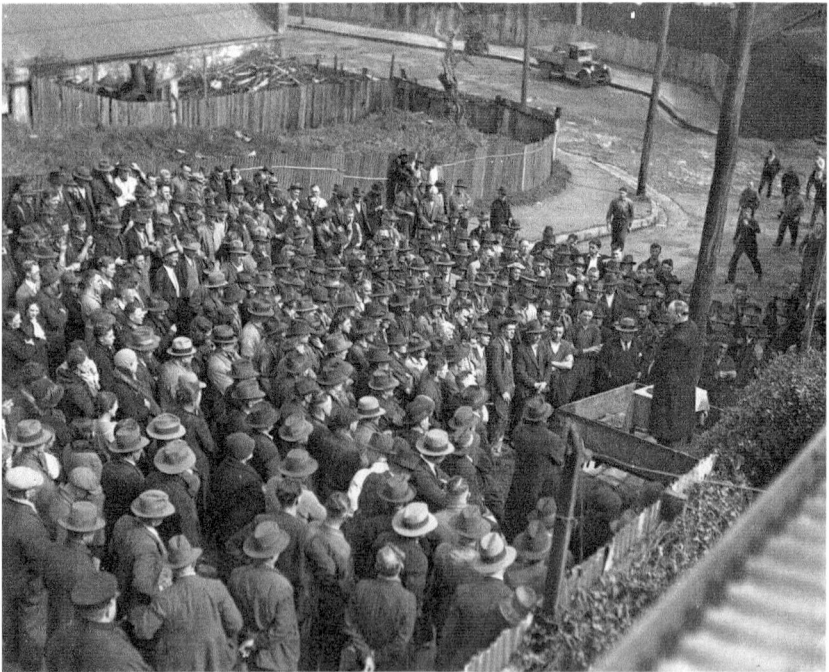

NSW Premier Jack Lang addresses supporters outside the Eveleigh railway yards in Sydney, 1934. These railway yards were a major industrial site and a major source of labour militancy (Dixson Galleries, State Library of New South Wales, DG ON4/351).

The real reason for the hatred of Lang lies deep in the psyche of the ruling class. The Bolshevik revolution of 1917, and the adoption in 1921 of 'socialisation' as Labor's official objective, had not faded from conservative memory. Lang's enemies were well aware, too, of overseas developments, especially the victory of Mussolini's fascists over the Italian socialists, and the defeat of the British General Strike of 1926 by secret paramilitary forces assisting the government. In their minds, then, Lang was the Australian expression of the international breakdown of respect for order, a leader whose populist ranting and unpredictability would unleash forces that threatened decency, loyalty to the throne, and private property. Whipped up by conservative politicians, fear of the dangerous masses was not a new feeling among Sydney's propertied classes; it went back in time to the mobilisation of working people from which the Labor Party emerged in the 1890s.

And the response by conservatives, their rejection of democracy and the embrace of authoritarian solutions, was not new either, as the English writer, D.H. Lawrence, discovered when he visited Australia in 1922. In Lawrence's novel *Kangaroo*, one of the characters is describing a secret army:

> There's quite a number of us in Sydney – and in the other large towns as well – we're mostly diggers back from the war – we've joined up in a kind of club – and we're sworn in – and we're sworn to *obey* the leaders, no matter what the command, when the time is ready – and we're sworn to keep silent until then. We don't let out much, nothing of any consequence, to the general run of members.
>
> Why, the plan is more or less this. The Labour people, the reds, are always talking about a revolution, and the Conservatives are always talking about a disaster. Well, we keep ourselves fit and ready for as soon as the revolution comes or the disaster. Then we step in, you see, and we are the revolution. We've got most of the trained fighting men behind us, and we can *make* the will of the people, don't you see: if the members stand steady. We shall have 'Australia' for the word. We stand for Australia, not for any of your parties.

Lawrence almost certainly met the leaders of such a secret army, although this was not understood until recent research showed that

THE

Gu...

SUNDAY, NOVE...

IF REVOLUTION

Foreword by CANON HOWARD LEA, Rector of St. ...

A S a man of peace I warmly commend this vision to the thoughtful consideration of all readers of "The Sunday Sun".

We are living in a fool's paradise.

We are refusing to face facts.

Ostrich like, we are burying our heads in the sandhills of our own making.

This Sunday before Armistice Day is a fitting day on which to sound this trumpet call.

Supine indifference is our great danger. In our midst are men and women, white hot with zeal for a cause which they hold will bring in the golden age. Contempt adds fuel to their fire. Cheap denunciation pours oils upon it. Hunger, poverty, injustice feed its flame.

Meanwhile we in inaction, we ta whence comes it? batant, but from

This vivid article shows some of t ror and misery and slaughter that Revolution would mean to Sydney- historian might see it, looking ba 1993. It is a grim possibility to whi appear to give little thought.

The ordinary
The ordinary
"Where is the r
rouse the ordinary
not have been wr
(R

By HOWARD ASHTON

S TEADILY the falling off of industrial enterprise under the foolish rule of the dictatorship had resulted in more widespread unemployment. The rich had been taxed, since the Privy Council had given its judgment on the abolition of the Legislative Council, till they were no longer able to pay, and had either left the State with what little remained to them, or had sunk into a

last, when, dead and dying, they were burnt in their looted homes.

Of the lot of the young and attractive women of these unfortunate people in the hands of these criminals and scum of the city, a scum which always attaches itself to revolutionary forces, it is better not to speak.

S EVERAL attacks were made on the citizens' guard and the

Bakyarde, a famous pre-revolution leader, was dragged out of his limousine and kicked to death, and the former Dictator, seeing that the friend of the people was apt to be the enemy next morning, betook himself, like Cincinnatus, to his farm, where he was out of reach of the city

Hall and t
Government
Treasury, g

The Sun newspaper stirs up conservative fears in Sydney, 1931 (*The Sun*, 8 November 1931).

his path had crossed that of a prominent secret army organiser by the name of Jack Scott. Scott lived in Mosman (where it is likely that he entertained Lawrence), and was treasurer of the King and Empire Alliance in 1921. Lawrence's character, 'Kangaroo', the name bestowed on the leader of the Diggers' Clubs by its members, was clearly based on Sir Charles Rosenthal, the secretary of the King and Empire Alliance. This was the body behind the events described in Chapter 21, when over 100,000 'patriots' violently attacked Labor, socialist and Communist platforms in the Domain in May 1921. But the tradition of secret, paramilitary right-wing organising was already over a decade old by that time.

One source of this tradition can be found in the special constables who were enrolled whenever riots by the poor, or serious industrial conflicts, loomed. This tradition started in the 1840s and reappeared in the great strikes of the 1890s. A particularly impressive paramilitary mobilisation occurred during the 1917 General Strike in New South Wales, when a 'farmers' army' of over 7000 was assembled, provisioned and directed not only to perform the tasks of striking workers but also, armed with iron bars and the occasional pistol, to break up the marches and meetings of the striking workers. The same impulse to defend the interests of employers by force was seen during the police strike of 1923 in Melbourne, and the 1925 strike by British seamen that convulsed the main ports of Australia. It was during the seamen's strike that Jack Scott was given another opportunity to exercise his talents. He was in charge of a secret force that planned to kidnap the seamen's leaders and place them on a ship leaving the country.

Another source of the paramilitary tradition was hatred of the Sinn Fein and Communist enemies of the British Empire. There was a whole raft of secret outfits propelled by this hatred. We can date the origins of the first of them, the Australian Protective League, to just three weeks after the Bolshevik revolution in Russia. In Brisbane, the four weeks of violence sparked by the so-called Red Flag Riots, when armed vigilantes attacked Labor and left-wing buildings and marchers, can be linked to this body. During the 1920s this tradition was able to draw on the example of Italian fascism, which inspired an organisation called the Australian Legion. The influence of fascism also came via Britain

– and cricket. Several members of the Marylebone Cricket Club were prominent members of the British Union of Fascists (BUF), and after its 1925–26 tour there were branches of the BUF in several Australian centres. Apart from the King and Empire Alliance, other counter-revolutionary bodies in the 1920s and 1930s included the League of National Security, the Khaki Legion, and in New South Wales, the Old Guard. It was the latter's failure to respond aggressively to Lang's election that led to the formation of the New Guard.

The New Guard had access to arms and ammunition through sympathisers in army barracks, local drill halls and military camps. By March 1932, the Council of Action was ready to act. It had a plan to isolate the city by closing the main roads and railways with armed troops and cutting off the electricity by seizing Bunnerong power station, and then, under cover of darkness, to overthrow constitutional government. New Guard forces would occupy Parliament and the main government departments, and arrest the Premier, who would then be locked up in Berrima Gaol. Only the dismissal in May of Premier Lang by Governor Game, and the subsequent election win by the anti-Labor parties in June, prevented a right-wing coup in Sydney in 1932.

Australia is not usually thought of as a country marked by civil violence. Our uprisings against state power have been brief, small in scale, and outside the main cities – the Eureka Stockade of 1854, and the occupation of government offices in Darwin in 1918 and again in 1930. But as the story of the New Guard shows, Sydney came perilously close to an armed uprising to overthrow liberal democracy in the country's most populous state in 1932, and the danger came from the men of property, not the 'Reds'.

27

THE ANTI-EVICTION WAR

UNION STREET, ERSKINEVILLE

Sometimes radical history has to be dredged up from the archives; at other times a radical collective memory of stirring actions, exhilarating support and surprising victories remains alive for several generations. Then it inspires future artists and historians with radical possibilities. So it is with the anti-eviction war that convulsed the southern and western suburbs of Sydney in the first half of 1931.

In the 1950s, Lee Rhiannon was living in Newtown and attending the local public school. The future leader of the Greens in the NSW Parliament would listen as her parents and their friends talked about a huge eviction fight in Erskineville, at 143 Union Street, where a pitched battle took place between members of the Unemployed Workers' Movement (UWM) and the police in June 1931. She never forgot the sense of empowerment the story of that fight for dignity and justice gave them.

In the 1970s the Scots folksinger Alistair Hulett was living in Union Street and performing his songs about the struggles and desires of working people. After a gig one night at the Sandringham Hotel in King Street, Newtown, an archivist from the Mitchell Library told him about the history of the street Hulett lived in. With this and other sources, and using his imagination and artistry, Alistair created 'The Siege of Union Street', which he was often asked to perform.

His was not the first song about a string of events that have come to be known as the eviction wars. In 1999 Jocka Burns, who was a veteran of them, recorded for ABC Radio's *Hindsight* team one of the songs written at the time:

An evicted working-class family in Redfern, 1934, with their belongings on the footpath (L. Maitland, Dixson Galleries, State Library of New South Wales, DG ON4/871).

For we met them at the door,
And we knocked them on the floor,
Bankstown and Newtown,
We made the cops feel sore.
They outnumbered us ten to one,
And were armed with stick and gun,
But we fought well, we gave them hell,
When we met them at the door.

In the folklore of inner Sydney, this was the time when the kids started playing 'evictions' rather than 'cops and robbers'.

The Great Depression of the 1930s is, in popular memory, a time of resilience. We admire the way people coped with extraordinary unemployment (32 per cent at its height in mid-1932), endured dole queues, and suffered as they travelled the outback looking for work. The housing crisis, however, tends to be forgotten, except when romanticised in tales of adventurous 'moonlight flits'. We should recall that 57 per cent of the state's unemployed in 1931 were in the Sydney metropolitan area and that in Newtown and other inner suburbs almost 90 per cent of the people were renters. Because there was no rent assistance for the unemployed, every year of the Depression thousands of families were evicted for non-payment of rent. Houses then stood empty: in Sydney there were 11,000 empty dwellings in 1933 – there had been many more in 1931. Families thrown onto the street searched desperately for cheaper accommodation; inevitably some ended up in shanty towns, named, with caustic irony, 'Happy Valleys', set among the scrubby wasteland of La Perouse, Milperra, Ingleburn and Clontarf.

The unemployed possessed a quality often overlooked by historians of the Depression – militancy. The UWM was founded in 1930 and quickly grew to about 14,000 (in 70 branches) in Sydney. It was not a crowd of hotheads but an organised force of local people who had learnt their politics as activists in the trade unions. A typical male member was an ex-serviceman in his thirties. Local committees, controlled by the rank and file, campaigned for relief work, and reform of the dole system; they also gave food and material support to families, making sure that only genuine cases of distress were taken up. They soon discovered, however, that housing was a critical issue. As the inner-city landlords – some of whom were British companies – turned to the courts for ejectment notices, the UWM responded. At first they relied on picketing, lobbying and political pressure – and these peaceful tactics worked. By the middle of 1931 they had successfully prevented over 200 families from being evicted.

But in the middle of 1931, the landlords switched their strategy from using magistrates to using politicians, and the latter instructed the police to get tough with the picketers. The UWM now called for mass turn-outs to surround houses when families were threatened with eviction, and arranged for volunteers to move into the houses to protect the tenants, declaring that they would meet force with force. In this escalation there was an important role for women and children, who sustained the occupiers and kept a lookout for police attacks.

The new, confrontational stage of the struggle was not confined to Erskineville. Drew Cottle and Angela Keys discuss 13 major incidents of organised defence of families facing eviction in the first half of 1931: in Clovelly, Glebe, Surry Hills, Balmain, Annandale, Rozelle, South Granville, Lakemba, Newtown, Redfern, Leichhardt, Bankstown and Erskineville.

The house at 143 Union Street was a small two-up, two down terrace with a single-storey outhouse at the rear and a balcony facing the street. On 19 June 1931, behind doors barricaded with sandbags, and with an arsenal of stones and timber clubs, were 18 UWM members. Just before noon the police arrived – in force. They came by bus, car and motorcycle – perhaps about 60, of whom 20 immediately began to attack the house, firing at the UWM picketers on the balcony, while the rest provided backup and defence against a hostile crowd that soon grew to over 1000.

As a fusillade of bullets pushed back the defenders in the upstairs rooms, the police broke into the house from three directions: through the partition on the balcony from the next-door terrace, over the outhouse roof to enter through the back window, and by demolishing the back door and its barricade. This happened quickly, but the fighting in the downstairs rooms and passageway lasted longer. Fuelled by class hatred, it was a terrifying experience for both sides: a confined space, trigger-happy police shouting that 'Reds' should be shot, and defenders, with no way of escape, determined to give no quarter. The bullets from the police revolvers fired inside the house ramped up the terror; the flailing batons and clubs caused horrific injuries to police and picketers alike. Four of the defenders were admitted to hospital with head injuries. According to a report in the *Herald*, the back room:

> was absolutely bathed in blood. Practically every man in the room was bleeding from one or more wounds. Insensible men lay on the floor while comrades and foes alike trampled on them. The walls were spattered and daubed with bloodstained hands.

ANOTHER clash between police and anti-evictionists.—
General view of the crowd gathered before the fight at the house
(right) in Union-street, Newtown In the circle, the constable is
picking up empty shells of bullets fired in the fight. Below, the
constable facing the camera is exhibiting his injury.

Press photographs of the clash at Union Street in 1931, showing
police and anti-evictionists marshalling. In the circle, a policeman col-
lects spent bullet shells (*The Sun*, 19 June 1931).

After 20 minutes the police had beaten the defenders into submission,
but the horror continued. Arrested men were assaulted in the house, on
the way to the police station, and in the cells. And so the siege ended,
like many law-and-order triumphs, in an orgy of anti-Communist brutality.

Meanwhile the crowd of several thousand outside grew angrier as
what was happening to the defenders sank in. Insults and hoots met the
police as they tried to keep order on the street. From the back of the

AFTER THE CLASH to-day between police and unemployed at a two-storied house in Union-street, Newtown. Note the revolver in the officer's hand at left.

A newspaper photo pointing to a policeman hiding his revolver after the clash (*The Sun*, 19 June 1931).

crowd stones found their targets among the police. The police retaliated, drawing their weapons and charging into the front lines of the crowd, forcing it back beyond the police wagons and injuring people in the process. The crowd regrouped, and as the prisoners were driven off, rocks rained down on the wagons. The crowd had become a force in this struggle against eviction.

The partisan behaviour of the crowd, rather than the desperation of the defenders, ensured that the siege of Union Street would live in

Gentrified today, this terrace house was the site of the famous Union Street siege in 1931 (Nick Irving).

popular memory. The defenders were unquestionably courageous, but because the UWM tactic was to provoke a siege and threaten violence, the defenders were bound to fail as soon as the state brought its superior capacity for violence to bear. The people in the crowd, on the other hand, went home undefeated. Theirs was the biggest spontaneous demonstration of the 1930s.

Politicians are ambivalent about crowds. They love the terror crowds inspire in their enemies; they hate the loss of control of the people that a contentious, spontaneous crowd portends. Therefore they hasten to deflect it into safer, representative channels - and that is what happened in the wake of the eviction battles of mid-1931. Jock Garden, the mountebank populist who was still secretary of Labor Council, announced that he was a candidate for Labor preselection on the promise of preventing evictions. By August, the Lang Labor government had introduced laws to postpone ejectments for non-payment of rents. The movement declined. Too late the UWM discovered that the benefits of these laws for unemployed families were more symbolic than real.

In the 1970s, Nadia Wheatley completed a thesis that recovered the details and explained the significance for radical history of the struggles of the unemployed in the Depression. This chapter is largely based on her research. She discovered that this was a living history, part of a tradition of radicalism that deserved its own tribute, so she wrote *The House That Was Eureka*, a novel for younger readers, in the 1980s. In the next decade, Lea Redfern produced an exciting documentary about the same events for Radio National's *Hindsight* team, called 'Forever striking trouble'. In 2008, the National Play Festival included Sue Smith's *In the Violet Time*, in which a leading character joins the UWM and barricades his house against the police trying to evict his family. It is a tradition that still inspires.

28

THE DEFENCE OF
DHAKIYARR WIRRPANDA

In history, periods of serious challenge from below alternate with periods of passive acceptance of the status quo, and different groups of people raise the banners of resistance at different times. From the late 19th century to the middle of the 20th century it was militant trade unionists, inspired by anti-capitalist ideas, who were the main challengers in Australia. Accordingly, they were coerced and imprisoned by laws that sought to prevent them from importing books, circulating their propaganda by mail, speaking and collecting money in public places, marching on the streets, picketing unfair employers, going on strike in specified industries, belonging to 'unlawful' organisations or deregistered unions, resisting the eviction of families from their homes, and entering 'reserves' to expose the injustices suffered by Aboriginal workers.

No one has counted the arrests and gaolings of labour movement people in our country, but the numbers were significant – running into many thousands – and by no means confined to leaders or prominent agitators. Thus, in the seamen's strike of 1925 there were 946 warrants for arrest issued in Sydney alone. In the northern coalfields lockout of 1930, which only ended, one participant claimed, after 'a reign of terror' by the police, 90 miners from the village of Abermain were convicted of unlawful assembly. In the Sydney Domain, as a consequence of the Disloyal Organisations Act, there were arrests of sellers of Communist literature every week for almost the whole of 1934. After such episodes the mere threat of legal sanctions was intimidating. It was to counter this constant atmosphere of intimidation that International Labour Defence (ILD) was set up in 1932.

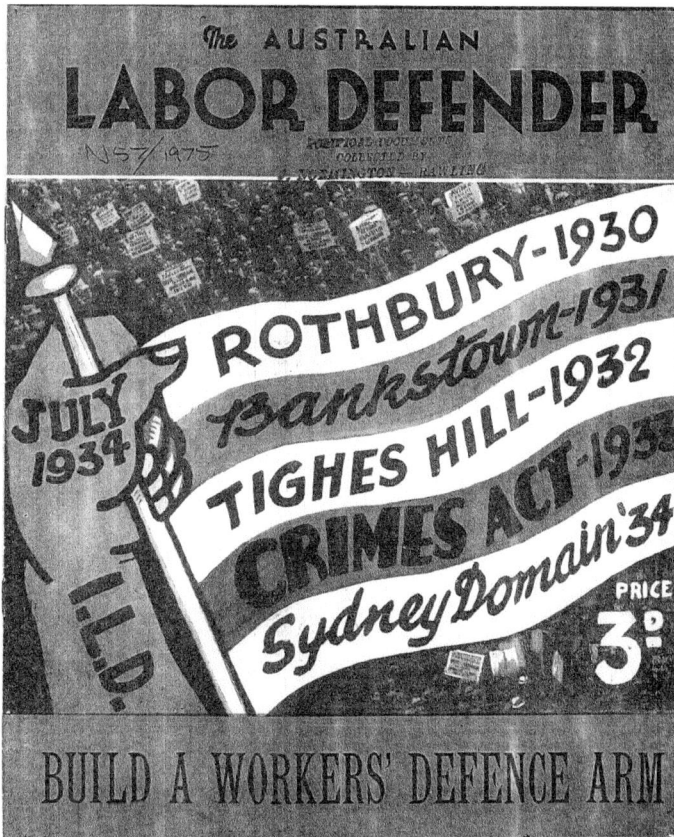

Front cover of the International Labour Defence organisation's journal, listing significant sites of bloody clashes between labour and capital in the 1930s (Noel Butlin Archives Centre, Australian National University Archives, J.N. Rawling Collection).

Initiated by the Communist International, the ILD operated as a network bringing together sympathetic lawyers with a handful of activists from the Labor Party's socialist left, the Communist Party, the remnants of the pre-war militant 'industrialists' in the trade unions, and middle-class humanitarians and civil libertarians. Amongst the latter was the future novelist Kylie Tennant, who wrote about the ILD in her autobiography and in her novel *Ride on Stranger*, calling it 'a thorn in the pants seat of justice'.

Author Kylie Tennant mischievously hams it up for the camera at a fancy dress party. Tennant was a fiery advocate for the International Labour Defence organisation in the 1930s (National Library of Australia, MS 7574).

She describes its officials at work in Trades Hall, 'huddled in shabby overcoats in a frozen room, because they could not afford a radiator. They ate ... at a sleazy little fish shop whose proprietor was a supporter and gave them free meals.' This was a reference to café owner Nick Zenodohos, who was raising money to aid political prisoners of the fascist Metaxas government in Greece.

By 1932, the ILD was in room 513 of Roma House at 537–43 George Street. With its tiled floors, frosted glass doors, and lift, this was a rather salubrious address for a Comintern front, but no doubt it was a good cover against random New Guard thuggery, for at street level the Catholic books and sacred artefacts of Pellegrini's gave the building an air of pious respectability. Staff conditions, however, had not improved much, as Nick's daughter, Della, an unemployed stenographer, discovered when she went to work in the office in 1932. Unable to pay her a wage, the ILD gave her the fare for the tram and a penny each day for the ILD lunch, which consisted of a stale pie from Sargent's across the road.

George Bateman was the secretary in 1932. Through his office, Kylie Tennant remembered, 'flowed the tide of human woe. Cast-off wives, evicted families, deserted children, the bereaved, the aggrieved, the penniless ... We lived on meat pies.' The work was neverending:

> Part of the duty of the [ILD] staff was to be out addressing meetings of Labour supporters night after night in little dusty halls all over the suburbs, 'putting the case' for this or that protest ... The Sydney of the [ILD] was a network of lawyers' offices, of bare wooden meeting halls, committee meetings, annual conventions, labour conferences ...

George was 'an old IWW man' from the north of England, who had been in 'quite a few gaols for his politics in the old country'. As secretary of the ILD he was arrested in the Domain in 1934 for selling Communist literature. The next week he was back again, this time chairing a meeting called to protest against the Disloyal Organisations Act. At 2.45 pm about 2000 opponents of the Act had gathered at Eddy Avenue. Refused permission to march, they walked in groups to the Domain, where a crowd of 5000 listened to speakers attack the state government's repressive Act. About 5.15 pm police began rough-handling literature sellers and attacking speakers. According to the *Workers' Weekly*:

> Jean Devanny, from the Anti-War Movement, then mounted the platform and spoke to the workers for about six minutes. A policeman climbed the platform and amid jeers and hoots from the indignant crowd threw her to the ground, where two more attacked her. Several more workers were then arrested trying to assist her.

The ILD's role was crucial in the campaign in 1934 to save an Aboriginal man – his name in the English language was Tuckiar – who was facing the death penalty after being convicted of murdering a policeman in the Northern Territory. A party of police had landed on Woodah Island and captured a group of Aboriginal women in the hope that they could be persuaded to give evidence against their menfolk on a different matter. Tuckiar released the women by spearing the policeman to whom his wife was chained, then disappeared into the bush. At Tuckiar's trial the missionary who persuaded him to give himself up said:

> the Aborigines were out of control. If a dictator could get the murderers, give them a public flogging, show them the power of the white garrison with a bayonet charge and big gun fire and the like, flog them and let them know that the next murderers would be publicly shot, it would be a lesson to them.

The judge was equally bloodthirsty, opining that the best thing to do with Aborigines who broke the law was to hang them. He ignored the obvious provocation represented by the capture of the women, and the possibility that under Aboriginal law Tuckiar might have been acting appropriately. Further, the idea that Aboriginal women were as entitled to the protection of the law as white women, who were excused the need to give evidence against their husbands, apparently never occurred to the court.

The ILD swung into action: 1000 letters were sent to sympathisers and a public meeting was organised. Held in King's Hall in Hunter Street on 7 August, the meeting heard speeches defending Aborigines against the statements of racist judges and missionaries, and calling for federal government intervention. The speakers included white activists such as Mick Sawtell and George Bateman, Aboriginal leader Ruby Duncan, Professor of Anthropology A.P. Elkin, and several clergymen.

The outcome for Tuckiar was both good and bad. The High Court commuted his death sentence and decreed that he should be returned in custody to his own country. Then his supporters in Sydney were disturbed to hear that on release from gaol he had 'gone bush'. They feared for his safety. As the Reverend W. Morley explained in a telegram of protest to the Attorney-General, Robert Menzies, public opinion in Sydney was:

> deeply concerned at published accounts of Tuckiar's alleged escape, [believing that] his present position was equivalent to the re-imposition of the death penalty.

In his home country, when he failed to return, his people concluded that Tuckiar had been killed by the police.

His real name was Dhakiyarr Wirrpanda, and he was an elder of the Yolngu people of Arnhem Land, where he has not been forgotten. In 2003, his sons and the descendants of the policeman met in Darwin. The Yolngu people and their friends had carried out a prolonged campaign, the result of which was the Northern Territory government acknowledging that in 1934 a miscarriage of justice had occurred. In a spirit of reconciliation, the Chief Justice of Australia unveiled a magnificent memorial to Dhakkiyar Wirrpanda – a group of ceremonial poles, made by his Yolngu people – outside Parliament House in Darwin.

It is not a comfortable thought that our state rules ultimately by violence or the threat of violence, but those who challenge the status quo, if they seriously undermine by word or deed the power of their rulers, soon discover that truth. The Aboriginal law that Dhakiyarr Wirrpanda invoked could not be allowed to prevail over the violence of the white invaders. So too with the militant workers defended by the ILD: their freedom of speech, freedom of assembly, and right to act against oppression had very definite limits in uncertain times. It is a lesson that the anti-globalisation protesters, mounting today's challenge to unbridled financial capitalism, are also learning.

29

THE NEW THEATRE

Michelle Arrow

Imagine, if you can amid Sydney's present-day concrete and clamour, that it is 1937, and you are sitting in the Conservatorium of Music, on Macquarie Street, watching a play. You love to go to the pictures – you go all the time with your sister – but this play is something else. It holds you breathless, rapt, until the end, this play about men who are killed in war but rise from the dead, who refuse to be buried because they have been robbed of the rest of their lives. It's called *Bury the Dead*, and it is the first production of the Sydney New Theatre League that you've ever seen. It's so good that you are determined to seek this theatre out, to become a part of it, so, after asking around, you head to 36 Pitt Street.

There, up some rickety steps on the second floor, budding socialist and aspiring playwright Oriel Gray found the first proper premises of the Sydney New Theatre. This discovery would change her life, for she would eventually become one of the theatre's most prolific local playwrights. Still in existence today, the Sydney New Theatre is probably the longest-running theatre in Australia. Springing from the Communist Party of Australia and inspired by British and American models, the New created a distinctively Australian type of workers' theatre, marked by its serious moral purpose and larrikin verve.

But before we explore 36 Pitt Street, we need first to detour up the street a little, to 233 Pitt Street. Today, the Pitt Street Mall has swallowed all traces of the original building, but back in August 1932, in the depths of the Great Depression, 233 Pitt Street was, briefly, the founding premises of the Sydney Workers' Art Club, the precursor of

Playwright Oriel Gray, whose plays and sketches were a mainstay of Sydney's New Theatre (Courtesy of Michelle Arrow, from her book *Upstaged: Australian women dramatists in the limelight at last*, 2002).

the New Theatre. Formed at the instigation of Communist activist and writer Jean Devanny, and led by artist George Finey, the club hosted art and drama classes, lectures, film screenings and literary evenings, all under the banner of 'art is a weapon'. The group moved to 36 Pitt Street (the former home of the Seamen's Union of Australia, and today the site of a luxury hotel), close to the bustle of Circular Quay, in October 1932.

The theatre group that developed there was soon dominating the activities of the club, giving performances every Sunday night on a tiny stage in the club's cramped auditorium. By the end of 1935, the group had staged 30 productions, including seven new Australian plays. They took over the club completely in 1936, launching their new name, the New Theatre League, with a production of American playwright Clifford Odets' *Waiting for Lefty*.

Premiering on 25 January 1936, the play was hugely successful. Its depiction of the hardship of Depression-era lives struck a chord with audiences, who delighted in its stridency, compassion and bold theatricality. Encouraged by the success of *Lefty*, the New was ready to strike out from the clubhouse, and they did so with a provocative play that sparked one of the most notorious and celebrated episodes in the New's history.

The New Theatre made its debut on a mainstream theatre stage at the Savoy with another Clifford Odets play, *Till The Day I Die*, on 9 June 1936. The Savoy, at 29 Bligh Street (now demolished), was a big step up for the group: a bigger theatre meant the possibility of a larger audience. The broader audience reached, combined with *Till The Day I Die*'s scathing indictment of Nazi tyranny, soon attracted the scrutiny of the authorities. Soon after the play opened, the German Consul-General wrote to the Minister for External Affairs, complaining that the play was an 'insult' to the German government. The Minister ordered an investigation, which was taken up by the NSW Chief Secretary, who had the power to censor live performances. He promptly banned performances of *Till The Day I Die*. This was a provocation irresistible to the theatre, which resolved to defy the ban.

On 22 July the curtain rose on their performance of *Waiting for Lefty* and a mysterious 'unnamed' play, in front of an audience heavy with press and police. The police eventually twigged that this 'unnamed' play was in fact *Till The Day I Die* and went backstage to stop the performance. Holding the police at bay, the cast asked the audience if they wanted the performance to continue. Of course the audience did; the police withdrew, and the play went on. While New Theatre secretary Vic Arnold was fined for the performance, the theatre continued to perform the play at their clubhouse for several years, exploiting a loophole in the Act that permitted 'private' performances, until the ban was lifted in 1941. The New milked the incident for all it was worth; the confrontation brought them more publicity than they could ever have hoped for.

However, the outbreak of World War II left the theatre in a bind. Having spent years passionately campaigning against fascism, Communists everywhere struggled to rationalise the Soviet Union's 1939 non-aggression pact with Nazi Germany. The Communist Party's subsequent denunciation of the 'capitalist war' was deeply unpopular: the party was banned in Australia from 1940 to 1941, and according to historian Robert Darby the Sydney New Theatre only narrowly escaped being outlawed as well. When German troops invaded the Soviet Union in 1941, the Communists were once again on the right side, and the New Theatre rode a new wave of public acceptance, which was consolidated by their increasingly nationalist outlook. By 1943, they had outgrown their Pitt Street clubhouse and swapped premises with the International Seamen's Club, moving to the third floor of 167 Castlereagh Street. This is the theatre's only inner-city premises still standing; today it's a gym, but former members can still trace out the lines of the stage and seating around the punching bags and dumbbells.

The Cold War was tough on the New Theatre. Membership and audiences dropped in this new world of anti-Communist paranoia and Australian Security and Intelligence Organisation (ASIO) surveillance. Many members worked for the theatre under pseudonyms; others had their phones tapped; their appearances, plays and activities were described and filed away in one of the 16 volumes of documents gathered on the theatre (and now housed at the National Archives). Wavering member numbers during the 1950s meant that much of the work of the theatre was performed by a small number of dedicated volunteers –

The New Theatre's second home: 167 Castlereagh Street today (Robert Irving).

all to produce shows that were poorly publicised (the *Sydney Morning Herald* famously refused to accept the theatre's advertisements from 1948 to 1961) and staged under circumstances that would have sunk many other less dedicated companies.

One play which struck a chord during these years (and probably kept the theatre afloat) was the nationalist folk musical *Reedy River*, which the company performed at hired venues across the city and suburbs. The New Theatre was without a permanent home in 1954, having been turfed out of Castlereagh Street, and shared space for eight years with the Waterside Workers' Federation (WWF) at 60 Sussex Street (now demolished). The WWF always had first priority over the space, of course, which led to much confusion and many cancelled rehearsals, and the performance space itself was extremely small. Nonetheless, Arthur Miller's searing Cold War allegory *The Crucible* had its Australian premiere on this tiny stage in 1958, and the theatre provided a space throughout the 1950s for left-wing writers to project their idealistic visions for Australia.

The New survived the toughest years of the Cold War, and entered the 1960s with a proud record of support for Australian playwrights and actors. The 1960s infused the group with new energy, and ensured that the New Theatre would continue to mix politics and performance in ways that inspired Sydney audiences – just as it had inspired Oriel Gray back in 1937. Today it owns its theatre on King Street, Newtown.

30

THE DAY OF MOURNING

THE AUSTRALIAN HALL,
150–52 ELIZABETH STREET

Living at a time when there was no television, and when radio was in its infancy, people in the first half of the 20th century liked to go out in the evening, looking for entertainment, education or action, and often they ended up in a hall. Sydney used to be a city of halls, and radicals were among their most frequent users. Before radicals act they need to talk – to each other and to their public. 'Going to the meeting' in a local hall or the back room of a pub was as habitual to radicals as buying their weekly groceries.

The southern end of the city, from Bathurst Street down to Central, was a radical precinct. Much of the action and debate described in this book took place in the halls or on the street corners of this small area. It was thick with halls. To take just one block in Castlereagh Street, between Bathurst and Liverpool Streets: in the early 1920s, radicals met at the Carrington Hall, which was next to the Protestant Hall, and also across the road in the Royal Foresters' Hall, and the hall over McNamara's bookshop, or in Leigh House or in Marx Hall further down the block.

Today, apart from the Protestant Hall, which became The Worker Building (derelict at the time of writing), they are all gone. So are most of the city's dispensary halls, the schools of arts, and the halls of the Buffaloes, Oddfellows and Masons. Some of the pubs have survived, but these days publicans dedicate any non-drinking space to poker machines or so-called sports bars.

One hall that has survived is the Australian Hall, at the southern end of Elizabeth Street – but it only survived as a result of a long campaign in the 1990s to save it. Even more remarkable is the fact that today it lives up to its radical heritage by commemorating Aboriginal struggles.

In 1905, a German social club, Concordia, built its first home on this site. When Elizabeth Street was widened in 1911 the club radically renovated and extended its premises, creating the sandstone-fronted building that still exists. As well as containing the Concordia Hall (used mainly for dancing), the club had dining rooms, a large bar, a double skittle alley, a library, a ladies' room, committee rooms, and 24 bedrooms on the top floor.

The radical phase of its history began with an act that many radicals at the time must have abhorred. In 1915, in World War I, the club was forced to close when the government, because of relentless anti-German hysteria in the press, interned over 60 of its members.

The Concordia trustees had to sell the building. In the late 1920s it became known as the Australian Hall. Earlier, a spiritualist church met there, and between 1920 and 1922, when it was known as Mrs Bishop's Concordia Hall, the newly formed Communist Party used it for regular Sunday night lectures. In the following decades the connection with the left continued. In the 1930s, it was where the supporters of former Premier Jack Lang, at that time in opposition to the 'official' State Executive of the Labor Party, held their meetings. In 1945 striking ironworkers from Mort's Dock in Balmain met there, and in 1946 it was the site of a meeting to protest British intervention against the Communist partisans in Greece.

The peace movement too has a connection with the Australian Hall, appropriately enough given the fate of the Concordia Club. In 1950 the 'Red Dean' of Canterbury, Dr Hewlett Johnson, addressed a conference of supporters of the Communist-led World Peace Council, which was calling for a ban on atomic weapons.

But the truly historic event associated with the Australian Hall, and the event that saved it from destruction, occurred on Australia Day 1938.

On 26 January 1938, a group of Aborigines stood in Park Street to watch the procession celebrating 150 years of white 'progress'. Dressed in thick worsted suits, with collars and ties, they sweltered in the boiling heat. Earlier, at Mrs Macquarie's Chair in Farm Cove, a different group of Aborigines had taken part in a re-enactment of Governor Phillip's landing. This was intended as a lesson in racial power. According to the official program, a group of first-fleet marines, coming ashore by boat, would 'put the Aborigines to flight', while Governor Phillip would land from the second boat. The Aboriginal actors had been brought from Menindee and kept isolated from the city Aborigines, especially from those watching the procession in Park Street, whose subservience was more in doubt.

The group of Aborigines in Park Street were also actors, but their stage was politics: theirs was to be a meeting of protest, an act that would put the Aboriginal view of the events of 1788 – and since. Some of these activists had been preparing in Sydney for months; others had just arrived from interstate or country New South Wales. Organised by the Aborigines' Progressive Association, their aim was to teach the white oppressors a lesson in popular power, for they were going to demand civil rights for all Aborigines. They were a formidable group of leaders: among them were Jack Patten, Bill Ferguson, Pearl Gibbs, William Cooper, Margaret Tucker and Doug Nicholls.

In the run-up to the sesquicentenary celebrations they had issued a pamphlet, 'Aborigines Claim Citizen Rights', with the help of Percy Stephensen, the editor of *The Publicist*. 'Inky', as Stephensen was called, had been an early member of the Communist Party, but he was now in his ultra-nationalist phase – this would end with his internment as pro-Japanese during World War II. He was bankrolled by W.J. Miles, who was also interned. It suited their anti-British views at this time to promote Aboriginal rights.

Also supporting the Aboriginal cause was the Communist Party. Tom Wright organised a meeting to raise funds at Mooney's Club, in the basement of 727 George Street, but the party kept most of the money and publicised the campaign as their own initiative. However, Bill Ferguson, the Aboriginal leader, deflated this claim by releasing the real story to the daily press.

After the procession passed it was time for Aborigines to reveal to whites the real meaning of the day for Aboriginal people. In Australian

AUSTRALIAN

Aborigines Conference

SESQUI-CENTENARY

Day of Mourning and Protest

to be held in

THE AUSTRALIAN HALL, SYDNEY

(No. 148 Elizabeth Street — a hundred yards south of Liverpool Street)

on

WEDNESDAY, 26th JANUARY, 1938

(AUSTRALIA DAY)

The Conference will assemble at 10 o'clock in the morning.

ABORIGINES AND PERSONS OF ABORIGINAL BLOOD ONLY ARE INVITED TO ATTEND

The following Resolution will be moved:

"WE, representing THE ABORIGINES OF AUSTRALIA, assembled in Conference at the Australian Hall, Sydney, on the 26th day of January, 1938, this being the 150th Anniversary of the whitemen's seizure of our country, HEREBY MAKE PROTEST against the callous treatment of our people by the whitemen during the past 150 years, AND WE APPEAL to the Australian Nation of today to make new laws for the education and care of Aborigines, and we ask for a new policy which will raise our people to FULL CITIZEN STATUS and EQUALITY WITHIN THE COMMUNITY."

The above resolution will be debated and voted upon, as the sole business of the Conference, which will terminate at 5 o'clock in the afternoon.

TO ALL AUSTRALIAN ABORIGINES! PLEASE COME TO THIS CONFERENCE IF YOU POSSIBLY CAN! ALSO SEND WORD BY LETTER TO NOTIFY US IF YOU CAN ATTEND

Signed, for and on behalf of

THE ABORIGINES PROGRESSIVE ASSOCIATION,

J. T. PATTEN, President.
W. FERGUSON, Organising Secretary.

Address: c/o. Box 1924KK, General Post Office, Sydney.

In 1938 white Australia celebrated the sesquicentenary of 'the founding of Australia'. In Sydney, the Aborigines' Progressive Association organised a Day of Mourning and Protest (Mitchell Library, State Library of New South Wales, Posters 1612).

The historic moment on 26 January 1938 when Jack Patten, President of the Aborigines' Progressive Association, moves the resolution calling for full citizen status and equality for Aborigines (Mitchell Library, State Library of New South Wales, Q059/9).

Hall, at 1.30 pm, Jack Patten called to order the 'Day of Mourning' conference. Apart from two white journalists, only Aborigines were allowed entry. The meeting endorsed this historic call:

We, representing the Aborigines of Australia, assembled in conference at the Australian Hall, Sydney, on the 26th day of January, 1938, this being the 150th Anniversary of the Whiteman's seizure of our country, hereby make protest against the callous treatment of our people by the whitemen during the past 150 years, and we appeal to the Australian nation today to make new laws for the education and care of Aborigines, and we ask for a new policy which will raise our people to full citizen status and equality within the community.

It took another 30 years before full citizenship for Aborigines was made possible by the referendum of 1967; a further 39 years before the Australian government would say sorry to the country's Indigenous people; and they are still waiting for the 'new laws' to right the wrongs of dispossession and discrimination that began in 1788.

That unfinished business makes the Australian Hall an icon to Aborigines and to all progressive Australians. It explains why a campaign to save the building began in 1992.

At that time the owners of the building, the Cyprus Hellene Club, wanted to pull it down to erect a high-rise office and apartment build-

The Australian Hall today, now owned by Aboriginal interests; the Aboriginal flag out the front has been tangled by the wind (Robert Irving).

ing. But there was a preservation order blocking the development. Then, unexpectedly, the NSW Labor government weakened the preservation order so that only the façade had to be kept, leaving the way open for the rest of the building, including the Australian Hall, to be destroyed.

At this point a coalition of Aboriginal activists, environmentalists and labour historians came together to save the building. For six years, through the courts and on the streets, the campaign to save the hall went on. There were rallies outside Parliament House and protest marches. The National Trust and the History Council – the peak body representing history in New South Wales – spoke in support of the campaign. The leadership provided by the Aboriginal History Committee, and the growing interest of Aboriginal activists in their history, led to the formation of the National Aboriginal History and Heritage Council – a group of Aboriginal activists dedicated to promoting the history of Aborigines since the invasion – which challenged the NSW government in the Land and Environment Court. As they said, 'There are few buildings in Australia – let alone New South Wales or Sydney – that can be identified as being associated with an event of this magnitude in Aboriginal history.'

Facing media criticism and damage to its reputation among conservationists, the government in 1998 at last retreated, reimposing a full preservation order on the entire building just before the court case was due to be heard.

A few months later the Metropolitan Local Aboriginal Land Council bought the building. Today the flag of Aboriginal Australia flies proudly at the front of this historic building.

31

WELCOMING THE NAZI TOURIST

SYDNEY TOWN HALL, 1938

When Australia followed the lead of Britain and declared war on Germany in September 1939, there were no outbreaks of patriotic fervour and enthusiasm like those that had greeted the outbreak of World War I. Instead there was little sense of being at war, and no sense of urgency.

Conservative governments had encouraged a mood of complacency in Australia during the 1930s with regard to political events in Nazi Germany and fascist Italy. Many leading Australian politicians and citizens publicly expressed their sympathy and admiration for the fascist leaders of the two nations. In 1938 federal Attorney-General Robert Menzies returned from a tour of Nazi Germany praising what he had seen and declaring: 'There's today a really spiritual quality in the willingness of Germans to devote themselves to the well-being of the state.' The following year Prime Minister Joseph Lyons rebuked the visiting internationally renowned English writer H.G. Wells for describing Hitler and Mussolini as 'criminal Caesars', and Hitler as a 'certifiable lunatic'.

Behind the scenes Lyons exerted pressure on Australian press owners and the ABC to tone down their treatment of Hitler and Mussolini. A vigorous Commonwealth censorship policy during the 1930s had blown the list of banned items out to some 5000 titles, including many left-wing books and pamphlets warning of the threats posed by Nazism and fascism ... *Mein Kampf*, Hitler's personal blueprint for the future, on the other hand, circulated freely.

In 1934 the Australian government attempted to prevent the prominent Czech anti-fascist writer and publicist Egon Kisch from entering Australia. Denied permission to disembark and enter the country at Fremantle, he jumped from the ship he was a passenger on in Port Melbourne, breaking a leg in the process, and landed on Australian soil, thereby complicating the Australian government's legal problems. A section of the Immigration Act allowed the failure of a test in any European language to justify the exclusion of undesirables. This was subsequently used against the incapacitated Kisch - Gaelic was the language cynically chosen in an attempt to outflank the writer's wide command of European languages. Predictably, Kisch failed the test; he was charged as being a prohibited immigrant and sentenced to imprisonment. Eventually he won a High Court challenge which argued that Gaelic was not a European language. The attempted ban generated a great deal of publicity, turned Kisch into a national celebrity, and attracted large audiences to his anti-fascist addresses around the nation.

Returning home from Europe in 1939, where he had visited Nazi Germany, and had sponsored 36 refugee German Jews for settlement in Australia, the Australian anti-fascist and future prominent leftist journalist Wilfred Burchett found it difficult to get the anti-fascist message across to fellow Australians. As he related in his memoirs (*At the Barricades*, 1980):

> To relate my German experiences of the past few months to anything within the comprehension of easygoing, tolerant Australians was very difficult. To talk of the Gestapo, concentration camps, and the lower depths of human beastliness while the blue smoke curled up and the lamb chops sizzled in a pan on a weekend picnic - it all seemed too fantastic, too remote and unreal. The cultured Germans could not behave like that ...

Unlike Kisch, the Nazi apologist Count Felix von Luckner had no trouble entering Australia. At midnight on 20 May 1938 he sailed his luxuriously appointed schooner *Seeteufel (Sea Devil)* into Sydney Harbour. On board were the Count, his wife, and seven crew members, one of whom was an undercover member of the Gestapo. They had sailed

Nazi apologist Count von Luckner and his wife on their yacht during their Sydney visit in 1938. Behind him are some of the residences of the Sydney elite who fêted him (A.J. Perier, 'On the deck of the German sailing boat', Mitchell Library, State Library of New South Wales, NCY6/258 (a)).

from Germany in April 1937 for a two-year voyage around the world, bankrolled by the German government. After being cleared by quarantine authorities, he anchored in Neutral Bay and later that day went to a luncheon hosted by the Royal Sydney Yacht Squadron.

The 56-year-old von Luckner was no ordinary yachtsman, *Seeteufel* was no ordinary yacht, and the world cruise was no ordinary civilian adventure. During World War I the Count had commanded the maritime marauder *Seeadler* which, disguised as a Norwegian timber carrier, had cruised the Atlantic and South Pacific oceans and sunk 14 unarmed merchant ships. In 1928 the Count's biography by American spin-doctor Lowell Thomas transformed the aristocrat into a world-famous personality and media star, a modern-day buccaneer.

Seeteufel was 88 feet long (nearly 27 metres), weighed 117 tons, had almost 4000 square feet (around 371 square metres) of sail, and a cruising range (it had auxiliary diesel engines) of around 10,000 km. Luxuriously appointed, the yacht had refrigeration, food for six months, a large supply of fine German wine, sophisticated radio receiving and transmission equipment, sophisticated photographic and hydrographic equipment, a film projector for showing German films, a plush book-lined stateroom with Persian carpets and oak furniture. Photos of Hitler and Goebbels and an autographed portrait of Nazi police chief Himmler were prominently displayed. Since the Nazis had come to power, von Luckner had made propaganda tours for Hitler, and this world voyage was one such. As he had explained to the Nazi press on the eve of departure, 'I am going as Hitler's emissary to the youth of the world.'

Sydney's rich and powerful fawned over the Count. During their 14-week stay in Australia the von Luckners were guests at their homes, rural estates and private clubs. Mr Mark Foy, retail doyen, was a Sydney friend, a fellow yachting enthusiast, and one of those businessmen who earlier in the 1930s had helped bankroll the quasi-fascist New Guard organisation (1931–35); so too was Captain James R. Patrick, owner of the stevedoring and ship-owning firm Patrick and Company, formerly a member of the New Guard's General Council and in charge of its Finance Department.

To Sydney journalists von Luckner described a rosy Nazi Germany. Hitler was a reasonable, friendly man, capable of enjoying a joke. The *Daily Telegraph* reported von Luckner as saying:

> His [Hitler's] democratic manner to the least important German subject, his anxiety to advance the poor instead of the rich, and his shunning of personal pomp are the secrets of Hitler's power in Germany.

Quizzed about the fate of the high-profile German Communist leader Ernst Thälmann, arrested in 1933 as part of Hitler's elimination of political opposition, the Count explained that he was simply in protective custody, for his own good, and enjoying luxurious accommodation in 'a beautiful villa' with tennis courts and a bowling alley. Von Luckner failed to name this top-notch resort. Thälmann was eventually executed in Buchenwald concentration camp.

Not everyone was persuaded by this nonsense. Since the tour had been announced in early 1937, an array of organisations nationally, including trade unions, Trades and Labour Councils, the small but energetic Communist Party, Labor Party branches, and the Movement Against War and Fascism (MAWF), which had been established in 1934, lobbied the Australian government to ban the *Seeteufel* from entering Australian waters.

As the Count headed for Sydney, Lloyd Ross, NSW Secretary of the Australian Railways Union and National President of MAWF, hit the airwaves, telling 2KY Sydney radio listeners that von Luckner was a 'fascist lecturer' preparing Australians to support Hitler when he 'marches into Switzerland, Belguim, Czechoslovakia and Soviet Russia'. Anti-Luckner feeling was so strong that there were mass meetings of Sydney railway workers at the huge Eveleigh railway workshops in June and July 1937, soon after he began his world voyage – to great fanfare, and with Australia on his itinerary.

As far as these workers were concerned, von Luckner's forthcoming visit was a fascist propaganda tour. Fascism, they explained in motions to the federal government, 'is responsible for the murder of thousands of Trade Union, Labor Party, Jewish, and Church leaders'. German fascism 'has nothing in common with our ideas of justice'. Von Luckner represented a political viewpoint that 'must be seriously challenged'; his tour would serve as 'a rallying point for fascist elements in Australia'. If the federal government did not prevent the tour from taking place, the railway workers would authorise their union leaders to organise 'through the Trades and Labour Council an anti-Fascist campaign, commencing on the arrival of von Luckner'.

In a deal brokered through the German Consulate in Sydney, a small Sydney public relations agency organised a national speaking tour for the Count, who would travel by car, rail and air, beginning at the Sydney Town Hall on the evening of Monday, 6 June 1938. Hiring that particular staid, iconic symbol of civic power proved difficult: the majority of the City Council's Labor aldermen supported the anti-fascist cause and opposed the hire, and the nervous Lord Mayor sought Prime Ministerial advice before accepting the Count's booking.

Opening night, the first of four Town Hall appearances, and the first leg of an extensive NSW tour. The Count was nervous. There were at least 100 protesters outside the Town Hall, along with a large police presence. Protests had commenced the morning after his yacht moored in Neutral Bay. Everywhere the Count went there were protesters, many of them young people, carrying anti-fascist signs or wearing anti-fascist slogans sewn onto their clothing. His recent trip to Canberra and a warm, private meeting with Prime Minister Lyons had been gratifying; as von Luckner later told an interviewer, he and Lyons seemed to be of similar mind.

The Count had a fixed smile as he strode onto the Town Hall stage. Before him was an audience of 400, many of them formally attired. In the front rows he recognised friendly faces from Sydney's elite. As for the rest, it was a bedlam; boos, slogans and taunting political questions greeted his appearance. Von Luckner waved his arms and appealed for quiet. 'I have travelled 17,000 miles,' he began. There were scuffles in the audience as his supporters clashed with anti-fascists. Among the protesters were members of Sydney's Jewish community; for them von Luckner was a symbol of Nazi anti-semitism, and the freedom of entry to Australia extended to him was in stark contrast to the anti-refugee policy of the Lyons government, which had drastically curtailed Jewish immigration.

A confetti of anti-fascist leaflets filled the air. Sixty uniformed and plainclothes police waded into the audience, and 30 protesters were removed. A young woman was dragged away, but not before she unfurled a banner reading 'HITLERISM MEANS MASS MURDER OF WOMEN AND CHILDREN'. Von Luckner continued his speech, and likened himself to Sir Francis Drake. The rhetorical device had won over American audiences – there he had compared himself to American naval hero John Paul Jones and the Wild West's Buffalo Bill. Sydney's anti-fascists erupted with a torrent of abuse and pandemonium ensued; anger and frustration reddened the Count's face and his smile disappeared.

Von Luckner struggled through his address, ending with the observation that 'Britain is the head and brains of Europe; Germany is the

Three people were arrested at this anti-von Luckner demonstration outside Sydney Town Hall on 6 June 1938 (*Daily Telegraph*, 7 June 1938).

heart.' But one troubled night at the Sydney Town Hall was enough. The scheduled tour of New South Wales was cancelled and the Nazi emissary confined himself to selected 'invitation only' audiences. When he moved interstate, anti-fascist protests continued. In Melbourne police dispersed crowds of protesters with baton charges. In Queensland the Count found sympathetic audiences among the large Italian and German immigrant communities, and fascist salutes were not uncommon; however, at Innisfail there were 1200 protesters outside one of his talks. When the Count sailed from Cairns on 6 September 1938, and finally left mainland Australia, the *Seeteufel* flew the swastika flag – it was the first ship to ever fly the flag in the port, claimed proud propagandists in *Die Brücke*, the weekly magazine which had been published since 1934 (in English and German) by the German-Australian Chamber of Commerce and the German Alliance of Australia and New Zealand.

One of the charges von Luckner faced from critics while in Australia was that he was a Nazi spy, a deduction based on his maritime past and speculation about the real purpose of his current voyage. Britain's Director of MI5 was also curious, and alerted Australian intelligence authorities. Throughout von Luckner's Australian tour he and his crew were under surveillance by the Commonwealth Investigation Branch and Naval Intelligence. For the Australian spooks there was much of interest, including the possibility that the *Seeteufel* crew was gathering maritime intelligence, the Count's periodic reports to German Foreign Minister von Ribbentrop, and a long and apparently important meeting in a suite of the prestigious Hotel Australia in Sydney with a German manufacturer of bomber aircraft, fresh from Japan. But the intelligence data gathered was inconclusive. Surveillance did generate a list of people of German and Italian origins who seemed to be pro-fascist. Following the outbreak of war this list was apparently used by authorities as a guide for rounding up people for internment.

32

KEN COOK AND THE JAPANESE COLLABORATORS

THE GRACE BUILDING, 77–79 YORK STREET

Drew Cottle and Shane Cahill

Guests and visitors to the elegant art deco Grace Hotel can view in its marbled and tiled foyer a detailed illustrated display of the building's history. They learn of the Grace's dashed expectations with the onset of the Depression following its construction as an office building in 1930, its struggle to attract tenants during the rest of the decade, and like Australia itself, its salvation in early 1942 when the Supreme Commander of Allied Forces in the Pacific, General Douglas MacArthur, took over the premises, bringing it financial security at last.

But what the chronology fails to reveal is that the man who promised he would return to the Phillipines and wrest it back from the Japanese who were sweeping towards New Guinea and Australia was taking up residence in a building which had housed, since 1933, none other than the Japanese Consulate-General as a major tenant.

This omission also denies us the chance to see first-hand a prime location in a unique story of intrigue, courage and treachery. For it was up these marble staircases and in these panelled lifts that an enigmatic figure in Australian history, Ken Cook, made his way, masquerading as a Japanese sympathiser and agent while engaging in counter-espionage that revealed both the extent of Japanese plans to absorb Australia into its empire and the identities of some of the prominent Australians they

The Grace Building: from this building the Japanese Consulate-General operated its intelligence network during the 1930s (Mitchell Library, State Library of New South Wales, ON2/145).

believed would co-operate in its administration and policing. And it was to the Japanese consulate staff in these same offices on the 10th floor that pro-Axis Australian intelligence officers revealed Cook's true identity and intentions in an act of callous betrayal.

A neighbour of the consulate on the 10th floor was the Retail Traders' Association of New South Wales, whose members, including C. Lloyd Jones, the Chairman of David Jones Ltd, were among the most vociferous advocates of a strong trade relationship between Japan and Australia in the 1930s.

The Consul-General and his staff were responsible for overseeing the activities of all Japanese nationals in Australia, for gathering information on Australia and for co-ordinating the cultivation of Australians who were considered sympathetic or amenable to Japan's case for trade and territorial expansion ... which included separating Australia from its British imperial connection and enticing it – or forcing it, if necessary – into the Japanese imperial orbit.

The consulate managed a major espionage program. While this is not unique in the world of diplomacy, not all nations which gather intelligence data via their diplomatic staff end up at war with their hosts. Successive Japanese Consul-Generals and senior officials had backgrounds in military intelligence, disguised behind veneers of bland commercial interests or cultivated ineptitude. With almost no Australians able to speak or read Japanese, it was not difficult for the consulate to maintain tight security. Mixed in among the legitimate inquiries and requests for material, the consulate sought and obtained information on Communists and Jews in Australia, Australia's financial reserves in London, and strategic details about infrastructure (such as coastal defences, harbours, ports, airfields, power and water supplies) – information that might be useful to an invading military force.

The most important organisation established by the consulate was the Japan-Australia Society, which was founded by the Consul-General, Prince Tokugawa, on Armistice Day 1929 (11 November). The society was an exclusive – by invitation only – organisation and its members were academics, conservative politicians and the owners of the pastoral, retailing, shipping, stevedoring, milling, banking and insurance interests that were benefiting from the rapidly expanding trade between the nations. Identical bodies were established across Asia and proved to be the breeding grounds for the puppet leaders and administrators who took control of their countries when they fell under Japanese rule from 1942. Weekly luncheons were held at the Hotel Australia in Castlereagh Street, and the Consul-General entertained regularly at his palatial Point Piper residence, Craig-y-Mor.

Japan emerged as a major player in the Australian economy during the Depression, rescuing it from its lowest ebb in 1932–33 and allowing Australia to maintain its repayments to its British creditors. Japan's purchases in Australia were in large part used to clothe and feed its army as it set about taking over Manchuria and then invading China. The Australian businessmen who benefited from Japanese trade were under no illusions that their continued good fortune depended on continued Japanese military and territorial expansion, and indeed eagerly anticipated further Japanese incursions into China, as a series of articles – based on Japanese briefings – in the *Sydney Morning Herald* praising Japan's mission in Asia revealed. The articles were produced by Major Jack Scott, a Great War veteran, insurance broker, Japanophile, member of the distinguished Street legal family, and a key player in the Australian paramilitary organisations that flirted with fascism during the 1930s. Later he joined Military Intelligence.

The Commonwealth government also turned a benign gaze on Japanese expansion, partly funding a lavish publicity volume published in English and Japanese language editions – *Japan, Australia and New Zealand*. It was written by Ken Sato, a Japanese journalist and public relations man working in the Japanese consulate, and Charles Cousens, Sydney's leading radio personality, who left his high-profile position for a year to work on it. Interviewed in Osaka, Japan, by Australian journalist Denis Warner after the end of the war, Sato claimed that had Japan become the conqueror of a vanquished Australia, he (Sato) would have organised a puppet administration – under Japanese control – using the Australian business and political contacts he had made years earlier.

As for Cousens, he served as an Australian army officer in the war against Japan. Captured during the capitulation of Singapore, he was taken to Tokyo, where he made propaganda broadcasts over Radio Tokyo, wrote radio scripts and trained Japanese broadcasters. Following the defeat of Japan, Cousens was arrested and charged with treason by Australian authorities; the charge was dropped in late 1946.

Members of the Japan-Australia Society were called upon by Japan in November 1937 to reject Chinese claims that atrocities had been committed at what the world called the Rape of Nanking, which had occurred during Japan's undeclared war on China. This they did. Sir Thomas Gordon, for example, of Birt & Co., which represented Japanese shipping interests in Australia, talked directly to Cabinet members and newspaper editors; he soon reported back to Japan that only a few malcontents were still making anti-Japanese statements. Japan's entry into the Axis in September 1940 failed to move the members of the Japan-Australia Society to wind the society up.

British intelligence decided it needed to find out the exact nature of the relationship between Japan and Australia, in business and political terms, and where it was heading. An Australian, Ken Cook, was

Two spies: Ken Sato, Japanese operative; Ken Cook, Australian operative (*The Home*, September 1935; courtesy of Drew Cottle, from his book, *The Brisbane Line: A reappraisal*, 2002).

recruited; he was keen to help resist the rise of Japan, having witnessed Japanese militarism at work in China first-hand when working out of Hong Kong as a journalist. After being taught the basics of espionage and intelligence-gathering, he contacted the Japanese Consulate in Sydney – notionally to seek advice on patents – and began to build an identity as a Japanese sympathiser. He did this under the name of Ken Easton-Cook, and as a theatre owner, having prevailed upon his wealthy family to buy him a theatrette in Kings Cross. He became fluent in Japanese, and established his *bona fides* with the Japanese by setting up a short-lived pro-Japanese organisation ... but he lost all his Australian friends in the process. Cook provided reports of his work to Australian military and naval intelligence authorities.

Japanese consular officials understood that if it came to war between Britain and Japan, Australian businessmen and politicians would support Britain. Nonetheless they saw it as in their interests to weaken that support as far as possible. During the late 1930s the Japanese stepped up their efforts to gain prominent Australian sympathisers and Cook was told that they were focusing on finding Australian collaborators who would assist them, and that they believed Australian politicians 'were not above accepting bribes'.

Unfortunately for Cook, the Australian intelligence community harboured some people with pronounced right-wing, and in cases openly pro-Axis, sympathies. They betrayed Cook to some of the Japanese consular staff and an attempt was made to strangle him on board a Japanese ship. Cook maintained his composure and other more senior Japanese staff expressed their confidence in him. However, Cook subsequently ceased his intelligence activities.

Australia followed the US and Britain in freezing Japanese assets in July 1941, in a bid to halt the Japanese advance into Southeast Asia. Although trade between Australia and Japan virtually ceased, and most Japanese businessmen and their families returned home, the consulate stepped up its efforts to win Australians over to the Japanese cause. Some of the Australian rich and powerful continued to sit on the fence and the Consul-General and his staff continued to host members of the Japan-Australia Society at lunches and dinners until days before the Japanese attack on Pearl Harbour.

Finally, when war became inevitable, Craig-y-Mor's chimneys belched out smoke continuously for a while as the consulate's most sensitive records, including assessments of Australian sympathisers and potential co-operators and collaborators, were destroyed.

While the Japanese strike force was steaming towards Hawaii, the consular staff assembled with the Japanese businessmen who remained in Sydney for a farewell dinner and group portrait at the Hotel Australia. With the outbreak of war the Japanese were placed under a loose form of detention – which scrupulously observed diplomatic courtesy and respect – prior to being repatriated by sea to Japan, via a neutral port in Mozambique, in a swap for Australian diplomatic personnel in 1942.

At the conclusion of the war, preliminary Australian security investigations of Japanese consular materials that had survived destruction and been seized by authorities at the outbreak of war with Japan revealed significant Japanese pre-war intelligence activity in Australia and pointed to evidence of fifth-column activities by prominent Australians. However, the postwar politics of the American-led rapprochement with a defeated Japan prevailed. America worked hard to stabilise its influence throughout the Pacific region, and a full investigation was never conducted.

As the Cold War took hold, the pre-war appeasers and courtiers of fascism re-emerged in a new guise, as staunch anti-Communists, and the pre-war world of Australia's Japan lobby was quietly pushed aside. However, in 1954, at the Petrov Royal Commission, the silence was broken when the sensational 'Document J' became public: it revealed the pre-war connections between the Japanese consulate and prominent business and political figures, and the argument that had Australia been invaded by Japan during World War II, co-operators in a Japanese-occupied Australia would have emerged from among these people. These claims were not rigorously examined by the Petrov Royal Commission and the document was consigned to archival secrecy until its public release by the Hawke Labor government in 1984. One of the sources of information in 'Document J' was Ken Cook.

33

THE BATTLE OF
BLIGH STREET

They came up the hill from Sussex Street, a hundred or so wharfies marching from their union hall on the radical fringe of the city to the centre of the financial district. Their mission was to disrupt a public meeting of the Australia First Movement in the Adyar Hall in Bligh Street.

It was February 1942. In Europe, Nazi Germany seemed poised for victory; in Asia, its fascist ally, Japan, seemed unstoppable. Pearl Harbour had been bombed, Singapore had fallen, and that afternoon's papers had carried the frightening news of a Japanese attack on Darwin.

Earlier that day, 'Sydney heard the banshee wail of air-raid sirens in the first daylight raid test in Australian history' – and the results were farcical, exposing the abysmal level of planning by the authorities. There were no sirens in many parts of the metropolitan area, only a quarter of the wardens turned out, shelters in the city were inadequate, and in the pubs the drinkers thought it was a huge joke. But some on the political left thought the situation called for urgent action.

Back in 1936, a strange advertisement had appeared in the *Sydney Morning Herald*:

> Wanted, a young man, not more than 35 years of age, of good personality and education, not necessarily University, willing to actively devote the whole or part of his time to 'Australia First' political propaganda (having as its object the formation of a new Australian political party). He would need to Australian-born of British Aryan stock ...

Behind the advertisement were W.J. Miles, a wealthy businessman from the North Shore, and P.R. ('Inky') Stephensen, a writer and publisher. Both of them had anti-establishment histories rooted in contempt for liberal principles and the capacities for self-government of ordinary people – histories that were the perfect seedbed for fascism.

The term 'Australia First' was coined by Miles during World War I to indicate his opposition to conscription and the ruling-class sideshow of 'imperial federation', a scheme dreamed up in the late 19th century by British conservatives to make the parliaments of the British settler colonies subordinate to the British Parliament. In the 1920s he added fascist corporatism to Australian chauvinism, ideas which he passed on to Stephensen when he became Stephensen's financial patron in the 1930s. On his deathbed in 1941 Miles ran a sweep for his friends on when he would die. A cold and rigid man, he was not missed by his daughter, Bee Miles, the eccentric but life-affirming woman who used to recite Shakespeare on Sydney's streets in the 1950s.

The volatile 'Inky' Stephensen became a Communist in the 1920s. In Oxford as a Rhodes Scholar, he picketed with fellow Communists during the General Strike of 1926. Subsequently he became a publisher and a crusader against censorship, helping D.H. Lawrence publish an English edition of the banned *Lady Chatterley's Lover*. Returning to Sydney in 1932, he spent several lean years publishing Australian writers at a time when Australian literature was unknown to readers and spurned by the main commercial publishers. He came to Miles's attention when he wrote a vigorous defence of the distinctiveness of Australian culture. Miles put him on his payroll. Stephensen's conviction that European civilisation was decaying made him susceptible to Miles's ideas.

With money from Miles and contributions from Stephensen, a monthly journal, *The Publicist*, appeared in 1936 to prepare the ground for the Australia First Party. Miles ran it from the Publicist Bookshop at 209A Elizabeth Street, in the old T&G Building on the corner of Park Street. *The Publicist* was openly sympathetic to Japan. It drew together the visible and noisier part of the publicity-shy pro-Japanese crowd and the appeasers in the daily press, mainstream politics and business.

The journal's philosophy was fascist, a concoction of rabid nationalism, anti-semitism and hatred of democracy and the left. It argued that

Australian author and intellectual Percy Stephensen, the front man for the Australia First movement. He was interned during World War II for his political activity (Mitchell Library, State Library of New South Wales, P1/s [BM]).

Australia should isolate itself from the war that was looming in Europe, and when Australia entered the war on the side of the Allies it took on the role of softening up the public for an Axis victory. After the Japanese attack on Pearl Harbour, *The Publicist* demanded a separate peace between Australia and Japan.

The left had observed Stephensen's drift to the right. On the day war broke out in 1939 someone painted a large sign on the window of the Publicist bookshop: 'Nazi HQ'.

The Australia First Movement was launched in October 1941. It held regular meetings, one of which was announced for the Adyar Hall on 19 February 1942. There were about 100 Australia First supporters in the hall when the wharfies arrived. They joined other trade unionists who had come for the same purpose. 'Ladies and Gentlemen' was all that the first speaker managed. Immediately, someone called from the audience, 'This is a fascist meeting', and then there was pandemonium. Amid stink bombs and a hail of rotten eggs, chairs were smashed and used as weapons; plaster flew off the walls and pillars of the hall.

On stage, well-known Australian writer Miles Franklin was helped to escape through a rear door, while the main speaker, Stephensen, was hit on the head with a water carafe. He fell to the ground, where he was kicked and punched. The undercover police at the meeting did nothing. The uproar and fighting continued for half an hour before two uniformed constables arrived, but by then most of those involved in the fighting had departed.

The meeting resumed, but when Stephensen, bloodied but defiant, responded to further interjections by inviting a wharfie onto the platform, in the expectation that he would make a fool of himself, the biter was bit. The speaker was surprisingly well informed, and explained how the fascist quislings of northern Europe had opened the gates to Hitler. He showed that the Australia Firsters, extolling the superiority of Japan over Australia's effete democracy, were playing the same role. He provided details about the Japanese government's having paid for trips to Japan by the Walshes (Adela and Tom), once on the left but now members of Australia First.

There was more uproar. A woman who had been expelled from the Hotel, Club and Restaurant Union hit an organiser from that union over the head with an umbrella. He was arrested, as was James McLaughlin, a waterside worker, who shouted, 'This is a fascist meeting and these people are Japanese agents.' It was time for the last of the anti-fascist disrupters to retire, which they did, but they took with them Australia First's membership receipt book.

When McLaughlin was brought before the Central Police Court next day, charged with offensive behaviour, he told the magistrate that he was an Australian who had tried three times to enlist. His three

Adyar Hall, Bligh Street, site of the 19 February 1942 clash between the pro-fascist Australia First organisation and militant anti-fascist trade unionists (Mitchell Library, State Library of New South Wales, NCY 1/826).

brothers had joined the army. One was killed in Crete, another was presumed lost in Malaya, and he did not know where the third was. He said the views expressed by the people holding the meeting were repugnant to him, and they were damaging the war effort. The magistrate said that if McLaughlin thought that people were doing something subversive he should report it to the proper authorities. He found the offence proved but discharged McLaughlin without proceeding to conviction.

Perhaps the 'proper authorities' received the Australia First membership book, for within a month, Stephensen and 15 other members of the movement were arrested and interned without trial for the duration of the war – thus did the government regain the initiative. At a postwar inquiry no evidence was produced that Stephensen and the other internees were plotting against the state. Scholars now agree that Stephensen and his associates were sad proponents of unpalatable ideas, which in turn led to their becoming victims of gross infringement of their civil liberties.

It is important to realise, however, that the Australia Firsters were only the visible and eccentric part of the quisling iceberg. Their internment may have prevented acts of treason by showing the wealthy supporters of Japan that our government would not hesitate to use the force of the state against them.

34

FRED WONG AND THE CHINESE SEAMEN'S UNION

175 HAY STREET

When Japan entered World War II, and British and Dutch ships sought safety in Australian ports, their Chinese, Indian and Indonesian crews were stranded in a country that regarded them as prohibited 'coloured' immigrants. Their struggle for equality with Australian workers, their part in the Allied war effort, and their contribution to anti-imperialist campaigns after the war should be better known, for by their struggles these seamen punched holes in the 'great white walls' of Australian racism.

In 1945, Dutch filmmaker Joris Ivens was also marooned in Australia, not wanted in either Hollywood or his homeland because of his left-wing politics. He decided to document the boycott by Indonesian seamen and Australian maritime workers of the Dutch ships carrying weapons and supplies from our ports to defeat the new Indonesian republic. In the film *Indonesia Calling* he shows Dutch soldiers on the troopship *Stirling Castle* refusing to listen to pro-republic demonstrators. Then, in the climax of the film, another ship, the *Patras*, is leaving Sydney harbour, followed by an open launch from which a man shouts 'Indonesia Merdeka' to the Indian crew who are leaning over the side. The *Patras* noses out into the open water, slipping away. Then its engines are shut down and it returns to the harbour – it is a victory for freedom ('merdeka') and international solidarity. This powerful film was smuggled into Indonesia (with commentary in Malaysian), but was never screened in the Netherlands.

The man in the open boat was Fred Wong, the President of the Chinese Seamen's Union. Born in Cobar, Wong Gar Kin was drawn into radical politics by the Japanese threat to China. The Japanese government, after annexing Manchuria, launched a full-scale invasion of China in 1937. In Sydney's Chinese community, where Fred Wong had many contacts through his business as a greengrocer, there was growing frustration at the reluctance of the Nationalist Chinese government to co-operate with the Chinese Communists against the Japanese. At the same time the Australian Communists were calling for a boycott of Japanese goods, as part of a broader strategy to mobilise the working class against fascism.

The first opportunity to bring together patriots in the Chinese community and the left of the labour movement came when 36 Chinese seamen deserted from the SS *Silksworth* in Newcastle in October 1937. The *Silkworth* was a British ship chartered to a Japanese company to carry Australian produce to the Japanese puppet state in Manchuria. Its crew were in dispute with the captain over the actions of a Japanese officer who, while drunk, had beaten a Chinese seaman. Arriving in Newcastle, the crew heard the news of the Japanese 'Rape of Nanking': the slaughter of thousands of civilians in the capital of Nationalist China. Incensed by their inability to obtain justice from the captain and fired up by resentment at the part they were being forced to play in support of Japanese aggression against their country, the crew walked off the ship and sought help at Trades Hall.

As non-white workers, the Chinese seamen ran the risk of imprisonment and deportation. Would Trades Hall be a safe haven? Although many labour organisations, including the Labor Party, were officially against any weakening of the white Australia policy, workers' struggles could modify rank-and-file racist attitudes, as subsequent events were to show.

When the 36 met the secretary of the Newcastle Trades Hall Council he reported that he had 'never met better unionists'. Meanwhile, in Sydney, Fred Wong had joined a 'Hands Off China' committee formed by the Trades and Labour Council. The strategy was to prevent the ship from sailing and thus draw attention to the exploitation of the Chinese seamen and the tacit support of the Australian government for Japanese aggression. If the crew 'disappeared', delaying immigration proceedings against them, the ship would be prevented from taking on a replacement crew. Accordingly, six of the Chinese seamen were hidden in the homes of Australian workers, reappearing from time to time to make statements to the press through interpreters arranged by Fred Wong. After a long struggle the crew were permitted a discharge with back pay and a promise of repatriation to China.

For Fred Wong and his friends in the Chinese community the experience of working together with militant unionists was repeated a year later in the notorious *Dalfram* dispute in Port Kembla, when waterside workers refused to load pig-iron for Japan. As a greengrocer, Fred Wong was able to organise the collection and distribution of food to the families of the workers on strike. He also persuaded Chinese seamen to donate money to the strike fund. Out of these experiences came the Chinese Youth League, set up in 1939 to unite the revolutionary nationalists and facilitate co-operation with the Australian left. Fred Wong became its first President.

The Chinese Youth League, which celebrated its 60th anniversary recently, had important welfare and cultural functions. It staged plays and Cantonese operas, many of them with pointed messages for exploiters within their own community. It was one such opera that brought tensions to a head in 1943.

By this time Japan had attacked Pearl Harbour, captured Singapore and bombed Darwin. As a result there was a sudden increase in the number of Chinese seamen – to nearly 2000 – in Australian ports. With most of China occupied by the Japanese, they could not be repatriated. Moreover, their families depended on their wages, which had not been paid since their ships sheltered in Australian ports, and the Australian government, which promptly commandeered the ships, was now expecting them to go back to sea in a war zone, on wages far less than those received by Australian and British merchant seamen. So they refused to work. In Fremantle, military guards attempting to terrorise the strikers shot dead two Chinese seamen. In Sydney, after several arrests, the Chinese seamen met with the leaders of the Seamen's Union of Australia, and formed the Australian branch of the Chinese Seamen's Union, in the rooms of the Chinese Youth League at 66 Dixon Street. Fred Wong was again the first President.

At the inaugural meeting a play was performed urging seamen not to throw their wages away on opium and gambling. The leaders of the union saw this as part of their welfare function, but they also knew that penniless and addicted members were unreliable fighters for better conditions at sea and, ultimately, for Chinese independence. Naturally the gambling houses were incensed, and their thugs began to intimidate union members, threatening to destroy the union's premises. Arthur Locke Chang, who was a member of the union, recalled the story of what happened next:

> An urgent meeting was called at the Chinese Youth League premises, when Stanley Wai, General Secretary of the Chinese Seamen's Union, urged the crowd to take firm action against the bosses of the gambling houses. That night a group of seamen led by Stanley Wai and K.Y. Tong, the head of the Shanghai Group, went up Campbell Street and played fantan. They placed their bets on the centre of the square, which was unorthodox, as this meant whichever way the result went, 1, 2, 3 or 4, the banker had to pay out. When their bets were refused, the seamen smashed up the joint.

The next morning, surprisingly, a great calm prevailed over Chinatown, especially around Paddy's Market. Premises of the Chinese Youth League and the Chinese Seamen's Union were more crowded than usual, and Fred Wong and Mr Lai happily went along to sell opera tickets and collect donations for famine relief, as they had done many times before in support of China's war effort.

During the war the Chinese Seamen's Union secured better wages and conditions for its members, organised labour brigades that worked on civil construction (including the Warragamba Dam), and often provided lodgings, food and friendship for stranded workers. Its members marched with Australian workers in Sydney's May Day processions. When the war ended, however, hundreds of its members returned to their homeland to fight for a new China. As the union weakened, the shipowners lost no time trying to reimpose the racial division of labour. The Chinese seamen fought back, but their union was only capable of providing welfare and creating propaganda for the seamen.

A meeting of the Chinese Seamen's Union in Sydney's Trades Hall during World War II (Mitchell Library, State Library of New South Wales, NCY31/544).

It was more successful, however, when it turned its attention to the postwar struggles for national independence by former colonial peoples. It organised support for the Indonesian seamen who, like the Chinese seamen on the *Silksworth*, were refusing to work on ships owned by a colonial power. It arranged for meals in Chinese restaurants for the Indonesian seamen, and collected money for Joris Ivens' film.

In 1948 the Chinese Seamen's Union still had an office in Hay Street. It shared the office with a company called Asian Airlines Ltd, which was an ambitious attempt to form an airline to trade with China and to carry medical and other supplies to parts of Indonesia and Malaya controlled by the independence movements fighting the Dutch and British colonialists respectively. The main investor was Clarence Campbell. He had a long history in the Labor Party left, and was the nominal owner of Marx House, the Communist Party headquarters at 695 George Street. Fred Wong also held shares in Asian Airlines, as did

175 Hay Street, Sydney today. It formerly housed the headquarters of the Chinese Seamen's Union and Asian Airlines (Robert Irving).

a number of other Chinese Australians. The company bought a Catalina flying boat from the Australian government, and reportedly had an option to purchase 11 more.

Opponents of Communism saw this development, along with all struggles for national independence, as part of the 'red menace'. Having received reports from a spy in the company, the Commonwealth security service began to feed misinformation about the company's investors and its plans to conservative politicians and the press. All the investors were described as Communist, which Campbell and others vigorously denied. During a Civil Aviation inquiry into the company, press photographers harassed Campbell, who unwisely scuffled with one of them. Next day there were photos on page 3 of the *Sydney Morning Herald* of Campbell's 'attack' on the journalist. The company's fate was sealed:

The symbol of the Chinese Youth League of Australia, one of the founders of which, Fred Wong, founded the Chinese Seamen's Union (courtesy of the Chinese Youth League of Australia, from its publication *60th Anniversary Magazine*).

Indonesia was still too dangerous to fly to, and then the British government refused the company permission to land in Singapore.

But the heart went out of the company when Fred Wong met a mysterious death in July 1948. He had gone to Lake Boga, in Victoria, in the company's flying boat, and there he and the pilot had been working on other Catalinas. When the dinghy they were working from capsized, the pilot swam to safety but Wong, although a competent swimmer, drowned.

On the wall of the Chinese Youth League at 10 Dixon Street this scroll commemorates Fred Wong:

> Happiness of human race not yet attained,
> Ordinary folk have responsibility.
> Spirit of our President undying,
> Great righteousness prevails forever.

35

'BARGING' AT THE GPO

IMPERIALISM AT BAY

Admiral Lord Louis Mountbatten, Supreme Commander of South-East Asia Command, decked out in naval uniform and wearing six rows of medal ribbons, was all smiles as he stepped from his open limousine. The great-grandson of Queen Victoria moved through the press throng and an adoring, mainly female, crowd and entered Sydney's General Post Office (GPO). It was 3 pm on Friday, 29 March 1946. The landmark Classical-style building in Martin Place, between George and Pitt streets, was still in wartime mode, minus its imposing clock tower, which had removed in 1942 for fear of becoming a Japanese bombing target or providing them with aerial navigation assistance.

Mountbatten had recently flown to Australia from his Singapore headquarters. The doting Australian press enthusiastically greeted his arrival, dubbing him 'the Playboy Prince': 'tall and handsome, his dark hair touched with grey, [he] will charm Australians', the *Sydney Morning Herald* had fawned. Mountbatten had met in Canberra with Prime Minister Ben Chifley and Cabinet, and was now headed for a special meeting in the office maintained by the Minister for Supply and Shipping on the first floor of the GPO building. In particular he wanted to meet with representatives of the two major Australian maritime unions, the Waterside Workers' Federation (WWF) and the Seamen's Union of Australia (SUA), and discuss matters relating to the future of Asia.

A group of high-powered men eventually gathered in the Minister's suite for the meeting: aside from Mounbatten and his party, there was the Minister for Shipping and Supply and his Departmental Secretary; the Commonwealth Director of Shipping; Albert Monk, Secretary of

Postwar Sydney: GPO, Martin Place, where Mountbatten met with unionists in 1946. The clock tower is still missing; it was removed during World War II to prevent it becoming a landmark for possible Japanese air attacks (Mitchell Library, State Library of New South Wales, GPO 1–36585).

the Australian Council of Trade Unions; the Secretary and Assistant Secretary of the NSW Trades and Labour Council; and representing the maritime unions, Ted Roach (Assistant General Secretary, WWF) and E.V. Elliott (Federal Secretary, SUA).

Mountbatten wanted the maritime unions to lift the ban on Dutch shipping that had been imposed in September 1945 in solidarity with Indonesian independence. Eventually involving 31 unions, the ban had tied up Dutch ships and their cargoes in Australian ports, denying Dutch colonial authorities access to supplies vital to their postwar reoccupation of the Netherlands East Indies (NEI), present-day Indonesia. As far as Mountbatten was concerned, the release of the Dutch ships would relieve British ships that were currently assisting the Dutch – they were needed for Britain's imperial interests elsewhere in Asia.

The ban had been imposed following the proclamation of a Republic by the Indonesian independence movement in August 1945, and the subsequent call for Australian trade union assistance against the re-establishment of Dutch colonial rule in the NEI. The Australian government had hosted the exiled NEI government, along with its paraphernalia of empire, during the war, after the Dutch abandoned their colony in the face of invading Japanese forces in 1942, leaving the struggle against invasion to nationalist forces. Australia was therefore a crucial staging post for the Dutch reoccupation of their colony. The nationalist request for Australian trade union assistance and the subsequent ban reflected the close relationship the maritime unions in particular had developed with thousands of Indonesians, many of them nationalists, who had also been displaced by war and exiled in Australia as political prisoners and/or employees of the Dutch.

This relationship had developed primarily through contact between Indonesian seamen and the SUA dating back to 1941. Some 5000 Indonesian seamen passed through Australian ports during the war, and many sought help from the Australian union in relation to general welfare matters, wages and conditions. Despite being exiled in Australia, Dutch authorities thumbed their noses at Australian wages and conditions, expecting Indonesian maritime workers to continue to labour in exile under substandard colonial conditions, and for wages massively out of kilter with those of their Australian counterparts. Since the 1920s the NEI colonial administration had tried to suppress trade unionism among Indonesian workers, with the result that Indonesian trade union sentiments and inclinations tended to be radically nationalist.

As far as the SUA was concerned, seafarers were seafarers, irrespective of nationality or race, and exploitation was exploitation. The union willingly assisted the Indonesian workers, and in 1944 helped establish the Indonesian Seamen's Union, headquartered in Woolloomooloo. This union was headed by a 17-year-old Indonesian seaman. In later life, as Tuk Subianto, he became a prominent Indonesian trade union leader; however, he disappeared in the bloody anti-leftist purge of 1965 –66 led by the Indonesian military.

Mountbatten's GPO meeting failed to dint union resolve: the ban would continue until such time as the Indonesians indicated that it should be ended. That night Mountbatten recorded in his diary that his talk with the union leaders had been 'a good barging match'. Behind his back, in Singapore, critics who thought he was a bit soft when it came to putting the boot into Asian nationalism called him a 'champagne socialist'.

Elliott and Roach had not been pushovers; they were both tough, forthright, skilled negotiators who saw no place for colonialism in the postwar world. Within the next five years Roach would serve 11 months in jail for his trade union activities. A former itinerant labourer turned wharfie, he became a national figure in 1938 when, as leader of the Port Kembla Branch of the WWF, he led the Pig-Iron Dispute: Port Kembla wharfies refused to load pig-iron destined for Japan onto the British tramp steamer *Dalfram*, arguing that the pig-iron would help Japanese militarists, then in the process of invading China, and that soon it would be Australia's turn to face the military might of Japan. For his aggressive role in trying to break the ban and maintain the pig-iron trade with Japan, Robert Menzies, then the Attorney-General in the conservative government, earned his unsavoury lifelong nickname, 'Pig-Iron Bob'.

Elliott was a former railway worker turned seaman who became national leader of Australian seamen in 1941. A seasoned internationalist, Elliott believed that trade unions had the right and duty to take political stands, and to campaign on international issues; the responsi-

Two legendary maritime trade union leaders: E.V. Elliott (left) of the Seamen's Union of Australia, and Ted Roach (right) of the Waterside Workers' Federation. Both had substantial roles in the boycott of Dutch imperialism post-World War II (Mitchell Library, State Library of New South Wales, ON 173 for Elliott; and Butlin Archives Centre, Australian National University Archives, Z248-82 for Roach).

bility of Australian trade unionists did not end at the nation's coastline.

While bound by pledge and protocol to help reinstate the NEI government, the Australian Labor government did not use its full range of police and martial options against the boycott; it should be noted that during the 1949 coal strike, however, it did use both troops and gaol terms. In the United Nations the Australian government supported the cause of the Indonesian Republic. The government's soft approach to the boycott generated withering, at times hysterical and racist, political and media criticism: an Asia without European overlords was a dangerous, uncertain place; government foreign policy was being dictated by militant trade unions. These criticisms drove nails into the Labor government's postwar coffin, and helped pave the way for the political manipulation of a fear of Asia that helped keep conservative governments in power for over 20 years.

The Dutch ban was finally lifted when the sovereignty of the Indonesian Republic was satisfactorily assured late in 1949. Overall the boycott affected – in Australia – 13 Dutch naval vessels, including an aircraft carrier, 8 Australian corvettes transferred to the Dutch, 2 Royal (British) Navy troopships, 3 Royal Australian Navy ships, 36 Dutch merchant ships, 8 oil vessels, 450 small vessels (power and dumb barges, lighters, surf-landing craft) essential for stevedoring work in Indonesian waters, over 1000 motor vehicles, tonnes of warehoused munitions, uniforms, food, and other essential military supplies, and many Dutch aircraft (delayed at Australian airports). It was, and to date still is, the biggest trade union boycott action in Australian history.

36

MARGARET STREET RIOT, 1947

On 20-21 July 1947, Dutch imperialists launched a full-scale military offensive against the fledgling Indonesian Republic, formerly the Netherlands East Indies (NEI). As far as Dutch authorities were concerned, it was a 'Police Action'. To others, it was what it really was: an offensive to curtail and cripple the republic by denying it access to vital food and fuel supplies, control of lucrative plantations, and access to key deepwater ports.

After World War II, anti-colonialism swept through much of the world as subjected peoples struggled for national independence. Commenting on the Dutch 'Police Action', Indian nationalist leader Jawarahlal Nehru got to the heart of the matter: 'Foreign armies on Asian soil are an outrage to Asian sentiment,' he declared, 'an astounding thing that the new spirit of Asia will not tolerate.'

During 1942 the NEI government had been forcibly exiled to Australia by invading Japanese forces. The government-in-exile set up office in Brisbane. In August 1945 Indonesian nationalists had proclaimed the Indonesian Republic. Since then members of 31 Australian trade unions, led by maritime and waterfront unions, had hampered Dutch authorities by boycotting Dutch shipping in Australian waters, and strategic supplies on Australian soil that were intended for the restitution of Dutch colonial rule.

Among those concerned about the 'Police Action' were students at Sydney University. As war mobilisation and austerities ended, student life at Australian universities underwent what education historian Alan Barcan has described as:

a remarkable renaissance ... resuming the flowering of academic and student life interrupted in early 1942 by national mobilisation. Student newspapers became larger and more adventurous; student magazines reappeared. Once more, revues were staged and commemoration celebrations and downtown processions were held. The National Union of Australian University Students arranged intervarsity drama festivals and debates, and organised its first student congress, in Hobart in the 1946-47 vacation.

Peace brought with it an influx of students, especially ex-service men and women who were beneficiaries of a variety of Commonwealth and state scholarship and financial assistance schemes. Many among this ex-service generation had radical ideas, and were eager to help build a better world than the one that had, within 45 years, delivered the Great Depression, fascism, two World Wars and the atom bomb. In 1946 there was a record enrolment of 3600 first-year students at the University of Sydney; a third of these were ex-service personnel. Social reform was in the air as the Commonwealth Labor government of Ben Chifley constructed the welfare state; there was a fragile, uneasy, but working relationship between the Australian Labor Party and the Communist Party of Australia. It was an atmosphere conducive to student radicalism.

On Friday, 25 July 1947, Sydney University students gathered in the centre of Sydney to protest against the 'Police Action'. Their decision to protest downtown was radical. Traditionally, Australian university students constituted a privileged, predominantly male, elite. The general expectation was that they would, in a conservative and compliant manner, though not necessarily diligently, eventually gain degrees. Graduation entitled them to a useful, possibly leading, role in Australian society, especially in the professions. University clubs facilitated student social and cultural activities; the focus was on the campus. Political controversy was not encouraged – campus political clubs only made their appearance in the 1920s. The Act of Incorporation which established Australia's first university (Sydney) in 1850 neatly expressed this tertiary ideal: the university was an expedience serving 'the better advancement of religion and morality, and the promotion of useful knowledge ...'

In the history of Australian universities, off-campus student political protests and demonstrations had been rare. Historian Mick Armstrong claims that the 'first sizeable [student] presence on a left-wing demo … occurred in Melbourne, [with] a contingent of sixty-five students marching in an anti-war demo in August 1934'. In June 1940, following the entry of Italy into World War II on the side of Germany, 300 Sydney University students took to the streets, chanting racist slogans as they rampaged through Sydney smashing the windows of Italian-owned

The Kembla Building in Margaret Street, home of the Dutch Consulate and site of the 1947 demonstration of students and young workers in support of the newly formed Indonesian Republic (three doors down from Pfahlerts Hotel) (City of Sydney Archives, SRC 7756).

shops. In April 1944 a large body of students (estimated at between 500 and 1000), marched from the Sydney University campus downtown to the offices of the Commonwealth Censorship Department, protesting against wartime press censorship restrictions.

The 25 July Margaret Street demonstration was the first significant Australian student protest in support of an Asian independence struggle. The decision to protest followed a campus meeting earlier that week. The speaker was an American woman, K'tut Tantri (also known as Surabaya Sue), a resident of Indonesia and an English-language nationalist broadcaster and resistance fighter. The meeting resolved to elect a student committee to plan an anti-'Police Action' protest. The Sydney University Labour Club, the strongest political club on campus, bringing together an array of Communist and non-Communist social-ists, led the initiative; it had been active in support of the Indonesian Republic from the outset in 1945.

The protest began modestly in a corner of Wynyard Park, off Mar-garet Street, about 100 metres from the office of the Dutch Consul-General in the Kembla Building (since demolished). Initially the gather-ing was small, about 70 people. They were addressed from the pedestal of a park monument by Labour Club identities, an organiser from the Communist Eureka Youth League (Hal Alexander), and the Assistant Secretary of the Sydney Branch of the Waterside Workers' Federation (Ted Roach), who had recently returned from Indonesia. The Dutch 'Police Action' was denounced, a protest resolution was carried, and a deputation of seven was elected to carry the resolution to the Consul-General's office.

In an orderly, restrained, earnest fashion, the deputation, escorted by fellow protesters, moved off, keeping to the kerb and the footpath edge, leaving plenty of room for pedestrians, and the roadway clear for the sparse 1947 city traffic. Student numbers had grown, eventually reaching an estimated 300. Protest placards and banners denounced the Dutch, and called for mediatory intervention by the United Nations; the Australian flag was evident. Student David Armstrong, years later an internationally recognised philosopher and local Cold War conserv-ative warrior, carried a placard proclaiming 'WE HAVE NOTHING AGAINST THE DUTCH ... IN HOLLAND'.

When the students reached the Kembla Building, they were confronted by an enormous police presence, also numbering about 300. As the student deputation moved closer to the building's entrance, the police went into action: without warning, they moved against the students, manhandling them, and forcibly removing placards, banners and flags. It was early afternoon, and curious onlookers and workers on their lunchtime break dramatically swelled the number of people in Margaret Street. All up, about 3000 people were crowded tightly into the protest area.

The degree of violence was exacerbated by the intervention of aggressive male roughnecks, wearing oddments of army clothing, black polo-necked jumpers, lumber jackets, and cloth caps. Their anti-student violence, including bashing students and hitting them with confiscated placard/banner supports, was not reduced or slowed by the uniformed police presence. Initially some protesters believed that these thugs were pro-Dutch supporters enlisted by Dutch authorities to intimidate pro-Indonesian supporters, a tactic Dutch authorities had previously employed in Australia. As it turned out, they were members of the notorious 21 Squad, a plain-clothes fighting unit of the NSW police force which used brawn, guns and 'verbals' in their fight against crime. Some of its leading members were themselves corrupt, it was later found, straddling both sides of the law.

Police arrested 14 students; they released one regarded as being too young to be charged. Subsequently, 13 students were charged with offensive behaviour and/or assault. Police had anticipated arrests being made, as a holding room had been established on the ground floor of a nearby building. Dick Klugman was one of those arrested. The 23-year-old science graduate and medical student was taken into custody while noting down the identification numbers of uniformed police engaged in violence. In later life Klugman became a Sydney doctor, federal Labor politician and law reform advocate, and was one of the founders of the NSW Council for Civil Liberties. Of those arrested, Klugman was one of two found not guilty.

Also arrested was arts student and Communist, Bob Walshe a 23-year-old ex-serviceman who was the President of the NSW Council of Reconstruction Trainees, an outfit representing the ex-service

Police seizing banners from students outside the Dutch Embassy in Margaret Street (*Sydney Morning Herald*, 26 July 1947).

beneficiaries of the postwar Reconstruction Training Scheme. Walshe was targeted and arrested by two plain-clothes police in Margaret Street. Before literally being thrown into the holding room, he was isolated, pinned against a wall by the larger arresting officer and bashed in the lower body by the smaller officer. His experience was not unique in the annals of Sydney policing. The following day the *Sydney Morning Herald* summed up the Margaret Street protest with its front-page headline: 'WILD FIGHT IN CITY. Demonstration broken up'.

Sympathetic elements within the Sydney legal world rallied to support the students, providing bail funds and free legal defence. The trials of those arrested, during which many of the accused displayed their ex-service lapel badges, found all except two guilty, but with convictions not to be recorded.

In Wynyard Park during the demonstration in support of the newly formed Indonesian republic: press photo in *The Daily Mirror* captioned 'Girls join with men' (*Daily Mirror*, 25 July 1947).

The events in Margaret Street reverberated: during the week after the demonstration, over 1000 students and staff gathered on the iconic front lawn of Sydney University to condemn police behaviour and demand an inquiry into 'the methods used by the police'; in Wellington, New Zealand, students emulated the Sydney protest; in Melbourne 1000 students met, condemning both the Margaret Street arrests and the Dutch 'Police Action'; and in India, the All-India Student Federation called a national student strike.

For some student leaders Margaret Street was part of something greater than a protest against one injustice. Late in 1947 Bob Walshe published a 46-page booklet titled *Student Work for Progress*, an introduction to student organising, campaigning and leadership. Walshe argued that students should not be content to passively do their academic work; indeed, they should reject the role of being 'ivory tower' exclusives focused on 'intellectual detachment from a mundane world'. Rather, students should both study and engage vigorously with the world.

According to Walshe, if students realised they had the potential to exercise political and social power, and if they organised, then collectively they could help build a better world. They could work towards changing society, engage with major issues like peace, and help the advance 'of progressive ideas and the defence of democratic liberties'. Also, collectively, students could protect and advance their own interests regarding the conditions they studied under. It was all a matter of practicality, of 'organisation and agitation' – what Walshe termed 'student action'. Part of this, Walshe argued, involved getting 'rid of the prejudices that women can't organise' and 'such nonsense' as the notion that the social interests of women 'are limited to husband-hunting'. The 'mid-Victorian conception [of the] essential inferiority' of women had to be eradicated, and women had to be allowed 'fully into active participation in student organisation'.

During the 1960s, galvanised by the Vietnam War, these realisations would dawn on another generation of students and be dramatically acted on.

37

DOROTHY HEWETT AND THE REDFERN REDS

LAWSON SQUARE

Lawson Square lies on the oldest European route out of Sydney: the track to Botany Bay which escaping convicts took in 1788, hoping to secure a passage to freedom on the French ships of Captain La Perouse. In time this track became Botany Road, and the section that ran along the edge of the workers' suburb of Redfern was renamed Regent Street.

The radicals of this suburb might draw strength from its history, tracing their refusal to conform back to the convict and rebel after whom it was named. Dr William Redfern had been sentenced to death as a leader of the mutiny of the British Navy in 1797 at the Nore. The origins of this mutiny lay in over a century of deteriorating conditions for naval seamen, who were tyrannised by the officers, fed rotten food and nauseating drink, and denied their pay. By 1797, in the middle of a war with France, when revolutionary ideas were in the air, they had had enough.

The mutiny spread through the fleet. Seamen took over the ships, elected delegates, chose one of their number as president and set up 'a floating republic'. William Redfern, a young surgeon's mate on HMS *Standard*, advised the crew 'to be more united among yourselves'. After the mutiny was suppressed, the pay and rations of the seamen were improved, but the leaders were court-martialled, and 29 were hanged. Redfern was reprieved because of his youth, and instead transported to Sydney, where he soon made a mark as a skilled and caring surgeon. Pardoned, and rewarded for his service to public health with 100 acres (around 40 hectares) of land in what would become the suburb of

Redfern, he became one of the first leaders of the ex-convicts, the 'emancipists', who were struggling to claim civil and legal rights from the British government.

Lawson Square, running off Regent Street, was named after another republican, the rebel poet Henry Lawson.

By the late 19th century, Redfern was an industrial workers' suburb, surrounded by breweries and boot factories, the largest railway workshops in the southern hemisphere at Eveleigh, and the factories of South Dowling Street and Alexandria. About 90 per cent of its residents were tenants, many of them paying rent to overseas landlords, such as the Scottish and Australian Land Company. Pubs, of which there were 35 in 1903, catered for their social life. By the middle of the 20th century, Redfern's houses were in very poor repair, and thus a favourite demolition target for philanthropic advocates of slum clearance and Housing Commission bureaucrats. In the 1950s, Merv Lilley, boarding in Redfern between stints as a seaman, found that:

> its residents were fiercely resentful if any outsider called it a slum.
> Redfern provided a refuge for the outcasts, the victims of the big
> city: the lame, the halt, the blind, the drunks, the simple, the mad,
> the unskilled, the old and the Aborigines. The derelict terraces were
> shelters for the methos; the population contained a fair percentage of
> petty crims. In such areas tolerance is about the only virtue, and the
> Redfernites practised it like a religion.

On the western boundary was the railway line, which was what made Lawson Square a key thoroughfare for the people of Redfern. It connected them to the Redfern railway station, and by crossing the bridge over the line at this point, to the suburbs of Chippendale, Darlington and everywhere further west. For over a century, Lawson Square's strategic position has attracted political agitators. The earliest entry for the site in *The Labour Heritage Register* is for 1895, when the Unemployed Labour Conference chose the corner of Redfern Street and Botany Road for its mass meeting.

Another form of dissent appeared in the square a few weeks later. The Irish Nationalists, most of whom worked and lived in Redfern and the inner suburbs, chose the western end of the square outside the railway station as the assembly point for a procession. From here, with banners and bands, they marched into the city via George Street to welcome their hero, Michael Davitt MP, at the Grosvenor Hotel. A socialist as well as a nationalist, Davitt was the founder of the Irish Land League. As a young man, he spent eight and a half years in British gaols for his participation in the Fenian movement, which aimed to create an Irish republic. Now he was on a world tour to promote Home Rule for Ireland, the cause that had led to his election to the British Parliament. Returning to Britain he wrote a book, *Life and Progress in Australasia*, in which he honoured the contribution of the Irish rebels of 1798 to the struggle for democracy in New South Wales.

By this time Redfern was politically Labor. The state's first Labor Premier, boilermaker 'Honest Jim' McGowen, represented Redfern from 1891 to 1917, when he was succeeded by another boilermaker, William McKell, who also became the Premier of New South Wales and later Governor-General of Australia. Federally, Redfern was part of the South Sydney electorate, which became a safe Labor seat after 1906, when it was represented by Chris Watson, a compositor who had been Labor's first Prime Minister in 1904.

The Socialists too were well established in Redfern. In 1907, urged on by local businessmen, the police began prosecuting speakers from the International Socialist Party, who were drawing large crowds to the Redfern Street corner. But the party fought back, persuading the Redfern Council to intercede with the police to stop the harassment. In 1931, the local 'Socialisation Unit', part of a movement that briefly committed the NSW Labor Party's annual conference to 'socialism in our time', was holding mass meetings in Lawson Square.

However, these examples of 'respectable' radicalism are only part of Redfern's story. When Jack Beasley was the Communist Party's organiser in Redfern in the early 1950s, he was told that '500 armed Redfernites' had been ready, in 1931, to support Labor Premier Jack Lang in his showdown with the City of London bondholders. According to Beasley, 'The story may not have been true but they didn't tell that kind of story about any other working-class suburb.' No doubt the Premier would have been aghast had he known. The Communist Party's leadership too had difficulty controlling its Redfern branch. Merv Lilley noticed this larrikin style of radicalism:

> The Redfern Communist Party branch was unique of its kind: strongly
> regional, anarchistic, easy-going but resentful of 'the heads', whether
> the capitalist bosses or the Central Committee in Marx House in the
> city. They knew what was best for Redfern, and the rest of the Party
> were impractical theoreticians who couldn't fight their way out of a
> paper bag and knew little about the tough practicalities of Redfern
> politics.

The local queen of the underworld, Kate Leigh, was 'always good for
a donation to Party funds', according to Lilley – perhaps because her
rival, Tilly Devine, the Madam of Darlinghurst, was rumoured to vote
for the Liberal Party. The 'heads' in Marx House were deeply suspicious of the criminal connections of the branch for the very good
reason that a criminal record made one vulnerable to police pressure.

By the 1940s, Redfern was truly part of Sydney's 'red belt'. There
were Communists elected to Redfern's municipal council, and the party
branch had its headquarters in the Henry Lawson Memorial Hall, a
former billiards parlour, at 103 Regent Street, looking across Lawson
Square to the railway station. In faded paint you could read – until
recently – the words, 'Australian Communist Party', high up on the shop
front. Next door on the left was the soup kitchen and op-shop run by
the Catholic Church, and on the right was the London Tavern – three
buildings offering ways to understand and satisfy Redfern's collective
desires: succour, combative politics and conviviality.

On the other side of Redfern, near the Mounted Police barracks,
author Dorothy Hewett and her partner squatted in a deserted house
at 65 Marriott Street in the early 1950s. While she lived there it was a
centre for the activities of the South Sydney Section of the Communist
Party. In the backyard shed a flatbed press printed hundreds of illegal
leaflets; in the front room she typed up the stencils: 'Dark figures knock
on our front door late at night, picking up their copies of *Tribune* (the
Communist newspaper) for sale at branches and factory gates.'

Since its election in 1949, Robert Menzies' Liberal government had
been trying to ban the Communist Party, and in 1951 the government
had to win a referendum to alter the Australian Constitution to allow

The Billiards Parlour at 103 Regent Street in 1940. It became the Communist Party's Henry Lawson Hall (Mitchell Library, State Library of New South Wales, GPO 1–23509).

this. As the likelihood of a victory for the 'Yes' vote increased, the Communists burnt their literature in backyard fires and adopted clandestine methods. Hewett became a secret courier, meeting the district organiser in Moore Park each week to hand over the party funds, hidden under a pillow in her baby's pram, 'while the methos slept under the Moreton Bays'. The Communist Party was relieved, and surprised, when the referendum was defeated.

Before she was sacked for being eight months pregnant, Hewett worked in the Alexandria Spinning Mills. What she learnt there about gender and politics became the basis for her great working-class novel. At the annual meeting of the Textile Workers' Union she had demanded equal pay for women workers but the male leadership ignored her. Knowing she would be sacked if the boss knew she was a Communist, she organised other members of the Redfern branch to distribute an

Dorothy Hewett's house (middle) in Marriott Street, Redfern. She squatted in this house and organised clandestine Communist activities in the community and the local sewing mills (Nick Irving).

illegal bulletin at the factory gates . It opened with her then partner's words: 'There's a name for a man who lives off women.' The title of the bulletin, 'Bobbin Up', became the title of her novel.

In December 1992, to launch the Year of the World's Indigenous People, Labor Prime Minister Paul Keating made a speech in Redfern Park to an Aboriginal audience. Some of the audience would have come from 'The Block' of Aboriginal Co-operative Housing at the western end of Lawson Square. In this speech Keating famously called for an act of recognition by Australians of European descent:

Recognition that it was we who did the dispossessing. We took the traditional lands and smashed the traditional way of life. We brought the diseases. The alcohol. We committed the murders. We took the children from their mothers. We practised discrimination and exclusion. It was our ignorance and our prejudice. And our failure to imagine these things being done to us. With some noble exceptions, we failed to make the most basic human response and enter into their hearts and minds. We failed to ask, how would I feel if this were done to me? As a consequence we failed to see that what we were doing degraded us all.

It was a noble speech, and honourable in its desire to promote inclusion. However, the sentiment is never enough. For over 100 years politicians have been addressing working-class audiences in Redfern and

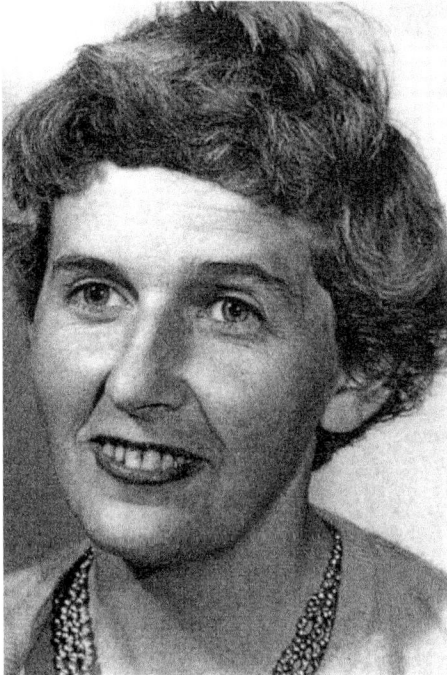

Author Dorothy Hewett, photographed in 1959 for the publication of *Bobbin Up* (courtesy of Kate Lilley, from Dorothy Hewett's book, *Wild Card*, 1990).

promising them inclusion. The reason they have had to repeat this message has been the stubborn refusal of a (changing) section of the working class to believe them. Given their continuing marginality, why should the most oppressed people accept that the politics of representation will work for them? Like the Redfern Reds, they embrace a style of politics that leads either to larrikin defiance or to violence. Neglected, unrecognised, their grievances mounting, and tormented by misconceived philanthropy and government paternalism, some of the oppressed will always opt for the militant, confronting politics of direct action that works because of its unpredictability and capacity to ignite popular anger. Just like the mutinous sailors at the Nore.

On a Sunday in February 2004, soon after midnight, in Lawson Square, a section of the Aboriginal community attacked hundreds of policemen and women, many of whom were injured. Twelve hours earlier a young Aboriginal boy, T.J. Hickey, had died after being chased through the streets of Redfern by a police wagon. In the days that followed many members of the Aboriginal community were arrested.

Today, radical Redfern is disappearing. Gentrified terraces, up-market dwellings and corporate offices advance over the suburb, dispersing its recalcitrant and sporadically mutinous white and black citizens. This process looks inevitable, but is in fact the result of political decisions; it is government that makes a particular kind of market-based society possible, and in this instance the major parties agree. Our rulers, having decided that Sydney must be one of the 'global' cities of finance capitalism, encourage the spread of concrete and glass but ignore its consequences for the city's heritage. In the pubs and halls, shops, factories and houses of Redfern are vital traces of its radical past; they should be marked and examined. Their disappearance is a significant loss for the city's social heritage.

38

THE WATERSIDE WORKERS' CULTURAL COMMITTEE

Lisa Milner

If you walk down Erskine Street and around the corner into Sussex Strett, you will find a remnant of Sussex Lane running behind the old buildings on Erskine Street. On the site bounded by this lane and Sussex Street there is now a multistoreyed glass-fronted temple to business power, but until recently it was occupied by a more modest building of three storeys, the former headquarters of the Sydney branch of the Waterside Workers' Federation (WWF) of Australia. It was built in stages between 1914 and 1928 for the union by the state government, from whom the union leased the building until 1978.

In this building, a remarkable cultural experiment took place. For 30 years, this union made a major contribution to the artistic life of radical Sydney, hosting and encouraging activities that have been described as creating 'a workers' cultural heaven'.

In the early 1950s, the union was led by 'Big' Jim Healy, and ran on a unity platform of the Australian Communist Party and the ALP left wing. Under this leadership the union had a general philosophical commitment to the promotion of Australian culture. Membership was high and the economic position was favourable, and in 1952 the union renovated the building to provide a hall, canteen, art studio, facilities for film production and musical performance, and a reading room. Now, alongside its normal business, the union could host a wide variety of activities.

WWF Sydney branch building, 60–66 Sussex Street. The top rear rooms were occupied by the Film Unit and other cultural groups (Noel Butlin Archives Centre, Australian National University Archives, Z 432 Box 86).

The building's busy life was encouraged and supported by the actors, musicians and artists who, returning from World War II, could not find employment in their preferred field of work. Many of these went onto the wharves, where casual employment and flexible shifts were the norm, and workers could devote time to other pursuits. One wharf work unit, Gang 364, was composed of musicians, actors and artists, and was dubbed 'the Brains Trust'.

The success of this enterprise was helped by the fact that the building was next to the Sydney wharves. That was an important factor in the activity of the union, and in the lives of its members. It made it easy for unionists to stop in at lunchtime, or before and after work. They would go to the canteen, have a meal and socialise. Then they would come into the hall, where they knew there would be something to entertain them: a concert, recital, dance performance or lecture.

Harry Black was the Secretary of the WWF Cultural Committee, which sponsored the hall's activities. He observed that 'artists are beginning to realise that their best and most appreciative audiences are trade unionists'. A small library was established, with book exhibitions and talks by writers. Workers formed athletics, cricket, boxing, fishing, football and other sporting groups and teams. The first of the WWF's Women's Committees was established in the building. As well as feeding unionists in the canteen, the Women's Committee organised many functions. This group was particularly important in extending union activity to workers' families.

Live music was well liked, and a diverse range of local and touring groups performed in the hall. The Waterside Workers' Choir became very popular. Other acts included the Chinese Opera Company and the Margaret Walker Dance Group. A 1960 visit by American actor, singer and civil rights activist Paul Robeson went down very well with the wharfies. It was after his 'official' performances at the Sydney Town Hall that he came down to the wharves, and to the Sussex Street building. He said: 'I feel much better about performing here anyway. I can say things that I wouldn't think about saying in the Sydney Town Hall and I know that I'm amongst friends.'

During strikes, the hall also saw the formation of all-singing, all-dancing entertainment units. These groups gave performances in parks, factories, hotels, and on the back of flatbed trucks. These strike concerts played a very important role. 'Where they performed, we were able to link the art forms with the message that we were endeavouring to get across about the reason we were on strike. And we would link them very closely together,' said Harry Black.

A workshop was built on the top floor of the building for visual art. These art groups were popular with wharfies and their families, as were the resultant exhibitions held downstairs in the hall. For many years wharfies had been involved in the construction and painting of banners for May Day marches, demonstrations and other events, and their work in the art groups was an extension of these activities.

From 1953 to 1965, under the guidance of Rod Shaw, art group devotees, wharfies and non-wharfies painted a large mural on a wall of the union canteen, depicting the history and philosophy of the WWF. The mural has become a significant reminder of the union's continuing commitment to workers' cultural achievement; it is now housed at the Australian National Maritime Museum, across the water at Darling Harbour.

In 1953 an opportunity arose that allowed another type of cultural activity to extend to the wharves: Jock Levy and other wharfies established the Maritime Industries Theatre (MIT) in the hall. Levy observed that, for him, 'it had always been a sort of a challenge to us to get ordinary blokes working in the industry to come to the theatre'. As they did in other cultural projects, wharfies collaborated with the theatre experiment, particularly in set construction and stagehand work.

The MIT's performances set the precedent for radical theatrical work in the hall. The WWF enjoyed a longstanding alliance with the innovative, left-leaning New Theatre, whose member Betty Roland had written *War on the Waterfront* in response to the 1938 Pig-Iron Dispute. It played in Sydney to appreciative audiences – and to police, who stopped performances and arrested actors. From 1954 to 1968 the New Theatre staged over 30 productions in the hall under the auspices of the WWF's Cultural Committee. The wharfies' offer of space and support came at a time when performance space in Sydney was as scarce as hens' teeth.

An interest in cinema was also fostered on the waterfront. The Film Group scheduled film screenings at lunchtime, evenings and weekends. Feature films were shown alongside short works and cartoons. The Australian film *The Sentimental Bloke* (1932) was a favourite, especially after it was discovered that its director, Raymond Longford, worked as a night watchman on the Sussex Street wharves. The films were usually shown in the context of a stop-work meeting, a talk, performance or concert. And as in other creative spheres, people were encouraged to get involved: classes to learn film projection were organised when it was seen how popular the screenings were.

The popularity of films saw the establishment of the WWF Film Unit, one of the few trade union film groups ever established. The unit was formed in 1953 by wharfies Keith Gow and Jock Levy, who were joined in 1954 by Norma Disher. They produced 16 films all told, for the WWF and other groups. These works focused on industrial disputes, safety, housing shortages and other social and labour issues, all interpreted from a working-class viewpoint. The unit was assisted by the unionists, writers, artists and theatre workers who had gravitated

'We Film the Facts': WWF Film Unit van in a Sydney May Day parade during the Cold War (National Film and Sound Archive, 349889).

to, and honed their skills in, the other cultural groups operating in the Sydney building. A grassroots distribution and exhibition system was used; films were screened at union and community meetings.

The filmmakers used a room at the top of the Sussex Street building for all the writing, co-ordination, production work and editing. They also produced animated sequences and cartoons. These were made on an animation bench that they constructed in the building's basement; there were no steps to get down there, so they had to build a ladder. The proximity of the Film Unit's office, just upstairs from the hall, meant that the filmmakers were closely involved in the community of the WWF. 'There were so many wharfies when we were there, it was really buzzing with life,' Norma Disher recalled. 'A lot of them would come upstairs in the lunch hour and see what we were doing, telling us stories.' Wharfies were involved in the production process as cast, extras or helpers. Keith Gow said:

that was one of the wonderful things about that particular period of making films. One had this enormous support from one's fellow workers. They would rally around whenever they were needed for a crowd scene. It might be arranged in their lunch hour or when they were rostered off, but they would turn up in large numbers and do everything needed with the greatest of enthusiasm and generosity. It was overwhelming to get this kind of support and help from the rank and file of the union.

In the 1950s particularly - a period in which many Australians believed that a local, authentic culture was nonexistent - the activities of the Sussex Street building did much to keep our artistic practices alive. Importantly, the distinctions between producers and audiences began to break down, as filmmaking skills and tools were put into the hands of the people. The Sydney WWF branch's activities were replicated in other branches, and in other organisations. The Film Unit's work presented an alternative to the conservative, anti-Communist hysteria of the time, and is seen by many as one of the foundations of the tradition of alternative media in Australia.

With the election of the NSW Labor government in 1976 it became possible to negotiate the purchase of the building, and the union bought it in 1978. Now the WWF is known as the Maritime Union of Australia. Both its federal and its Sydney branch offices are just down the road at 365 Sussex Street, along with other labour organisations.

It's interesting to see that now, over 50 years after this burst of creative activity, the wharfies' union, the MUA, is once more trying to involve its members in artistic production. In 2005 the union organised a film competition for maritime workers - their task was to depict their union at work. The winners, Viron Papadoulos and Cooper Silk, won a trip to Cuba to film an international labour conference, and upon their return, began covering local union events. Today the Sydney branch of the MUA assists the work of the MUA Film Unit, inspired by the work of the old WWF Film Unit - just one example of the continuing legacy of all that went on in that old building in Sussex Street.

39

YOUTH CARNIVAL DEFIES MENZIES

THE CITY OF THE LEFT IN THE 1950S

In the early 1950s, just a few years after the defeat of fascism in a war that had killed over 60 million, the Australian government was preparing for another world war – this time against Communism. Elected in 1949, the conservative parties led by Robert Menzies immediately embarked on a major rearmament program and introduced conscription. By 1950, Australian troops were fighting Communist insurgencies in Korea and Malaya. The government followed a similarly aggressive program against Communists in Australia. Communist union leaders were gaoled, the Communist Party's offices were raided, and a secret plan was endorsed allowing troops to break strikes and round up Communists for internment.

In 1951, Menzies announced a referendum to alter the Constitution of Australia to give his government the necessary powers to ban Communism. This move had unexpected consequences: for a start, it meant the Communist Party now had allies in the non-Communist left. The desire for peace had already led to many on the left suspecting that anti-Communism was a cloak for warmongering, and the attempt to ban the Communist Party raised a new set of suspicions. Working-class activists worried that it foreshadowed an attack on trade unions; liberal intellectuals decried its undermining of civil liberties. Considering his options, the Labor leader in the Federal Parliament, Dr Bert Evatt, decided to mobilise the opponents of Menzies by campaigning for a 'no' vote on these grounds. When the referendum was defeated, by a small margin, the left – Communist and non-Communist – rejoiced.

Such a narrow victory brought home to the Communist Party the importance of the wider left in protecting its legal existence. By the early 1950s, the party had considerable influence in the left. Communist militancy in defence of wages and working conditions had won the party very significant support in the trade union movement; its nationalist cultural policy had attracted artists and intellectuals angered by the penetration of commercialised American culture; and its long-standing attention to Aborigines as workers provided political education for a group of important Aboriginal activists. But it had yet to regain the position it had held in the 1930s, when it was leading the resistance to fascism, of strongly influencing the wider left through an anti-war movement.

It was Audrey Blake, from the Eureka Youth League, the Communist Party's youth wing, who came up with the idea of holding a week

Audrey Blake, key organiser, at the opening ceremony of the Carnival (from Audrey Blake, *A Proletarian Life*, 1984).

of sporting and artistic events directed particularly to young people, and dedicated to peace. She had just returned from a Communist-run World Youth Festival in East Berlin. There had been 134 Australians at the festival, and most of them had had their trip paid for by community fundraising. A prominent member of the delegation was Ray Peckham, from Dubbo, whose passport, vetoed by the Aborigines Welfare Board, was issued only after a campaign by the Australian Aborigines League and left unions. Audrey's proposal was to build on community support for the Berlin delegation by having prominent sporting and cultural figures sponsor a similar festival in Sydney. A meeting in October 1951 endorsed the idea, and decided to hold a Youth Carnival for Peace and Friendship in March 1952.

There was an immediate rush of support for the Youth Carnival from the beleaguered left. The Australian Security Intelligence Organisation (ASIO) compiled a list of the Carnival's sponsoring bodies – it covered six pages. Scores of distinguished artists agreed to support the Carnival's cultural activities, among them Lloyd Rees (painting), Eleanor Dark (literature), Hal Lashwood (drama) and Margaret Walker (dance). Supporters raised more than £20,000 (over $600,000). A committee of full-time and voluntary organisers, including Ray Peckham, brought out a weekly newspaper, published over a million leaflets and posters, and lined up the hundreds of sporting venues and halls that would be needed for the thousands of people who were expected to participate.

But then the full force of ruling-class hostility struck. What hurt was not the Prime Minister's denunciation of the Carnival in Parliament, nor the complete blackout of Carnival news in the daily press, nor the proscription of the Carnival by the state executive of the NSW branch of the Labor Party; all of these were par for the course in the Cold War. Rather it was the use of state power that hurt. Visas were denied to overseas visitors. Censorship prevented overseas films from being screened. Then came the 'dirty tricks' – visits from ASIO agents and the Special Branch of the NSW police to local council officers to threaten them with exposure as Communist dupes unless they cancelled bookings of halls and sports fields for Carnival events: 17 of 18 councils gave in to this pressure. The sharpest blow was the loss of Harold Park for the opening ceremony. When a replacement was found, a privately owned picnic ground at Fairfield, 20 kilometres west of the city, the state Labor Minister of Transport refused to allow the organising committee to charter public buses and trains, and threatened to cancel the licence of a Fairfield private bus company if it transported people from the railway station to the picnic ground 7 kilometres away. As one of the organisers said later, 'until then I didn't realise how vicious the government could be'.

With just 12 hours for the job, a team of volunteers from building unions prepared the picnic grounds for the opening ceremony. Using hundreds of private cars and lorries, the organisers ensured that over 10,000 people could travel from the railway stations to see the opening ceremony's parade and concert. In the following week there were 156 major Carnival events. The closing march through the city was led

THIS IS THE STIRRING SIGHT THEY TRIED TO PREVENT

Crowd with banners at the Youth Carnival for Peace and Friendship opening at Fairfield in 1952. Powerful anti-Communist interests tried to prevent the Carnival taking place (*Challenge*, 19 March 1952).

by young Aboriginal workers, including Ray Peckham – he was later an organiser for the Builders Labourers' Federation and a leading activist for Aboriginal citizenship during the 1967 referendum campaign. The march included the 2364 delegates and thousands of supporters. One estimate is that there were 30,000 people in the Domain at the close of the march.

The Carnival revealed that there was a substantial left cohort in Sydney in 1952, and that there were places within the city that gave shelter to it. First in importance were the offices and halls of the left unions. The Carnival committee operated out of 36 Pitt Street, which the Seamen's Union vacated for them. Nearby, at 188 George Street, was the Ironworkers' Building where the exhibitions were held. Upstairs, the Sydney Trade Union Club hosted the billiards competition. The Aboriginal delegates presented a concert at the Waterside Workers' Hall at 60 Sussex Street. The Teachers' Union had a large building called Federation House at 166 Phillip Street, and it was one of the locations for the Carnival's film festival. There were also some events at Trades Hall in Goulburn Street.

Every night during the week the plays in the drama festival were presented at the New Theatre, which was then at 167 Castlereagh Street. Ethnic clubs were also important, especially as venues for films and concerts. The Russian and the Italian clubs had premises at 727 George Street (just a few doors from Marx House, at 695, the Communist Party headquarters until 1950), and the Chinese Youth League was at 66 Dixon Street. The table tennis competition was held at Szabados Academy at 399 George Street.

The working-class suburban arc to the south and west of the city, including the Aboriginal community at La Perouse, was also home to carnival events. Among important locations were the Capitol Theatre at Bankstown, the Town Halls at Paddington and Marrickville, and the Newtown Manchester Unity Hall. When the Carnival committee was refused permission to use some of these sites, the scheduled events went ahead under the auspices of sympathetic trade unions. Sporting events were held at ovals and parks in Redfern, Glebe, Kogarah, Ashfield and Coogee. The people of La Perouse hosted an exhibition of handicrafts, boomerang throwing, and a talent quest for Aborigines.

|| 1952 Carnival: cloth patch issued to participants (Irving collection).

In the century and a half since Britain had used military force to establish an overseas gaol on the shores of the harbour, Sydney had provided a series of spaces for radicalism. They were usually on the outskirts of the city, as business and official power dominated its centre. However, by the 1950s, through the organised labour movement, the radical left had established a significant presence in the city proper, a precinct in which radicals could move from offices to cafés to meeting halls to theatres to printeries and bookshops, with the occasional stop-off for a drink in a favourite pub. Its leaders could walk from Sussex or Goulburn streets to negotiations in Macquarie or Bridge streets with the state's men of power. This was an important moment in the history of radical Sydney. The Carnival of 1952 demonstrated that the left could use these spatial resources to defy the forces of anti-Communism with spirit and determination.

Of course this was just one of radical Sydney's moments, and just one kind of radicalism. In the 1960s there would be a different set of radical actors and places, a radical Sydney for the New Left, the student movement, and the new social movements. It was ushered in by the Oz trial.

40

P&O WALL FOUNTAIN

Hunter Street

The Tom Bass fountain-sculpture on the front of the Peninsula and Orient Line's building, on the corner of Hunter and Castlereagh streets, was part of a controversial legal battle that began in 1964 and ended in 1966.

It began with the cover of Issue No. 6 (February 1964) of *Oz* magazine, which featured a posed photograph of three males apparently urinating in the recessed wall sculpture.

A lengthy caption explained that the sculpture was an attempt to alleviate the 'severe drabness' of the P&O Building, which had been officially opened by Prime Minister Menzies earlier that year, and was in fact an:

> attractive bronze urinal set in the wall for the convenience of
> passers-by. It is no ordinary urinal. It has a continual flushing system
> and basins handily set at different standing heights. There is a
> nominal charge, of course, but don't worry, there is no need to pay
> immediately. Just P.&O. Pictured is a trio of Sydney natives P.&O.'ing
> in the Bass urinal.

Oz was a volatile, abrasive Sydney based monthly magazine of satire and social comment published from April 1963 to February 1969. The first issue was 16 pages of black and white letterpress; it sold for 1/3d a copy, and was launched on April Fools' Day 1963. Ferry terminals and railway stations were targeted by street sellers to catch Sydney's office and shop workers on their way to work. The sellers, many of them young female students in tight tops and short skirts, sold the

OZ

No. 6 ... FEBRUARY

On the corner of Hunter and Castlereagh Streets, Sydney, the P. & O. Shipping Line has completed its contribution to the Australian Ugliness—the P. & O. Building, officially opened by the Prime Minister in January. To alleviate the severe drabness of its sandstone facade, sculptor Tom Bass has set an attractive bronze urinal in the wall for the convenience of passers-by. This is no ordinary urinal. It has a continual flushing system and basins handily set at different standing heights. There is a nominal charge, of course, but don't worry, there is no need to pay immediately. Just P. & O. Pictured is a trio of Sydney natives P. & O'ing in the Bass urinal.

The controversial cover of *Oz* magazine, number 6, February 1964 (courtesy of Richard Neville).

entire intial print run of 6000 copies within three hours, necessitating a second printing. Subsequent prosecutions and associated publicity boosted sales. At its height *Oz* had a circulation of 40,000.

The three editors were young, articulate, middle-class men; Richard Neville, a recent Arts graduate, medical student Richard Walsh, and artist/designer Martin Sharp. All of them had a background in university student publications. In 1963 they raised capital of £50, which was considerable for the time, formed the company *Oz* Publications Ink Ltd, and boldly set out to publish what Neville later described as 'a desperate alternative to [Australia's] puritan hangover and monopolistic media structure'.

Oz did not espouse a systematic ideological theoretical position. Its mood was republican; its political-cultural thrust seemed to revolve around the idea that Australia could be more than a timid nation culturally subservient to both Mother England and the United States.

Freedom of speech, and opposition to censorship laws that tried to inhibit the arts and public discussion of ideas in Australia, were central concerns. In effect, *Oz* challenged the culture of fear, caution and passivity generated by the Cold War.

The satire was hit-and-miss, ranging from trite to brilliant. Targets included right-wing reactionary aspects of Australian politics and culture, especially racism and militarism. The magazine consistently opposed conscription and the Vietnam War. Organised religion, suburban life, consumerism, and Australia's love affair with British Royalty were also in the firing line.

During the 1950s and 1960s organised crime, crooked police and corrupt politicians increasingly became parts of Sydney life – all were the subjects of Royal Commissions in later decades. *Oz* courageously published material exposing aspects of this sordid underbelly, using material from journalists whose editors in the mainstream press refused to handle it.

After *Oz*'s first three issues, the majority of Sydney's printeries refused to print it, fearing legal prosecution. Maverick journalist Francis James came to the rescue with his presses. James was managing director of The Anglican Press, publisher of the independent ecclesiastical newspaper *The Anglican* (1952-70). He was a colourful, enigmatic personality. A Battle of Britain veteran, James had been shot down over Nazi-occupied Europe, imprisoned, and had then escaped from captivity three times. An early public critic of the Vietnam War, James used *The Anglican* as the platform for his opposition to Australia's involvement in the war.

Oz Issue No. 6 went beyond the pale as far as the authorities were concerned; police seized and destroyed newsagency copies of the magazine. The urinal photograph apparently offended sensitivities, as did the contents, which included a cartoon-strip satire on folksingers headed GET FOLKED, a report on the joys of marijuana, an article savaging the Catholic Church by American social satirist Lenny Bruce, whose stage shows had been banned in Sydney in 1962, and a Snakes and Ladders-type board game dealing with unsavoury aspects of the culture of the NSW police force.

The editors were charged under the NSW Obscene and Indecent Publications Act. It was not the first time for the young trio. After the launch of the first issue of *Oz* in 1963 they had already been found guilty of publishing obscene material and each fined £20. Now they were serial offenders.

On 23 September 1964 Stipendiary Magistrate Mr G.A. Locke, in the Court of Petty Sessions, found the trio guilty: Neville and Walsh were sentenced to 6 months' gaol with hard labour; Sharp, as art editor, got 4 months. The printer was fined £50, and the publisher was fined £100.

According to Locke, who was clearly outraged, the cover of Issue No. 6 was 'indecent' and the content was variously 'smutty', 'disgusting', 'blasphemous', 'filthy', 'childish', 'obscene', and 'grossly offensive'. He believed the whole magazine would 'deprave young people or unhealthy-minded adults so injudicious as to fancy it as literature, and so misguided as to cultivate the habit of reading it'. Bail was set at £100 pending an appeal.

Leading radio commentator Eric Baume, an early target of *Oz* satire, was jubilant about Locke's decision. As far as he was concerned, *Oz* was a 'dirty little rag with filth in it', and he was pleased the editors were on their way to gaol; 'to wipe *Oz* out will be one of the best things for the country'. The mass circulation Sydney evening newspa-

"DEPRAVED" MAGISTRATE ON ARTICLES

3 GAOLED: 'FILTHY PAPER'

OZ company

Three publishers of "OZ" magazine were sent to gaol a n d the printers were fined today for publishing an obscene publication— the February issue.

Mr G. A. Locke, S.M., in Central Court said the magazine contained articles which were filthy, disgusting, offensive, libellous and blasphemous.

He rejected the evidence of defence witnesses "with academic and o t h e r qualifications" who had said the magazine material was not likely to deprave.

Mr Locke referred to the evidence of Professor J. K. Stout that "four-letter words never corrupted anyone."

word is. Four letter words never corrupted anyone."

Mr Locke said the defence witnesses, experts in their own particular field, had claimed young people would not be depraved.

"That evidence is rejected," he said.

Sign of the times: Sydney press reaction to the trial of the three *Oz* publishers (*The Sun*, 23 September 1964).

per *The Sun* devoted its front page to the conviction. After a lengthy appeal process, the Appeal Court reversed Magistrate Locke's decision and quashed the convictions. In his summing up, Justice Aaron Levine pointed out that satire:

is an important part of the literature of protest dating back to ancient Rome and Greece and before, and satirical magazines such as *Oz* have no doubt been published wherever protest was thought necessary. And whilst it may be a necessary part of satire to be critical of human behaviour by using a wide variety of weapons, including shock, invective and even crudity, and techniques (such as) ridicule, lampooning and caricature, nevertheless, I cannot make it too clear that obscenity may not be used as a weapon.

However, in his opinion the Crown had failed to establish that anything in the magazine was obscene.

The prosecution of *Oz* generated a powerful national cultural response. Supporters raised defence money; there was a major benefit concert at the Sydney University Theatre featuring prominent Australian radio, television and stage performers. Major Australian literary figures, including the editors of most of the nation's intellectual journals, rallied to the support and defence of the *Oz* editors. Seventeen leading Australian experts in literature, criminology, journalism, education and art appeared in court as expert witnesses to testify to the literary and cultural merits of *Oz*. The appeal counsel team included the President of the NSW Bar Association, John Kerr QC, the future controversial Governor-General of Australia (1974-77).

As the 1960s progressed the atrocities of the Vietnam War became increasingly apparent, and the casualty and death tolls mounted. On campuses, in schools, in the suburbs and on the streets, the ranks of a vibrant anti-war movement swelled. There were New Left critiques of the war, capitalism and imperialism, a flood of cyclostyled (and later offset) alternative literature, and an urgency and excitement about organising for political change. In comparison, the satiric provocation of *Oz* seemed timid; its market was being eroded.

Richard Neville and Martin Sharp left Australia in 1966 and back-packed to London. The following year Neville helped establish London *Oz* (1967-73), with Sharp as Art Director. This *Oz* incarnation ran for 48 issues; it was a more politically robust, confronting, technically innovative publication than its earlier Sydney incarnation. During 1971 it was the subject of the longest-running obscenity trial in British history. The international impact of London *Oz* on underground and alternative publishing generally has been rated as second only to New York's *The Village Voice*. On the home front, Richard Walsh went on to edit

| The P&O fountain in Hunter Street today – 'park and pee' (Nick Irving).

the innovative and provocative Melbourne-based national weekly newspaper *Nation Review* (1972-81).

Sydney *Oz* was a seedbed for radicals. For many young people old enough to be sent to the jungles and paddy fields of Vietnam but not old enough to vote because they were not yet 21, it affirmed that if you had something to say it was possible to get it out, in and on your own terms, and that words and images could be bullets. On the Richter scale of rebellion, Sydney *Oz* was not a call to arms, but it was much more than a whisper.

41

NESTOR'S CELLAR: LEFTIES IN THE SKY WITH DIAMONDS

72 OXFORD STREET, PADDINGTON

The New Left of the 1960s and 1970s, which brought together political rebels and countercultural resisters, had great potential for making radical change. The message of liberation was delivered with style as well as purpose. A range of liberation ideals – sexual, political, racial – were melded into a powerful and joyful rejection of authority. Particularly in the United States, ruling-class figures, mocked with carnivalesque antics, were forced onto the defensive, and its warmongering government (which was preparing for a nuclear attack on North Vietnam) was checked by massive demonstrations for peace. But it was a highly unstable coalition. In the United States, discord split the leadership, mutual incomprehension drove the political and countercultural radicals apart, and government provocateurs manipulated the most militant into ever more desperate and counterproductive violence. In the 1970s, as the movement fragmented, international big business gave it the kiss of death wherever it had flourished by co-opting its rebellious mood into a commercial youth culture.

The psychedelic drug LSD (lysergic acid diethylamide) played a central part in the destruction of the movement. First synthesised in Switzerland in 1938, and valued for its therapeutic role in mental illness, LSD was of purely medical significance until the early 1950s, when it was taken up by the US Central Intelligence Agency (CIA) as a weapon against the Soviet Union and left-wing popular movements. The CIA was looking for a 'mind-control' drug for interrogation, espionage and social engineering (that is, controlling communities, possibly by spiking the water supply). Under its notorious MKULTRA project, which ran until the late 1960s, the CIA administered LSD without consent to thousands of soldiers, prisoners, patients, and even punters picked up by prostitutes. The British government had a similar, if smaller, program. In recent years, victims of these programs have forced their governments to pay them belated financial reparations.

The hippies, who advocated an apolitical style of cultural resistance, popularised LSD as part of their 'new way of seeing'. In fact, it was a delusion: a roiling, out-of-time delirium, whether drug induced or the product of loud music and strobe lighting, would never threaten the power structure. When Timothy Leary told the young to 'turn on, tune in, and drop out' he cut them off from the left's distinctive emphasis on the need for collective struggle against the impersonal structures of power that limit freedom – it is difficult to drop out if you are already poor, for instance – and from resistance to the dominant culture of individualism that supports those structures.

In the early 1960s Nestor Grivas owned a terrace house on the corner of Oxford and Comber Streets, Paddington. He lived on the first floor, a tailor ran a business at street level, and beneath the house there was a large space formed by Comber Street's descent from the Oxford Street ridge. Nestor worked at the Greek newspaper the *Hellenic Herald*, which was owned by his father. The years after World War II saw an upsurge of political and cultural radicalism that attracted Nestor and his brothers. Nestor was a member of the militant Seamen's Union; his brother Cecil was part of the movement to protect and develop an Australian culture, which at that time was a project of the Communist Party. Cecil performed in New Theatre's *Reedy River* (Sydney's longest-running amateur theatre production, seen by over 100,000 people), sang with the original Bushwhackers Band in the early 1950s, and, when it broke up, formed The Galahs, another band that specialised in bush ballads, with two of his brothers (but not Nestor).

Nestor's political leanings were anarchist rather than Communist. He was a member of the Sydney Anarchist Group and socialised with the Sydney Push, a bohemian group whose intellectual core was provided by the Sydney Libertarians. In 1958 the Anarchists and the Libertarians rented a meeting room on the second floor of 727 George Street, and called it Liberty Hall. It was in the same building that the offices of the Communist Party had been in in the 1930s and 1940s. In the basement was the Russian Social Club, where the Third Secretary of the Soviet Embassy, Vladimir Petrov, met the spy Michael Bialoguski (known as 'Diabolo' to his ASIO controllers) in 1951. Together they caroused, over the next few years, as part of an ASIO plot to cause Petrov to defect, which he did in 1954. There was plenty of carousing also at Liberty Hall, and visits from the police when bottles and rubbish rained down on the footpath of George Street. After a year the landlord terminated the lease.

It was then that Nestor Grivas offered the space beneath his house as the new meeting place. Volunteers dug it out to over six feet, installed steel beams, concreted the floor and bricked it up to make an entrance on Comber Street. It was completed in 1962 and was soon fulfilling its purpose despite its rudimentary facilities – an urn and a pie warmer – for there was a sense of opportunity on the political left. The thaw in the Cold War and the process of de-Stalinisation among Communists were softening the rigidities of past strategies. The changing composition of the working class, resulting from automation and a more highly educated workforce, challenged ancient shibboleths about class politics. Thirty-five years of mass immigration was bringing cultural issues – especially how to communicate with non-English speaking militants – to the fore. And the affluence of the long economic boom was encouraging people to think of themselves as middle class and to question the need for censorship and authoritarian control in their private lives.

One sign of this redirection of non-Communist left activity was the formation of New Left clubs. The Sydney one met every month at the cellar on a Thursday night. Among those involved were Professor Henry Mayer, from the University of Sydney, who led a discussion in November 1962 on problems of the press, Jim Thorburn (the club's secretary, who managed the Pocket Bookshop), the writer Frank Moorhouse, and the journalist Richard Hall. After about a year the club moved its meetings to the Rose, Shamrock and Thistle, almost opposite, where the atmosphere was more congenial. The Sydney Anarchist

Group continued to meet on Monday nights: there would be an open editorial meeting for its journal, *The Anarchist*, followed by discussion of specific topics, current and past. Jack Grancharoff, a Bulgarian exile from Communism, was a moving force, as was Irishman Bill Dwyer. Economist Dave Clark delivered a paper on workers' control of production and film critic John Flaus brought the group up to date on kibbutzim in Israel.

The cellar today, from Comber Street, showing the back entrance (Nick Irving).

Also using the cellar was a group of Sydney Libertarians. Since the early 1950s the Libertarians had been propagating a philosophy of permanent protest against the servility of modern life and the moralistic defences of that servility, derived from the teachings of Sydney University professor John Anderson. Believing that political activity was pointless, their critics dubbed them 'the futilitarians'. The new questioning and stirrings on the left, however, attracted the support of some Libertarians, especially because the hedonistic and promiscuous lifestyle of the Push was no longer so distinctive – youthful permissiveness was becoming a generational marker. It was this group of Libertarians who met at the cellar. Papers by Germaine Greer, Liz Fell and Roseanne Bonney signalled the appearance of a feminist awareness. In 1966, George Molnar announced that a Libertarian Study Group would meet at the cellar to thrash out a more sympathetic approach to 'meliorism', the idea that society can be improved by human effort. Within a few years some Libertarians, including Wendy Bacon, Rick Mohr and John Murphy, were leading activists against the state's obscenity laws, and there were prominent Libertarians resisting the redevelopment of Victoria Street, Kings Cross.

In the United States, LSD was taking over the youth counterculture by 1967 – 30,000 hippies attended the first Be-In at San Francisco's Golden Gate Park. In England, the Beatles released 'Lucy in the Sky with Diamonds', which was understood to describe the effects of an LSD trip. This was also the year in which the drug culture became a presence in Sydney. The Free University, set up by radical students in a terrace house in Darlington, offered a course in 1967-68 just called 'Drugs', led by the future Minister of Education in a conservative state government, Terry Metherell. In effect, it popularised the drug culture.

At the University of Sydney, the editor of *Honi Soit* (the student newspaper) was the future right-wing pundit Keith Windschuttle. In October 1967 an American in a business suit turned up at the paper's office with information about how to manufacture LSD. The two of them then wrote an article together. Windschuttle wrote the sections attacking the state government's intention to make possession of the drug illegal; the American wrote the passages praising LSD. It was published with Windschuttle as the sole author. At this time the CIA was working closely with major drug dealers to promote the use of LSD within the anti-war movement, according to *Acid Dreams* (Martin A. Lee and Bruce Shlain, 1985). Perhaps Windschuttle was unwittingly drawn into this plot.

At the cellar, Bill Dwyer began to sell LSD in 1967 – from a steel cage with curtains so that only his hands were visible. He brought in mattresses, music and strobe lights to intensify the psychedelic effect, and sometimes there were crowds of 100 or so turning up. His rationale was that 'anything that can have a man incarcerated deserves inquiry by anarchists', but he was indifferent to the disruptive effects his promotion of the drug was having in the anarchist community. He knew that undercover police were buying LSD from him but boasted that his supplier had police protection. Police infiltrated the anarchist group and attended a picnic Dwyer organised at Wattamolla, where drugs were taken. Finally, in October 1968, the police arrested Dwyer for selling and several of his followers for possessing drugs at the cellar and at Wattamolla. After serving 12 months in Goulburn Gaol Dwyer was deported to the United Kingdom.

That was the end of the cellar as a meeting place for radicals, but not for the alternative community. Clem Gorman used it as a rehearsal space for the Australian Free Theatre Troupe, Leon Cantrell made experimental films there, and there were poetry and play readings. Meg Clancy remembers Melbourne's Australian Performing Group taking a production of John Romeril's *A Nameless Concern* to Sydney and performing it at the cellar, where boards had to be placed between the performing space and the outside lavatory because it was spewing effluent. The boards, she said, sank under the ghastly tide.

The cellar was closed in 1969. The New Left clubs had already fizzled, the Free University was running out of steam, and the anarchist group dissolved. Nestor sold his house, bought a farm, and died in a motor accident. Drugs became an illegal industry, and prospered. In the mid-1970s the anarchists regrouped, and successfully established a bookshop in Newtown.

42

POLITICAL BOLT-CUTTING

SYDNEY UNIVERSITY'S FRONT LAWN

The Sydney University 'front lawn' was designed to display the striking sandstone faux-Gothic building of Australia's first university (established in 1852) and its dominating clock tower. To a great extent the lawn is now unable to fulfil its original purpose, because of population and traffic growth and fundamental changes to the surrounding urban/city environment.

Today the front lawn is iconic, pleasant, decorative, and provides excellent photo opportunities. Over time it has been used as an improvised venue for campus meetings that university authorities have tried to discourage by frustrating or refusing access to regular venues, or when numbers involved have exceeded indoor capacities. The lawn is recessed in front of the clock tower, one side banked by a low retaining wall of stone, creating a stage and an audience pit. As a venue it is functional, dramatic and theatrical.

During the 1960s and early 1970s, the front lawn was the venue for many meetings opposing the Vietnam War and conscription. One afternoon in April 1972 it was the scene of a dramatic, unplanned incident that grabbed national political and media attention, symbolically capturing a rising national mood of anger, defiance and rebellion. By the end of that year this mood would significantly contribute to the election of the Australian Labor Party, led by Gough Whitlam, to national government, ending 23 years of rule by conservative coalition governments.

On Monday, 24 April 1972, around lunchtime, Michael Matteson left a secret interview with a couple of journalists in a Sydney city loca-

All quiet on the front lawn: the front lawn of Sydney University in the 1970s. It was a regular site for huge anti-war meetings during the Vietnam War (© State Government of New South Wales through the Department of Justice and Attorney-General, reproduced with the approval of the NSW State Library).

tion. He got into the back seat of a waiting car and hid under a blanket. Matteson was in his early twenties, long-haired, quietly spoken, thoughtful, introspective, articulate. He had been a Sydney University student until 1968, and since then had been a labourer on the Sydney Opera House ... until he went 'underground' in 1971.

Matteson was an anarchist who drew on the work of the Russian champion of absolute liberty, Michael Bakunin (1814–76), and the Spanish anarcho-syndicalists of the 1930s; he advocated non-violence. He was also an Australian political criminal who had been eluding capture for well over a year. His arrest was high on the agenda of the Australian

Commonwealth Police (now the Australian Federal Police). Federal authorities wanted him because he had refused to co-operate in any way with the National Service Act. For a start, he had publicly refused to register for National Service (conscription), and Commonwealth law required all males to register for National Service in the January or July preceding their 20th birthday.

As Matteson's car headed towards Glebe, just before 2 pm, its driver noticed that they were being followed. Subsequent evasive manoeuvres failed to shake the pursuing vehicle, which was breaking road rules so as to maintain contact. Heading up Parramatta Road, Matteson's car had to stop – there was a red traffic light – near Sydney University. Matteson attempted to exit from the car he was in, but before he could, he was pounced on by the two occupants of the chase vehicle. They handcuffed themselves to Matteson, telling him that his life on the run was over.

As the traffic lights turned green, Matteson told his capturers (Commonwealth police, as it turned out) to pull their legs inside the car, and told his driver to enter the grounds of the university. There was no time for the police to do otherwise. Worse still, from the police point of view, they had abandoned their own car and in the heat of the chase had not informed their colleagues of their whereabouts or of developments. In the moment it took Matteson's driver to move into first gear and let out the clutch, the captors became the captives.

Matteson opposed Australia's involvement in the Vietnam War and the system of conscription which had been brought in to support it. Australia's involvement had begun in 1962, with the deployment of 30 military advisers, and had escalated to full military commitment in April/May 1965 with the despatch of an infantry battalion of the Australian Regular Army to South Vietnam. In November 1964 the National Service Act was hastily passed: it allowed the conscription of 20-year-old males for a two-year period of military service; in May 1965 the Act was amended to make conscripts liable for service overseas. These young men were minors, legally speaking, because a person only became an adult at the age of 21 in those days. Conscription was not universal, either. It was selective: there was a twice yearly draw of birth-dates using a lottery-marble system which became known as 'the lottery of death'. The first death of an Australian conscript in Vietnam was in May 1966. During the war 15,381 conscripts served in Vietnam: 200 were killed and 1279 were wounded.

Initially, public opinion supported military involvement and conscription. Early critics tended to be dismissed, and called un-Australian, troublemakers, Communists. Over time this changed dramatically. Against a background of escalating anti-war and anti-conscription rallies and protests, mounting media criticism of the war and rising battlefield death and injury tolls, public opinion turned. By 1971 the conservative Australian coalition government was disentangling Australia from the nightmare of Vietnam without admitting that its involvement had been a mistake, and without apologising to the nation. The federal ALP Opposition had tapped into the groundswell of discontent and was heading for victory in the December 1972 federal election. After Gough Whitlam became ALP leader in 1967, the party hardened its general opposition to the war, promising in October 1969 to bring Australian troops home and in 1971 to repeal the National Service Act.

Matteson was prominent in the draft resisters' movement, a national coalition of people and organisations formed against this background of rising opposition to the war and to conscription. The movement brought together people actively opposing conscription and sought to increase and intensify resistance to the National Service Act, so that it would eventually be inoperable. Since 1965, a number of individuals had challenged and resisted the Act – and been punished by the penalties it allowed, including 2-year gaol sentences. The new mood aimed to replace this individual approach with mass resistance to the Act by young men eligible for conscription. This would force the government to arrest, prosecute and gaol resisters on a large scale, creating a critical mass of political prisoners: it was hoped that up to 400 would become martyrs to the cause, providing a rallying focus for activists and politically embarrassing the government. 'Radical militancy' was the key.

Draft resisters did not intend going quietly into the night of prison. Instead, the strategy was to stay free for as long as possible while nonviolently inflicting maximum political damage on the government. A national underground was established, made up of supporters and 'safe houses'. The traditional organisational tactics of clandestine outfits were used. Matteson, who had been underground for some 18 months, changed his place of residence an average of every three days.

Intelligence, daring, imagination and media savvy characterised the resisters; they became adept at making public appearances and then disappearing back into the underground. Matteson, for all his quietness and gentleness, was dramatic, and developed a Scarlet Pimpernel reputation for his ability to appear in public and yet elude significant efforts by both state and Commonwealth authorities to apprehend him.

But now, a day before Anzac Day 1972, Matteson was handcuffed to two Commonwealth police officers in a car entering the grounds of Sydney University. Both the driver and Matteson shouted 'Commonwealth police! Draft resisters! Help!' before stopping under the clock tower. There Matteson clumsily exited the car, police in tow. For the officers it was hostile territory; though considerably embarrassed, they managed to avoid inflaming the situation. In 1968, two NSW Special Branch officers (Special Branch were really political police), including the Branch Head, had been detained on campus by a large crowd of students for two and a half hours – the officers had been apprehended spying on a campus anti-war meeting. This incident eventually involved a police siege of the university and humiliating media coverage for the police.

As word of Matteson's arrest spread, a crowd gathered. People poured from campus eateries and Fisher Library, and were joined by a revved-up audience leaving at the end of a Billy Thorpe concert in the nearby Great Hall. The press got word too and journalists arrived. Eventually between 1000 and 2000 people assembled, surrounding Matteson and the officers.

Now the prisoner wanted his freedom. The officers were asked for their handcuff keys; they claimed they did not have them. The Gordian knot problem was solved with bolt-cutters procured from the Fine Arts Department. With the cutting of the handcuff chains, during which the police had to be restrained, the crowd parted and a runner guided Matteson, with the cuffs still on his wrists, away from the front lawn. At the same time the crowd again closed around the police officers, before escorting them off campus.

Matteson found sanctuary in the Philosophy Department, where his escape from campus was organised. Eventually a small convoy of cars,

Michael Matteson holding the handcuffs he was wearing when he escaped from custody. Photographed in a safe house after his escape, Matteson obliged the press with an interview and made a political point (*Sydney Morning Herald*, 24 April 1972, by K. Berry. Fairfax Photos).

with Matteson in one, left the university grounds, peeling off in different directions as they did. A suspected pursuit vehicle was spotted, and Philosophy academic George Molnar slewed his red sports car to a stop across its path, hopped out, opened the car's bonnet and feigned engine trouble. Later, in a 'safe house', Bob Pringle, a leader of the militant NSW Builders Labourers' Federation, cut the case-hardened steel handcuffs from Matteson's wrists; anti-racism activist Sekai Holland, in later life a heroic campaigner for democracy in her Zimbabwean homeland, administered first aid, as Matteson's arms were blackening and numb from the tightness of the cuffs.

The next day, Anzac Day, Matteson's escape was one of the main media stories. The following day the *Sydney Morning Herald*'s editorial dealt with the issue: yes, draft resisters had the right to seek the abolition of conscription, but Matteson and the students had gone too far; they had humiliated the Commonwealth police, exposed the force as inadequate, then prevented police from carrying out their duty. Once arrested, Matteson should have taken it in on the chin and quietly accepted the consequences.

Many escapades later, and when he was ready (in November), Matteson forced Commonwealth police to arrest him publicly. He was sentenced to 20 months' gaol for refusing to agree to obey a future call-up notice and for escaping from custody. Matteson was one of seven political prisoners freed by the Whitlam government in December 1972, during its first days in office. At the same time conscription was ended, and some 2200 conscriptees awaiting induction into the army were informed that they were no longer required. And 23 draft resisters emerged from underground.

43

THE SIEGE OF
VICTORIA STREET

KINGS CROSS

In April 1973, on a tranquil residential street, a struggle that bridged the new middle-class activism and the older radicalism of working-class militancy began. It was a struggle that starkly revealed the violence at the heart of capitalist power. On one side of the conflict were crooks, stand-over merchants, property developers, dodgy politicians and police; on the other side, working-class residents, middle-class squatters and a militant trade union. The conflict had its roots in the changing class character of the city, and so was intense and brutal. For the next three years, residents were terrorised, their homes vandalised; one activist was kidnapped, another was murdered.

It happened on Victoria Street, which runs north from Kings Cross to Potts Point on the escarpment above Woolloomooloo. For many years it was part of working-class Sydney, its elegant two and three-storey terraces offering rooms for itinerant workers, its Victorian mansions subdivided into flats. But in the early 1970s a property developer bought the houses between 55 and 115. Three hundred working-class tenants then stood in the way of his plans to erect three 45-storey towers with hundreds of expensive apartments.

To understand the momentous nature of these events we have to recall the history of residential social difference in Sydney. Until the first decade of the 20th century there were many enclaves of middle-class residents in the inner suburbs south of the harbour, but when the labour movement consolidated its power in the early 20th century the social character of Sydney changed very rapidly. The employers and professionals living in places such as Darlinghurst, Paddington, Glebe and Balmain – where the labour movement mobilised, sometimes with menacing aspect – fled to safer conservative suburbs; flats and boarding houses sprang up in their abandoned homes and the newspapers branded their former communities as 'slum suburbs'. Meanwhile, the northern and eastern suburbs became the acme of residential desirability. For the first half of the 20th century the agitators, bohemians and intellectuals of radical Sydney were reaching out to a city that had never been more spatially class divided. The inner city was working class, Labor, and turbulent.

In the 1960s the middle class rediscovered the inner suburbs. Professionals purchased and renovated terraces in Paddington, Annandale, Glebe and Balmain. What could be more desirable for these slums? The process was called 'gentrification', a term that lightly mocks these same professionals, but entirely ignores the political and demographic upheavals, not to speak of the pain, and sometimes terror, that was involved for working-class residents.

'Gentrification' also neglects the political complexity of this middle-class return. Cheap rents in the 1960s and 1970s made terrace houses attractive to a young middle-class generation that could afford to leave the parental home – a liberating experience in itself. Many of the young people were students, especially after the Whitlam Labor government abolished university fees. The most radical of them became supporters of the New Left, because it led the opposition to conscription and the campaign for student power in the universities and high schools. Their political understanding was crucially affected by where they were living – in areas of working-class Sydney. They could connect with inner-city working-class militants of an older generation, and with Aboriginal activists who encouraged them to apply their ideals of participatory democracy and equality to the needs and traditions of a local community. Soon there were 'movement houses' scattered through the inner suburbs, where feminists, socialists, gays, radical educationists, anarchists, members of Ananda Marga, underground journalists, performance artists, filmmakers and anti-racists practised an alternative politics and lifestyle.

'Gentrification' is also misleading about the changes to the built environment, for what was happening was not just a benign process, in which independent tradesmen and handy home-owners made pleasing renovations house by house, but a tornado of demolition followed by a tsunami of ugly construction. When the time came to defend the inner city's fast diminishing stock of cheap housing, the young radicals found a new cause, and they brought a more contentious politics than that of the gentrifying middle class into the resident action groups springing up in their neighbourhoods.

Meanwhile, a militant trade union was also making a contribution to the New Left. In 1961, labourers in the building industry purged their union of a corrupt and criminal leadership. Over the next 15 years the NSW branch of the Builders Labourers' Federation (BLF) brought a new kind of unionism to Sydney. Although it was associated in the public mind with Jack Mundey, Joe Owens and Bob Pringle, in fact this unionism was ultra-democratic, with rank and file control and limited tenure for office-holders. It encouraged women to enter the building industry and relied on workers' control of job sites to secure the safe working conditions demanded by the union. Most radically, however, it insisted that the union had a right to determine how the labour of its members was used, and a responsibility to use its industrial power to defend working-class interests in the community.

So the term 'green ban' entered the English language. It was coined in May 1973 by Mundey to describe action taken by the union in pursuit of these rights and responsibilities. The union imposed green bans to prevent the evictions of Aboriginal people in Eveleigh, to protect prisoners' rights, to force the reinstatement of a student expelled from a Macquarie University college because he was homosexual, to support a strike of Kings Cross strippers, to enable the introduction of a women's studies course at Sydney University, and to preserve public open spaces, most notoriously Kellys Bush in Hunters Hill. But the green bans that made the greatest public impact were those whose purpose was to defend the homes and historic places of inner Sydney – of Glebe, The Rocks, Woolloomooloo and Victoria Street.

Sydney in the 1970s was the crime capital of the southern hemisphere, according to international expert Alfred W. McCoy. This dubious distinction was only possible because organised crime was at the centre of a web of corruption that trapped greedy police, businessmen and politicians. In the 1960s and 1970s, criminals such as Abe Saffron made huge profits from illegal gambling and from the drug trade operating in the strip joints and clubs of Kings Cross. Abe Saffron's son has revealed recently that his father paid weekly sums of between $1000 and $5000 to the Liberal Premier, Robin Askin, and the Police Commissioner, Norman Allen. In return, they went soft on the activities of Sydney's criminal syndicates, and turned a blind eye to the connection between syndicate bosses and leading developers. Frank Theeman, the developer of Victoria Street, was a close friend of Saffron and of James Anderson, the manager of several clubs in Kings Cross owned by Saffron. It was Premier Askin who made it possible for Theeman and other developers to plan the destruction of inner Sydney – by sacking the Labor-dominated Sydney City Council in 1967.

The siege of Victoria Street began in April 1973, when Theeman's company started to evict the tenants from his properties, using a notorious stand-over man, Joe Meissner, and a corrupt former cop, Fred Krahe, as enforcers. Bricks were thrown through windows, and wrought iron, locks and stained glass were removed to make the houses uninhabitable. Many tenants left but some remained, effectively squatting in their own homes. Within a few days they had formed an action group to patrol the buildings and publicise their case for a form of development that would retain low-cost housing and protect a historic streetscape. The secretary of the group, Arthur King, approached the NSW BLF, which decided to impose a temporary green ban on the site. Then Arthur King disappeared. Days later he reappeared, terrified; he packed up his belongings and resigned. He had been abducted, blindfolded, locked in the boot of a car and threatened with a knife. The use of thugs from the criminal underworld to terrorise the activists would continue, culminating in the death of crusading newspaper owner Juanita Nielsen in 1975.

There were more dramatic scenes before her death. Four weeks after the evictions had started, merchant seaman Mick Fowler returned from his ship and found that his belongings had been removed. Enlisting the aid of fellow seamen and builders' labourers, he repossessed his

Anti-developer demonstrators frustrate police actions during the Victoria Street struggle, 1974 (City of Sydney Archives, SRC 14791).

room, ejecting three security guards and vowing that he would resist by force any attempt to evict him. Elsewhere on the site terrorism continued, and more of the original tenants departed, especially after an Aboriginal girl died in a mysterious fire in one of the houses. The residents' action group recruited people from the activist wing of the Sydney Libertarians, and their drinking mates in the Push, to join the squat. Soon co-operative forms of living complemented the organising of collective resistance. Fences between the houses were removed, and there were Sunday general meetings of the 60 of so squatters, who organised co-operative child minding, film shows and a food co-op with a rotating cooking roster. A sympathetic weekly report in Juanita Nielsen's news-

'For Need not Greed': demonstrators make their point from the roof of a building scheduled for demolition (*Australian*, 4 January 1974. Newspix).

| The same building today (Nick Irving).

paper, *Now*, documented it as 'one of the first publicly visible examples of the urban squatting movement in New South Wales'.

This went on for six months, as the struggle ebbed and flowed. Mick Fowler won an injunction to stay in his room. Theeman released a new plan that envisaged incorporating some of the houses and building a 10-storey development behind them. The National Trust endorsed this scheme, but it ignored the need for working-class housing, so the squatters rejected it. The conservative state government was re-elected in November after a 'law and order' campaign in which Theeman poured money into a media blitz against the BLF and the squatters. Just before Christmas the government finally established that squatting was illegal, and the courts upheld Theeman's right to evict.

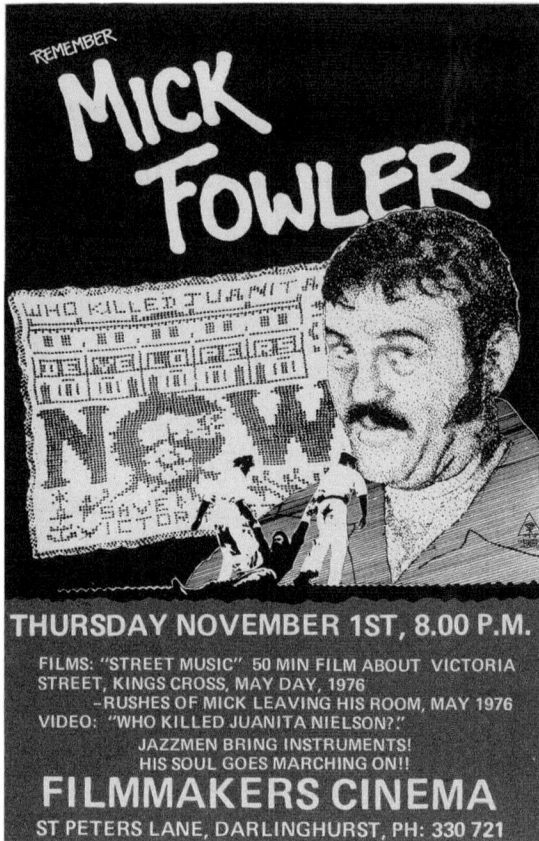

Poster celebrating the life of Mick Fowler, trade union militant, seaman, musician, Victoria Street resident, and one of the anti-development activists (courtesy of Chips Mackinolty; Collection, Powerhouse Museum, Sydney).

On 3 January 1974, 30 of Theeman's thugs, assisted by 250 police, raided the houses, using axes, sledgehammers and crowbars to physically evict the squatters. A huge crowd gathered. Two squatters clung precariously to a chimney for 17 hours. For two days the fight continued; the police made 54 arrests. After the squatters were forced out, the houses were smashed up by hired goons and fenced off to prevent further access. Mick Fowler, however, stayed put – he was the sole remaining legal tenant, and was supported courageously by Juanita Nielsen's newspaper and the BLF. And the union's green ban was still in place, protecting the whole site. Theeman, unable to begin construction, was bleeding millions of dollars.

It took two more years before he got his way. The green ban was lifted in October 1974, after a long intrigue between developers and union movement rivals, sooled on by the media, and facilitated by the state government, culminated in the takeover the NSW branch of the BLF. Then it was time for Juanita Nielsen to be neutralised. In July 1975 she went to a meeting in the Carousel Club, owned by Abe Saffron, to discuss his offer to advertise in her newspaper. She was never seen again. Much later, two employees of the club were convicted of conspiracy to abduct her. Finally, in 1976, Mick Fowler lost his case in the courts and was evicted. That was the end of the struggle for low-cost housing on Victoria Street.

In 1979, tower blocks rose on the site, and Mick Fowler, then in Western Australia, died. A plaque in Victoria Street commemorates his stand for housing based on 'need not greed'. A Memorial Lecture Series, sponsored by the NSW Greens, honours the courage of Juanita Nielsen.

44

THE CONSPIRACY AGAINST ANANDA MARGA

In 1978, there were Margiis living communally at 9 Queen Street, Newtown. A rambling former boarding house of 16 rooms, it was also the Australasian headquarters of their spiritual meditation and social action movement, which was called Ananda Marga, the path of bliss. From its offices on the first floor, Ananda Marga ran welfare, educational, relief and commercial activities. Its membership was about 500, but through its meditation centres and publications it reached and influenced many thousands more.

The Margiis of Queen Street were typical of the new radicals of the 1970s. They were younger and more highly educated than the radicals of the past, and they placed more importance on fighting the injustices of race and gender and the horrors of war than on organising for the dignity of labour. Like others of this generation, their political outlook was formed by the movement against conscription, the war in Vietnam, and the dead weight of conformity in behaviour and belief in our culture. The most radical of them were interested in neither the power games of political parties nor the reform of government. Theirs was a politics of defiance and rejection. The Margiis were part of this more extreme radicalisation, to which they brought a non-Christian spiritual underpinning, which included meditation.

The politics of their strand of political radicalism was summed up in June 1978 in a poster on the back cover of *Dharma*, one of the magazines associated with the Sydney Ananda Marga. In the psychedelic style common in the counterculture of the time, it showed a Margii of indeterminate gender and ethnicity drawing inner strength from meditation to subdue by force the demons of the world, under the slogan, 'Fight for Justice, Meditate for Peace'. This politics also accommodated revolution, which was both 'necessary and beneficial' when people were suffering from extreme exploitation, according to a statement in *Dharma* by Tim Anderson, the publicity officer for Ananda Marga in Australia.

Tim Anderson was a university student in Melbourne when he discovered Ananda Marga. He suspended his studies and embraced its life

'Fight for Justice, Meditate for Peace': 1978 Ananda Marga propaganda (Sydney), advocating an idealised mix of militancy and meditation (back cover of *Dharma*, June 1978).

of spiritual meditation and social activism, soon spending all his free time with the movement. In 1977 he visited India to meet its founder, P.R. Sarkar, affectionately known as Baba to his followers. Sarkar had developed a system of spiritual yoga, based on Vedic and Tantric philosophies, which he joined to a politics of social liberation. The message of Ananda Marga, which Sarkar founded in 1955, was 'self-realisation and service'. In 1959 he formulated the socio-economic theory of his movement, calling it PROUT, which stands for Progressive Utilisation Theory. It envisages a decentralised, community-based world economy of self-sufficiency for the poor; economic democracy; small business; and limits on the accumulation of wealth. There was also a spiritual dimension to PROUT. Its appeal to the new radicals of the 1970s was reinforced by Sarkar explicitly positioning PROUT as an alternative to both Communism and capitalism.

In India, Ananda Marga grew rapidly in the 1960s and 1970s, especially in West Bengal, where it became a serious challenge in some parts of the countryside to the Communist government. It had other enemies: conservative Hindus resented Ananda Marga's rejection of the caste system, and the Congress Party felt threatened as Ananda Marga entered public life. But the violent confrontations between mobs of supporters and opponents of the organisation, and the murderous attacks on Ananda Marga monks and nuns, were in fact part of a more general crisis of civil society in India. Sarkar was arrested and gaoled without trial in 1971, and, in 1975 the country's central government, declaring a state of emergency, banned Ananda Marga. It was not until 1978, after the end of the emergency, that Sarkar was found innocent of the charges and released.

During Sarkar's imprisonment, Margiis around the world campaigned to 'Free Baba'. Their actions were confronting, sometimes violent, but the violence was often provoked. Moreover, later evidence showed that much of the violence attributed to the Margiis was either instigated by security personnel associated with the Indian government, or the work of persons with no connection to the movement. This was true also in Australia, where there were local prejudices working against the Margiis. Cold War anti-Communism, the lifeblood of the spook community, was almost a spent force. The mid-1970s conservative government of Malcolm Fraser needed something that would persuade the community that it was necessary to move the security services to a counter-terrorism footing – the government already intended to give them wider powers. At the same time, the security services needed a defence against the successful campaign against 'the political police', which had been aimed not only at the Australian Security Intelligence Organisation (ASIO) but also at the police Special Branches in the states. Reforms and accountability were imminent. In this situation Ananda Marga, already labelled a terrorist group by the Indian government, was a godsend to Australian conservatives.

From 1976, state and Commonwealth police spied on Ananda Marga and harassed its members – there were 37 incidents reported by *Dharma* between September 1976 and August 1978. ASIO and the NSW Police Special Branch placed several informants in the organisation in 1977 and 1978.

It should come as no surprise, then, that immediately after a bomb exploded on 13 February 1978, killing three people outside the Hilton Hotel in George Street, where the Indian Prime Minister was staying, the media, politicians and security officials called it terrorism. Some immediately suggested that it was the work of Ananda Marga. At a

A secret surveillance photograph, taken by NSW Special Branch, of Tim Anderson outside Ananda Marga headquarters in Queen Street, Newtown in the 1970s (courtesy of Tim Anderson).

press conference, Tim Anderson rejected the suggestion, pointing out that Ananda Marga did not support violence. As the weeks and months went by, it was clear that the police could not produce evidence to link the bombing to Ananda Marga. In fact, many people were saying that the deaths resulted from a bungled operation by ASIO, which had planned for a bomb to be placed ... and discovered before it exploded. Then, a strange and fortuitous development switched the public's attention back to Ananda Marga. It also proved that there was an official conspiracy against it in Australia.

Just after midnight on 16 June 1978, 25 police surrounded 9 Queen Street. Led by Detective Sergeant Roger Rogerson (a notoriously corrupt cop, later gaoled), a posse of Armed Hold-Up and Special Branch detectives smashed open the door of the house and rushed to an upstairs room. There they handcuffed Tim Anderson, who had been sleeping, and planted evidence on him. They took him to Criminal Investigation Branch (CIB) headquarters, where he was assaulted and verballed – that is, the police concocted an unsigned interview to incriminate him.

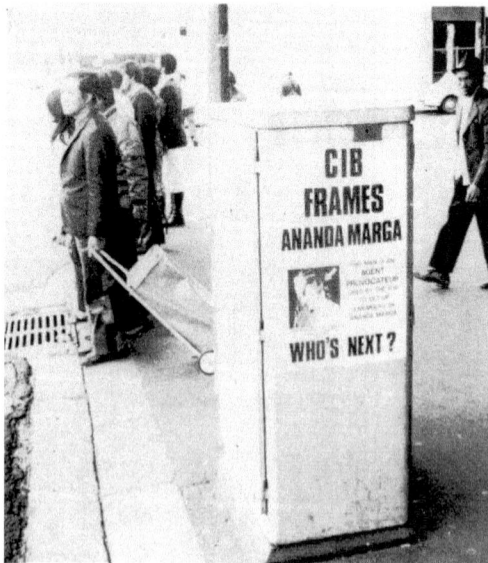

Poster in the city: 'CIB frames Ananda Marga' (*Dharma*, September 1978).

Then he was charged with conspiracy to murder the leader of a neo-fascist outfit called the National Front. Earlier that evening, two other Margiis - Paul Alister and Ross Dunn - had driven to the National Front leader's home at Yagoona to paint anti-racist slogans. They too were arrested and taken to CIB headquarters, where they were assaulted and verballed and charged with the same offence.

A fair trial for the three Margiis was becoming impossible. The media reported the conspiracy case as if the real story was that Ananda Marga was responsible for the Hilton bombing; the prosecution fuelled this by questioning the three about the bombing. After two trials, Alister, Dunn and Anderson were sentenced to 16 years in gaol. A campaign to free the Yagoona Three began, and seven and half years later, after a judicial inquiry, they were freed, with pardons. The inquiry found that the evidence against them had been fabricated, in the main by a person recruited by Special Branch to spy on Ananda Marga.

As the years passed, the police were still unable to bring charges related to the Hilton bombing, so the official conspiracy against Ananda Marga continued. Four years after his pardon, Tim Anderson was awakened one morning by the police and informed that he was under arrest - for the Hilton bombing. This time there were two sources for the police case, one who claimed to have planted the bomb at the Hilton under Anderson's direction, and the other a career criminal facing a lifetime in gaol who testified that Anderson confessed to the bombing. Their evidence was unbelievable, but a jury again convicted Anderson. He was gaoled in 1990. His legal team appealed, and in 1991 the NSW Court of Criminal Appeal threw out the evidence and quashed Anderson's conviction.

Tim Anderson spent seven and a half years in prison for crimes he did not commit. He was framed not once but twice, because he (and Alister and Dunn, who served seven years) belonged to an organisation that had been labelled as terrorist to serve the interests of conservative politicians, security officials and media controllers. The release of Cabinet documents confirms that before the Hilton bombing ASIO assessed Ananda Marga as dangerous to the country's security. Despite this, the government refused to ban it. Perhaps it was more useful to the conservatives to have this allegedly terrorist organisation legal and active.

Ananda Marga will always be wrongly associated, for those who were around in the 1970s, with the bomb that exploded in a garbage bin outside the Hilton Hotel in George Street in February 1978 – a crime with which it had no connection. It should also be remembered, however, for its radical social activism, its welfare services, its non-violent culture of meditation and self-realisation. Progressive Margiis were involved in feminist, environmental and anti-racist politics. When the official conspiracy bared its teeth on the night of 16 June 1978 the Margiis were engaged in the kinds of actions that are traditional in radical circles. Paul Alister had just returned from organising Ananda Marga's Kings Cross soup kitchen for homeless people. Earlier that day, Tim Anderson had discussed a graffiti raid on the home of Robert Cameron, leader of the racist National Front. That was why Dunn and Alister were heading to Yagoona – in a car stolen by Richard Seary, a recent recruit who turned out to be a police spy. They were unaware that on the back seat Seary had placed a bag containing the makings of a bomb. When the car arrived at Cameron's house, the police were waiting. So the nightmare began.

45

COMBATING THE 'GREATEST SOCIAL MENACE'

DARLINGHURST POLICE STATION

Two officers separated the prisoner from the others in the paddy wagon and took him into the police station, then along a long corridor to an empty room. The prisoner, a young man of 25, was alarmed, because he could not see much beyond outlines; he had lost his glasses when he was being arrested.

The bashing commenced. There were two police officers, landing blows to the head mainly, accompanied by the taunting mantra 'You're not so smart now, are you?' The prisoner had been arrested when trying to help fellow citizens felled by the police, and had protested against the treatment being meted out in the name of law and order. Now he was propped against a wall; blows were administered in such a way that he was systematically rolled around the walls of the room, starting from the door he had entered, and back again. It was classic thuggish policing, the walls acting as silent weapons of assault, allowing a possible future police legal defence that any injuries sustained were self-inflicted.

Then came a punch to the solar plexus. The prisoner collapsed and an officer went to work on one of his legs, apparently trying to break it, at which point the prisoner started to convulse, lost control of his bladder and pissed himself. Whereupon the bashing ceased and the prisoner was placed in a cell by himself.

Now the prisoner was alone physically, but not alone otherwise: he was one of 53 people violently detained that night, in one police

Darlinghurst Police Station 1978 (top left), where police bashed and terrified Mardi Gras participants and supporters while in custody (City of Sydney Archives, CRS 48/1798).

operation, and charged with resisting arrest, assaulting police, causing malicious damage, using unseemly language, disobeying reasonable directions, and so on.

As the prisoner struggled with his pain and fears, a noisy crowd assembled outside the police station. They were concerned about those who had been arrested, some of whom, once they had been bailed out, were taken by friends to hospital because of injuries they had incurred while being arrested, and afterwards in police custody.

This was Darlinghurst Police Station, Sydney, during the early hours of Sunday morning, 25 June 1978. Earlier that night, on Saturday, 24 June, the prisoner and the 52 others jammed into cells, had been participants in Sydney's first Gay Mardi Gras. At the time, homosexual acts were criminal offences in New South Wales. Homosexuals were often the targets of police violence, harassment, and entrapment.

The 53 arrested were an almost equal mix of males and females, ranging in age from 17 to 47, many in their mid to late twenties; in terms of occupations, a wide range was represented – unemployed people, students, teachers, nurses, a journalist, a company director, labourers, secretaries, clerks, a physiotherapist, a waitress, and a serving member of the Royal Australian Navy.

Despite growing political and public support for homosexual law reform, and increasing tolerance nationally, and probably in response to almost a decade of sustained and effective public activism by gay and lesbian rights groups and organisations, a powerful anti-gay back-lash was being engineered in New South Wales by the Sydney hierarchy of the Church of England and the right-wing Christian moral organi-sation the Festival of Light (formed in 1973), both of which opposed the decriminalisation, and acceptance, of homosexuality. The shadow of the 1950s in regard to homosexuality still clouded the state; in 1958 the obsessively anti-homosexual NSW Commissioner of Police, Colin Delaney, described homosexuals as Australia's 'greatest social menace' as he worked to strengthen anti-homosexual laws and refine harassment methods. At the same time he apparently turned a blind eye to organ-ised crime as it was becoming institutionalised, and turning Sydney into what a later head of the Australian Bureau of Crime Intelligence described as 'a stinking city, one of the most corrupt in the world'.

The first Mardi Gras was a cutting edge radical concept. Many gay men and lesbians had created lifestyles of discretion in suburban social clubs and subculture city venues. The Mardi Gras, however, was confronting. It was about being openly gay and lesbian in the public domain; it was an innovative blend of parade, street party, street thea-tre, the public celebration of being gay and lesbian, and political pro-test. It was intended to be a pointed yet joyful climax to a day of political activism which had included a gay rights march through the

Police move with force against a participant in the first Gay Mardi Gras, Sydney, 1978 (*Daily Telegraph*, 26 June 1978, by John Sefton. Newspix).

streets of Sydney, estimated to have been attended by between 300 and 500 people, a rally in Martin Plaza, and a public forum on gay politics in Paddington Town Hall. It was all part of a day of global activism and celebration called for by the San Francisco Gay Freedom Day Committee to commemorate the anniversary of the iconic Stonewall Riots in New York (June–July 1969), when gay men, lesbians, transgendered people, bisexuals and male prostitutes came together to fight back against systemic police harassment.

With the necessary permission from city authorities granted, the Mardi Gras centred on Sydney's emerging gay precinct. The parade began at 10 pm in Taylor Square on Saturday night, with about 1000 people, and moved down Oxford Street towards Hyde Park; there was a small truck carrying a small sound system, some music, some fancy dress costumes, people walking, dancing, holding hands, smiling, joyful, chanting slogans such as 'Out of the bars and into the streets!', 'Ho! Ho! Homosexual!', displaying placards making points like 'Love has no discrimination', and inviting the Saturday night crowds to join in. Eventually there were about 2000 revellers.

When the procession reached Hyde Park the police decided the show was over. To prevent the planned speeches taking place they confiscated the Mardi Gras sound system and impounded the truck it was on. Anger swept through the crowd and aggressive chanting broke out; many of the participants broke ranks and made the impromptu decision to head up William Street to Kings Cross, Sydney's traditional home of bohemianism and sexual diversity.

The police called in extra forces from other city stations, blockaded the Cross and attacked Mardi Gras revellers. Film footage supports eyewitness accounts of a full-scale riot ensuing as police and Mardi Gras participants fought with fists, placards and garbage bins. The violence of the night may have been exacerbated by Kings Cross locals who joined in to settle old scores with the police. However, police had cast the first stone: they had removed their identification badges before making the 53 arrests. This was a tactic often used by Sydney law enforcers when they were about to ignore civil liberty laws.

The Mardi Gras 53 appeared in Central Court of Petty Sessions on Monday, 26 June. Police blockaded the court and prevented journalists and the public from entering, apparently ignoring the advice of magistrates to the contrary. It was a wet day, sometimes drizzling and sometimes pouring rain; 170 police confronted 200 supporters of the arrested who had gathered outside the court. The confrontation generated some violence when police linked arms and tried to confine the supporters to a contained forecourt area. One supporter left with her arm broken, but police denied knowledge of any injuries; six arrests were made. Next day the *Sydney Morning Herald* published the personal details of the Mardi Gras 53 – their names, ages, residential addresses, occupations. For some of those listed there were negative consequences, including employer victimisation.

Police responses over those June days touched a raw national nerve, transforming what had started out as a local celebratory minority event into one of national significance, and invigorating gay rights and law reform campaigns. Across the nation demonstrations and rallies were organised in solidarity with the Mardi Gras 53, and money was raised for their legal defence. Apart from the rough-house nature of the police response, wider legal issues were involved. Fundamental democratic issues were at stake: police had arbitrarily shut down a legal demonstration, and their actions outside the court on 26 June raised the disturbing question of whether or not they had actually contested the authority of the court.

Over the following months the NSW Labor government received negative, at times hostile, media coverage over the handling of the Mardi Gras and the legal fallout. Between October 1978 and late December 1979, charges against most of the Mardi Gras participants were dismissed or dropped. In May 1979 NSW law was changed to make it more difficult for police to prevent street marches and demonstrations. As for the Mardi Gras, it went on to mirror changing public attitudes and law reform regarding gay and lesbian citizens, growing to become an internationally renowned joyous, and still political, annual Sydney event, involving hundreds of thousands of participants and onlookers, and worth millions of dollars each year to Sydney's economy.

46

SURVIVAL DAY, 26 JANUARY 1988, KOORI REDFERN

THE EMPRESS HOTEL, REGENT STREET

Before the British invasion on 26 January 1788, the land from South Head to Botany Bay, and from Sydney Cove to the ocean, belonged to the Gadigal clan. Almost at its centre, in the area we know as Redfern, was a crossing point where the Gadigal people would meet as they moved through their country. Smallpox and bullets in the first three years of the invasion wiped out most of the Gadigal, but by the 1830s Indigenous people were gathering again in Redfern. From its farms and market gardens they could beg food and sugar bags to compensate for their stolen hunting and fishing grounds. On the Cleveland Paddocks, where Prince Alfred Park is today, the survivors of the clans met to socialise and hold corroborees.

Inevitably, as the invaders built their city, this form of Indigenous living disappeared from Redfern, but the railway, the streets of working-class housing and the factories that submerged the natural landscape also brought Aborigines in the 20th century back to Redfern. It was close to Central Station, where trains from the country deposited Aborigines displaced by the processes we call the privatisation of land and the mechanisation of farming. For these Aborigines, however, Redfern was a kind of solace; rents were cheap and jobs were available in the Eveleigh railway workshops or local factories.

So a new form of economic relationship with the invaders began. As urban wage earners, Redfern Aborigines rented (and sometimes bought) houses, sent their children to school, and barracked for South Sydney's Rabbitohs. As a doubly oppressed section of the working class they joined unions and voted Labor or Communist, and they got a response. From 1957, the Eveleigh Loco Central Shop Committee campaigned for a 'New Deal' for Aborigines; left unions in the metal trades, building and maritime industries did the same in the 1960s and 1970s. In 1963, with the support of building unions, Ray Peckham and Monty Maloney published *The Aboriginal Worker*. Out of this experience of militant unionism one type of Aboriginal leadership emerged, including Redfern's Chicka Dixon; this was the respectable, working-class face of Koori Redfern.

The other face was the politics of resistance, forged by having to cope every day with racism and white violence. Most Aborigines in Redfern did not acquire even the dubious security provided by white working-class life. Their rate of unemployment was two or three times as high as that of white workers, many were homeless, and their health was poor. These problems became critical when Redfern's Aboriginal population exploded in the late 1960s. This explosion followed the success of the 1967 referendum, which, among other things, transferred Aboriginal affairs to the Commonwealth government. Reserves closed and employers sacked their Aboriginal workers rather than pay them the same wages as they paid their white workers. These workers often ended up in Redfern, as did people who had been removed from their families, people seeking to escape the racism of country towns, and a young black intelligentsia looking to solve these problems by creating a form of power among the oppressed – Black Power.

There was 'a small urban war between the people and the police' consuming Redfern when Aboriginal writer Bobbi Sykes arrived in 1971. Every Thursday, Friday and Saturday nights the police would raid the Koori pubs on Regent Street. Father Ted Kennedy remembers 18 paddy wagons lined up outside the Empress Hotel on a Thursday night in 1970. Aboriginal activist Gary Foley writes:

> It was like a taxi rank. [The police would] come in and beat the shit out of everyone inside [the Empress], arbitrarily arrest anyone who objected, and when the wagons were full, they'd drive off and lock people up on trumped up charges.

Homelessness, a huge problem at this time, also made Aborigines vulnerable to arrest. Father Ted, who was influenced by the Liberation Theology developed by Latin America's radical Catholics, made the Presbytery of St Vincent's in Redfern available for the homeless. Many Aborigines squatted in 'empties' – terrace homes left vacant by developers. Led by the notorious 21 Division, a flying squad of detectives trained to break up civil disturbances, the police conducted regular brutal raids on these squats.

Since 1969 a small group of young Kooris, disillusioned by government indifference to Aboriginal affairs after the referendum, and inspired by the actions of the Black Panther Party in the United States, had been fighting back. This was another step in the movement to assert Indigenous control of Aboriginal organisations that had begun in the mid-1960s. At the centre of the philosophy of Black Power was self-determination. Economic independence – meaning land rights – was also important, but in Redfern at that time it was more of a symbolic

The former Empress Hotel, Regent Street, Redfern, a site that features significantly in the world of the Black Power militants during the 1970s (City of Sydney Archives, NSCA CRS 1133/374).

demand. Above all, Black Power meant direct action. By defending themselves on the streets, Kooris would determine who they were in a public way and what it meant to be a proud member of an ancient culture asserting its relevance in a modern urban setting.

They began with surveillance. At the Empress and elsewhere they would record police activity and the identification numbers of officers involved in attacks on Aborigines. They joined with courageous Catholic clergy and laity (the 'Holy Left') to do the same thing in support of squatters in abandoned houses near Redfern station. Then, having made contact with young progressive lawyers who volunteered their services, they organised to defend Aborigines in the courts. As a result, in 1970, Regent Street saw the Aboriginal Legal Service come into existence. It was 'Australia's first free, shop-front legal aid centre', and was followed soon after by the Aboriginal Medical Service. Meanwhile, the plight of the homeless remained dire, so in a striking act of political theatre, activist Bob Bellear led marchers from the St Vincent's Presbytery, with tools and brooms, to take over the derelict houses in The Block in the name of the Koori community. When the Whitlam Labor government was elected, the occupation of these houses was legalised and the Aboriginal Housing Company was born. 'Conceived, established and controlled' by Aborigines, and achieved by direct action, the existence of these organisations vindicated the strategy of Black Power.

By the time of the white celebration of the bicentenary of the invasion in 1988, Koori militancy was an irrepressible feature of black politics. Mainstream Aboriginal leadership and their white friends had organised a march through the city on 26 January behind the slogan 'We have survived'. From all over the country, delegations of Kooris, Nyungars, Yolngu and Anangu came, and the march from Redfern Oval was led by men from Arnhem Land and the Central Desert in traditional costume. There were 15,000 marching, including contingents of white sympathisers, notably several hundred gay men and lesbians – peaceful demands for 'justice' and 'hope' always attract the constitutional left. Charles Perkins, Secretary of the Federal Department of Aboriginal Affairs, marched too. Reaching Hyde Park, the crowd swelled to about 40,000, as leaders spoke of the need for reconciliation between blacks and whites.

Left activists Joyce Stevens and Adam Farrar with Black Power leader Gary Foley 'challenging the bicentenary' at an Invasion Day meeting, Sydney 1988 (*Tribune*, 3 February 1988, SEARCH Foundation/State Library of New South Wales).

There was also, however, an earlier demonstration, and an alternative model of Aboriginal politics on that day. At 7 am, 1000 Redfern radicals had gathered at the Aboriginal Legal Centre. Defying a police ban they marched to Mrs Macquarie's Chair in the Domain, where they blew a subversive raspberry in the face of the official pageant of tall ships and royal speeches. They had their own fleet of small boats flying the Aboriginal flag. From one boat a man dressed as Captain Arthur Phillip was rowed ashore by white seamen, but at this point the re-enactment literally became 'a world turned upside down', as defending Aborigines capsized the boat, 'drowned' the white men and saved Gadigal country from invasion.

As the tall ships passed, the jeering from the point grew louder: 'Go home, convict scum'; 'Land rights now'. Protesters waded into

At Mrs Macquarie's Chair, on 26 January 1988, Aboriginal activists protested against the white celebration of the Bicentenary (*Sydney Morning Herald*, 27 January 1988, Fairfax Photos).

the water to light flares and throw bottles at the parade of ships. They booed Charles and Diana, who were representing the Queen of the invading power, as they passed by on the admiral's barge. There were fights with white patriots. This was a noisy, smoky, defiant and dangerous part of Sydney that refused to join what the commercial media called 'our ultimate party'.

That night in Redfern its radicals held their own party. From 10 pm to midnight they reclaimed part of Regent Street as Aboriginal land, defying the police, who sensibly kept well away. The police had learnt the limits of their power earlier at the Regent (formerly the Empress) Hotel. A white man drove up the street, turned his heavy truck around and deliberately mounted the kerb to disperse a group of Aborigines outside the pub. Although reported to the police by the publican, who stated that he believed the driver was trying to kill people on the footpath, the police gave the impression that it was a minor matter and that the driver would be taken around the corner and released.

This was stupidly insensitive on the day Redfern radicals had declared their self-determination once again. Suddenly 300 drinkers poured out of the hotel to confront the police. Eight police were injured in an hour-long clash, during which a policewoman was beaten with her own baton and threatened with her own revolver by a Koori woman. The police retreated and the street party began. This forcible resistance and public celebration of difference was what the radicals of Koori Redfern understood as the ultimate means of survival.

47

THE 'INVISIBLE' MARITIME WORKER

MEMORIAL AT THE NATIONAL MARITIME MUSEUM

When colonial administrator Governor Arthur Phillip began Britain's conquest and development of Australia in 1788, he selected Sydney Cove, part of the largest natural harbour in the world, for his base of operations. In doing so he rejected the vulnerable, exposed, less inviting Botany Bay, which had been chosen earlier by British maritime explorer Captain James Cook.

Strategically, it was obvious from the outset: the colony of New South Wales was dependent directly or indirectly on shipping, seafarers and, as time went on, shore-based maritime workers (initially this work was done by convict labour). So it was for the future development of Australia, and so it remains. The majority of the exports and imports that sustain and nourish this island continent are now, as the exports and imports that developed the nation's wealth were, maritime reliant. No ships, no seafarers, no maritime workers, no ports, equates to no Australia as we know it; it's as simple as that.

Sydney is a port city – a city built around, and owing its origin to, a port. The streetscape of the central business district, despite its tunnels, one-way streets, alleys, lanes, and pedestrian-only contrivances, retains skeletal evidence of this. Backbone roads run inland from the former maritime hub of Circular Quay to what were general access and distribution routes. Remnant rib roads, many now blocked traffic arteries, link the harbour's bays with what were once thriving, bustling, areas of wharfage, finger piers, warehouses, other premises involved in maritime trade and commerce, and crowded communities of maritime workers who, by necessity, had to live near their workplaces.

A long – and still continuing – process of mechanisation since World War II has dramatically changed and helped improve working conditions at sea and ashore. Until then maritime work was labour-intensive, working conditions were primitive, often harsh and unhygienic, and the work was physically demanding. Large numbers of workers were required to crew ships, to load and unload them, to repair and maintain them. It was unromantic, unsung work that often stressed human bodies to extremes; exhaustion, death, injury (often crippling) and bodily breakdown (respiratory diseases were abundant, along with arthritis and hernias) were not uncommon.

The sea claimed lives as well, even in the modern period after steam and diesel power had replaced the old, injury-causing sail technology. The 20th century abounds with merchant marine casualties off the Australian coast: *Bombo*, foundered off the south coast of New South Wales in February 1949, 12 dead; *Kiama*, foundered off The Entrance, New South Wales in January 1951, 3 dead, 3 missing; *Birchgrove Park*, foundered off Broken Bay, New South Wales in August 1956, 10 dead; *Noongah*, foundered off Smokey Cape, New South Wales in August 1969, 21 dead ...

While maritime workers generated vast profits for employers and investors, they were poorly paid; they tended to be cut out of the equation. As historian Michael Cannon has written about Australian shipowners in his book *Life in the Cities* (1975), 'Nowhere in the psychology of these self-made men was there any place for the idea that lower-class families should share in the increased wealth of the nation.'

Confronting this attitude and contesting this power relationship, maritime workers began organising trade unions during the early 1870s in many of the ports that dotted the Australian coast. By 1902 the two largest sectors of the maritime workforce, the seamen and the wharf labourers (wharfies), had established their own national trade union organisations, the Seamen's Union of Australia (SUA) and Waterside Workers' Federation (WWF). Over the course of the century these unions successfully improved the wages and conditions of their members, and in 1993 they amalgamated to form the Maritime Union of Australia (MUA), a small union which, in 2009, represented some 11,000 men and women members (seafarers, stevedoring workers, divers and port workers).

Industrial gains were sometimes achieved by co-operation between employers, the unions and governments, but at other times, only by maritime workers taking some form of industrial action, such as going on strike. As a former WWF leader (1984–92) Tas Bull once observed as he reflected on maritime unionism: 'The waterfront has never been a Sunday school picnic. The bosses played it tough and the unions played it tough.' The word for unions playing it tough is 'militant'.

Both unions gained a reputation for militancy. This was compounded by the fact that they did not confine their activites to improving working conditions, but also campaigned separately or jointly on a wide range of national and international social and political issues. Sometimes their political actions controversially opposed policies of the government of the day, as in 1938, when Port Kembla (NSW) wharfies banned the export of war materials to Japan, when government policy supported this trade.

The sea acts as an internationalising agency, helping create an awareness and understanding of other peoples, cultures, nations, races. Waterfronts also do this, as they are the frontier between land and sea, places where ships and crews from all over the world can be part of any working day. One result of this is that maritime unionists tend to involve themselves internationally in industrial and political matters. An early example of this was in 1890, when Sydney wharf labourers sent a donation of £500 to support striking London dockworkers.

For Australian maritime unionists, humour has often been used as a political weapon, and over the years much maritime political protest has been couched in wit and satire. An example of this political style is the song *Bump Me Into Parliament* (sung to the tune *Yankee Doodle*), by seaman William (Bill) Casey, a socialist militant hailing from Manchester. Casey came to prominence in Australia during the anti-conscription campaigns of World War I, and went on to hold several official positions in the SUA from the 1920s onwards, including in Sydney; he died in office in 1949 as leader of the Queensland branch of the union.

Among seamen, Casey was known as the 'Seaman Philosopher'; he read widely in political philosophy and economics, developed formidable legal skills, all self-taught, especially in the areas of maritime and compensation law, was a combative and witty debater and had the ability to compose satiric political verse with apparent ease.

BUMP ME INTO PARLIAMENT

by Bill Casey

Come listen all kind friends of mine
I want to move a motion
To make an Eldorado here
I've got a bonza notion

Chorus:
Bump me into parliament
Bounce me any way at all
Bang me into parliament
On next election day

Some very wealthy friends I know
Declare I am most clever
While some can talk for an hour or so
Why I can talk for ever

I know the Arbitration Act
As a sailor knows his riggins
So if you want a small advance
I'll talk to Justice Higgins

I've read my Bible ten times through
And Jesus justifies me
The man who does not vote for me
By Christ he crucifies me

Oh yes I am a Labor man
And believe in revolution
The quickest way to bring it on
Is talking constitution

I think the worker and the boss
Should keep their present stations
So I will surely pass a bill
'Industrial Relations'

So bump them into parliament
Bounce them any way at all
Bung them into parliament
Don't let the Court decay

Maritime workers and their unions were an integral and visible part of the life of Sydney until the 1970s, when technological change began to shift port activity to Botany Bay and Port Kembla. Before then, maritime workplaces on the city foreshores were part of the Sydney cityscape, as were Woolloomooloo and The Rocks, suburbs where many maritime workers lived during the 19th and well into the 20th centuries. In political street protests and demonstrations, especially during the tumultuous Cold War days of the 1950s and 1960s, large contingents of wharfies and seamen were dramatically, theatrically present, and identifiably so, with union banners and placards. For much of the 20th century, Sydney's maritime unions provided staple fare for a mainly hostile media, and Sydney-based national maritime union leaders such as Jim (Big Jim) Healy (WWF General Secretary, 1937-61) and E.V. Elliott (SUA Federal Secretary, 1941-78) were well known public figures, variously loved, respected, and reviled. Healy and WWF Assistant General Secretary Ted Roach both served 5 weeks in gaol for contempt of court during the bitter 1949 coal strike, and Roach served another 9 months and 18 days, some of it virtually in solitary confinement, for contempt of court during a wage dispute in 1951.

Modern technology changed the nature of maritime work, and greatly reduced the number of people employed in the maritime industry; the process continues today. A major result of this is that Sydney maritime workers are not as numerous or as visible as they once were. In 2003 the NSW government announced its decision to end Sydney's role as a working port, thus freeing up foreshore land for development and government profit. By January 2009 the last cargoes had been discharged and general stevedoring operations ceased in Port Jackson.

But despite this large-scale disappearance of wharfies, maritime workers do still work the harbour and its precincts. They are engaged in mooring and unmooring, servicing tourist vessels, working ferries and charter vessels, boat handling, port authority work, and as divers. Organised maritime workers still have significant political and industrial clout; the Sydney branch of the MUA, for example, has over 2000 members in Port Jackson and Port Botany.

The power and solidarity of the MUA nationally became apparent in 1998 during the four-month 'War on the Waterfront' between the union and the anti-union Commonwealth government of Prime Minister John Howard. The Commonwealth's plan was to break the stevedoring power of the MUA by introducing non-union labour onto Australia's wharves and unleashing, for the first time, the anti-union provisions of the contentious 1996 Workplace Relations Act. Once it had established its union-busting credentials by taking some 1400 jobs away from MUA members, the Howard government then planned to break the power of Australian trade unions generally.

But the plan backfired: the methods employed by the government and its main allies, the National Farmers' Federation and Patrick Stevedores, were dramatic, underhanded and clandestine, reeked of thuggery, and were bankrolled by very deep purses; apparently even elements of the Australian Army were involved in the machinations. This was not a formula likely to produce public indifference, especially when the non-union takeover of the waterfront took place in the dead of night under the protection of balaclava-wearing security personnel clad in anti-riot gear and assisted by guard dogs. The struggle dominated media attention and galvanised a great deal of public support for the MUA.

Eventually the government's plan was thwarted by picket lines, mass public protests, inter-union solidarity, international solidarity actions, trade union media savvy, and legal action. There was also a flow-on effect; as historian Tom Bramble observed, for many outside the union movement the struggle 'gave an added fillip to their own campaigns [and] lifted the spirits of those campaigning on issues as diverse' as opposition to the mining of uranium in Kakadu National Park, and opposition to the privatisation of Melbourne University.

Commenting in 1998 on the historical invisibility of maritime workers, historian Frank Broeze observed that maritime workers:

> have often been repressed in Australia's historiography, not
> least because the militant wharfies and seamen who helped
> tame distance were living proof that Australia was not the
> country of conflict-free consensus that conservative orthodoxy
> preached for so long.

Two significant sites in Sydney challenge this invisibility. In April 1992 a memorial was dedicated 'to the memory of the sacrifices made by Australian and International merchant seafarers in contributing to Australia's prosperity and peace'. Located near the entrance to the National Maritime Museum, Darling Harbour, the memorial consists of two giant sailing ship anchors mounted on a large platform. The anchors are remnants of the *Vernon*, an old clipper that had been converted to a nautical school ship for delinquent and orphaned boys. Moored in Sydney Harbour (1867–92), the *Vernon* served its function until it was replaced by another vessel. All up, about 2500 'trainees' passed through the vessel, some of them going on to maritime careers. The memorial's plinth was donated by Broken Hill Pty Ltd (BHP) as a tribute to the crews of three BHP ships – *Iron Chieftain*, *Iron Crown* and *Iron Knight* – that were sunk during World War II off the NSW coast by enemy submarines; 86 lives were lost when these lumbering unarmed merchant vessels were stalked and destroyed in Australian waters.

On the northern side of the memorial is a plaque, added in 1994, in memory of all Merchant Navy seafarers 'who made the ultimate sacrifice during World War II'. One in eight Australian merchant seafarers was killed during this war, and part of the plaque is a map recording the vessels lost off the east coast of Australia from 1941 to 1944 as the result of enemy action.

Each year in September, on World Maritime Day (designated by the United Nations), Australian merchant mariners, past and present, gather at the memorial to celebrate and reflect upon the enormous contribution merchant mariners have made to Australia in war and peace. It is a solemn and moving occasion, as sacred to many participants as Anzac Day is to the general public.

Memorial plaque outside the Maritime Museum to the merchant seamen who lost their lives off the east coast during World War II. This is one of the very few Australian memorials acknowledging the contribution of merchant seamen to Australian history (Robert Irving).

The other site is 'The Hungry Mile', the name maritime workers gave to the mile of wharves that stretched along Hickson Road between Circular Quay and Darling Harbour, today a mix of hotels, casinos, restaurants, arts venues and training spaces and residential redevelopment. In its heyday it was a political and industrial site, the engine room of a great deal of the wealth of the state of New South Wales, and of the nation.

To this mile of wharves maritime labourers in the 19th century, and on into the 1940s, tramped each day, regardless of the weather, to find casual, low-paid work, because that was the nature of waterfront work in those days. If you were serious about finding work you had to live nearby in whatever lodgings you could afford or arrange, so that you would be on hand whenever work became available.

Waterfront employment was gained via the 'bull' system, one that many labourers despised, regarding it as humiliating and demeaning, as it pitted worker against worker. Under this system workers gathered daily in a public place and competed against each other for the available work; employer representatives personally selected those required. 'Bulls' were the strongest, and thus the favoured, workers. It was a system in which violence, favouritism and bribery were commonplace, and where trade union activists often found themselves on employer blacklists. The 'bull' system prevailed until a combination of factors, including determined campaigning by maritime unions and the wartime need of the Commonwealth Labor government to regularise manpower in an essential industry, ended the system during World War II. For many maritime workers, The Hungry Mile and their experiences there came to represent the essence of capitalism, and helped shape the direction and colour of their politics, and their relationship with employers.

In 2006 the NSW government invited the public to suggest names for the new Sydney precinct that was being planned for the 22 hectares of defunct maritime industrial land which included The Hungry Mile. The name Barangaroo was gazetted in 2007, honouring a prominent and powerful Indigenous woman from Sydney's early colonial history. The MUA campaigned to also have the name 'The Hungry Mile' officially associated with the area. In July 2009 the Premier of New South Wales, Nathan Rees, announced 'The Hungry Mile' as the official place name for the section of Hickson Road between the Munn Street overbridge and the Napoleon Street intersection; close to 600 metres, not a mile, but a permanent reminder of our maritime/political past.

During the late 1920s a Sydney wharfie, Ernest Antony, wrote a powerful and legendary poem titled 'The Hungry Mile'. Antony (1894–1960) was an itinerant worker, trade union militant and working-class poet. During his life he travelled throughout Australia seeking work. He laboured on the wharves and in the cane fields, drove mule and camel teams, cut timber, helped build wooden bridges and wharves, and pros-

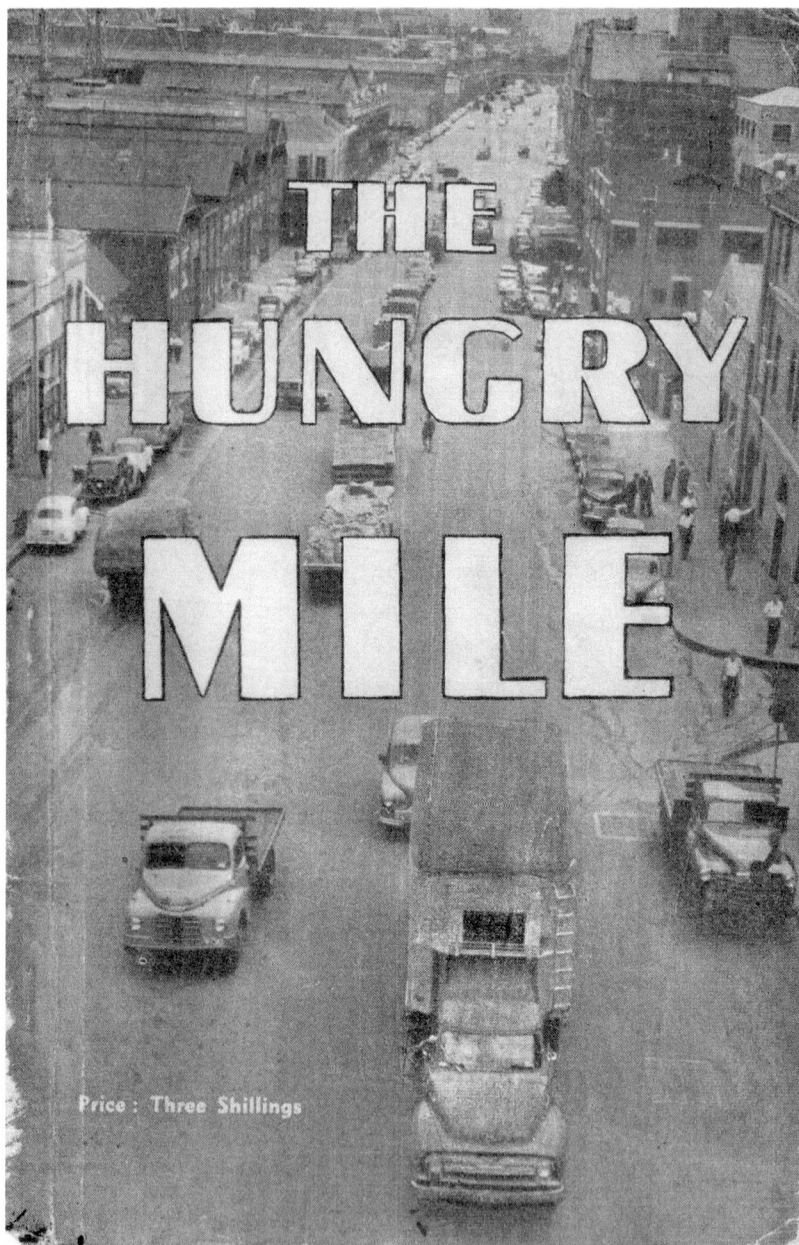

The cover of Tom Nelson's book, *The Hungry Mile*, an iconic trade
union publication (1957) that helped establish in the minds of maritime
workers their ownership of the area (Irving collection).

pected for tin and gold. During the 1920s and 1930s he contributed poems about political and industrial issues to labour movement publications, and published one book of his poems. For Antony, poetry was a political weapon.

THE HUNGRY MILE

by Ernest Antony

They tramp there in their legions on the mornings dark and cold,
To beg the right to slave for bread from Sydney's lords of gold;
They toil and sweat in slavery, 'twould make the devil smile,
To see the Sydney wharfies tramping down the hungry mile.

On ships from all the seas they toil, that others of their kind,
May never know the pinch of want nor feel the misery blind;
That make the lives of men a hell in those conditions vile;
That are the hopeless lot of those who tramp the hungry mile.

The slaves of men who know no thought of anything but gain,
Who wring their brutal profits from the blood and sweat and pain
Of all the disinherited who slave and starve the while,
Upon the ships beside the wharves along the hungry mile.

But every stroke of that grim lash that sears the souls of men
With interest due from years gone by, shall be paid back again
To those who drive these wretched slaves to build the golden pile.
And blood shall blot the memory out - of Sydney's hungry mile.

The day will come, aye, come it must, when these same slaves
shall rise,
And through the revolution's smoke, ascending to the skies,
The master's face shall show the fear he hides behind his smile,
Of these his slaves, who on that day shall storm the hungry mile.

And when the world grows wiser and all men at last are free,
When none shall feel the hunger nor tramp in misery
To beg the right to slave for bread, the children then may smile,
At those strange tales they tell of what was once the hungry mile.

The Hungry Mile (Hickson Road) looking south from High Street, scene of many bitter industrial/political struggles during the 20th century (City of Sydney Archives, SRC 11714).

RECOMMENDED READING

This book has presented history as a series of radical possibilities, as an account of refusals, challenges and alternatives in the past. It is also a way of thinking about the present in the light of the past. If this appeals to you as a way of doing history we would like to recommend some books and websites that we found useful.

First, here are some general overviews of important themes. As a pictorial history of working-class radicalism, Joe Harris's *The Bitter Fight: A Pictorial History of the Australian Labor Movement* (1970) has no equal. Australian history as a struggle for social justice is revealed in Stuart Macintyre's *Winners and Losers: The Pursuit of Social Justice in Australian History* (1985), and the lives of 12 of those who struggled are recounted in *Rebels and Radicals* (1983), a collection edited by Eric Fry. His 'Introduction' is a neglected statement of the approach to history that we embrace. The four-volume *A People's History of Australia Since 1788* (1988), edited by Verity Burgmann and Jenny Lee, is a collection of radical analyses of Australian society and culture by a wide range of authors, and much of it remains relevant and provocative. The often neglected rebellious and violent strands in our history are highlighted in Kevin Baker's *Mutiny, Terrorism, Riots and Murder: A History of Sedition in Australia and New Zealand* (2006). In print since 1989, John Pilger's *A Secret Country* is a radical/progressive discussion of Australia's history and culture.

There are several overviews of particular activist traditions. *First Australians: An Illustrated History*, edited by Rachel Perkins and Marcia Langton (2008) is a major achievement, brilliantly illustrated and authoritative. Gary Foley's *The Koori History Website* (http://www.kooriweb.org/foley/indexb.html), which contains over 3500 pages of source materials and essays, is especially important for its documentation of the Black Power movement. We also enjoyed Graham Willett's *Living Out Loud: A History of Gay and Lesbian Activism in Australia* (2000); Sandra Bloodworth and Tom O'Lincoln's (editors) *Rebel Women in Australian Working Class History* (1998); and Sean Scalmer's *The Little History of Australian Unionism* (2006).

For understanding the left of the labour movement in its formative years, two books by Verity Burgmann are essential: *'In Our Time': Socialism and the Rise of Labour, 1885–1905* (1985), and *Revolutionary Industrial Unionism: The Industrial Workers of the World in Australia* (1995). She is also the co-author with Meredith Burgmann of the only full study of Sydney's environmental labour activism, *Green Bans, Red Union: Environmental Activism and the New South Wales Builders Labourers' Federation* (1998). The labour, feminist and radical currents in the nation-building decade of the 1890s are brought to life by Bruce Scates in *A New Australia: Citizenship, Radicalism and the First Republic* (1997).

The proceedings of the national labour history conferences over the last 20 years are full of studies of working-class activism and social history. To find them, look up Australian Society for the Study of Labour History in your library catalogue. The publications of the Society's branches are also a wonderful source for this kind of history. The Sydney branch's *Hummer* has been digitised on the ASSLH website (http://www.asslh.org.au/branches/sydney/), but see also *Recorder* (Melbourne branch), *Illawarra Unity* (Illawarra Region branch), and *The Queensland Journal of Labour History* (Brisbane branch).

A short introduction to the history of activism on the conservative side of politics is Andrew Moore's *The Right Road? A History of Right-Wing Politics in Australia* (1995). He has also documented a secret, significant, little-known paramilitary response by conservatives to fears of radicalism, in *The Secret Army and the Premier: Conservative Paramilitary Organisations in New South Wales 1930–32* (1989). Richard Hall's *The Secret State: Australia's Spy Industry* (1978) remains the only accessible survey of the security responses of the Australian state to the types of rebellion and radicalism we have dealt with in our book.

To compare Sydney's history of radical sites with that of other cities, look at two earlier books from which we drew inspiration: Jeff Sparrow and Jill Sparrow's *Radical Melbourne: A Secret History* (2001); and Raymond Evans and Carole Ferrier's (editors) *Radical Brisbane: An Unruly History* (2004). Much of our knowledge of Sydney's radical sites was based on Terry Irving and Lucy Taksa's *Places, Protests and Memorabilia: The Labour Heritage Register of New South Wales* (2002).

The internet has become a great place for historical research. The *Australian Dictionary of Biography*, now online, is a major checking point (http://adbonline.anu.edu.au/adbonline.htm). Some of the websites with radical sources and commentary that we consulted frequently are: Reason in Revolt – Source Documents of Australian Radicalism (http://www.reasoninrevolt.net.au/); Bob Gould's site, OzLeft (http://members.optushome.com.au/spainter/Ozleft.html); Takver's Initiatives (http://www.takver.com/); Humphrey McQueen's stimulating writings (http://home.alphalink.com.au/~loge27/index.htm), and Tom O'Lincoln's considerable output (http://redsites.alphalink.com.au/).

SELECT BIBLIOGRAPHY

During research for this book the following journals/newspapers were variously drawn upon:

Aboriginal Worker
Australasian
Australian
Australian Highway
Australian Town and Country Journal
Australian Workman
Bulletin
Daily Guardian
Daily Mail
Daily Mirror
Daily Standard
Daily Telegraph

Home – an Australian Quarterly
Honi Soit
Labor Daily
Maritime Workers' Journal
Mirror
People
Socialist
Sun
Sydney Morning Herald
Tribune
Woman's Voice
Worker
Workers' Weekly

We also relied on information provided by correspondence or interviews with: Tim Anderson, Clem Gorman, Cecil Grivas, Alistair Hulett, Michael Matteson, John Maynard, Warren Smith, R.D. Walshe.

The following sources were drawn upon, and are grouped in the time frames/periods featured in our chapters. While some items listed may not directly relate to the period in which they appear below, they are linked to the relevant chapters.

BEFORE 1880

Andrews, Barry (1976) *Price Warung (William Astley)*, Twayne Publishers, Boston, MA.

Cameron, Robert S. (1986) *Robert Cooper of Juniper Hall: A Family History*, R.S. Cameron, Woollahra NSW.

Clendinnen, Inga (2003) *Dancing with Strangers*, Text Publishing, Melbourne.

Dawes, William, *The Notebooks of William Dawes on The Aboriginal Language of Sydney* (1790); high-quality digital images of each page of the notebooks, with accompanying transcriptions, are online at http://www.williamdawes.org/.

Flannery, Tim (ed.) (1999) *The Birth of Sydney*, Text Publishing, Melbourne.

Goodall, Heather (1996) *Invasion to Embassy: Land in Aboriginal Politics in New South Wales, 1770-1972*, Allen & Unwin, Sydney.

Grenville, Kate (2008) *The Lieutenant*, Text Publishing, Melbourne.

Hughes, Robert (1988) *The Fatal Shore: A History of the Transportation of Convicts to Australia 1787-1868*, Pan Books, London.

Irving, Terry (2006) *The Southern Tree of Liberty: The Democratic Movement in New South Wales before 1856*, Federation Press, Sydney.

Kruta, V. et al. (1977) *Dr John Lhotsky: The Turbulent Australian Writer, Naturalist and Explorer*, Australia Felix Literary Club, Melbourne.

Lawrence, Joan (1988) *Sydney from The Rocks*, Hale & Iremonger, Sydney.

Lohan, Rena (1996) 'Sources in the National Archives for Research into the Transportation of Irish Convicts to Australia (1791-1853)', *Irish Archives*, vol. 3, no. 1, pp. 13-28.

Mander-Jones, Phyllis (1966) 'William Dawes', *Australian Dictionary of Biography (ADB)*, vol. 1: 1788-1850, Melbourne University Press (MUP), Melbourne, pp. 297-98.

McKenna, Mark (1996) *The Captive Republic: A History of Republicanism in Australia, 1788-1996*, Cambridge University Press (CUP), Melbourne.

Meredith, John and Whalan, Rex (1979) *Frank the Poet: The Life and Works of Francis MacNamara*, Red Rooster, Melbourne.

O'Lincoln, Tom (2005) *United We Stand: Class Struggle in Colonial Australia*, Red Rag Publications, Melbourne.

Perkins, Rachel and Langton, Marcia (eds) (2008) *First Australians: An Illustrated History*, Miegunyah Press, Melbourne.

Pybus, Cassandra, (2009) '"Not fit for your protection or an honest man's company': A Transnational Perspective on the Saintly Dawes", [online] *History Australia*, vol. 6, no. 1, April: 12.1-12.7.

Reece, R.H.W. (2005) 'MacNamara, Francis (c.1810-1861+)', *ADB*, Supplementary Volume, MUP, Melbourne, p. 256.

Smith, Keith Vincent (2008) 'A Few Words From William Dawes and George Bass', *National Library of Australia News*, June, pp. 7-10.

— (2001) *Bennelong: The Coming in of the Eora: Sydney Cove 1788-1792*, Kangaroo Press, Sydney.

St Leon, Mark (2005) *Circus in Australia: Its Origins and Development to 1856*, Mark St Leon and Associates, Sydney.

Tench, Watkin (2009) *Watkin Tench's 1788* (ed. and intro Tim Flannery), Text Publishing, Melbourne.

Whitaker, Anne-Maree (1998) 'Swords to Ploughshares? The 1798 Irish Rebels in New South Wales', *Labour History*, 75, pp. 9-21.

1880 TO 1929

Beasley, Margot (1996) *Wharfies: A History of the Waterside Workers' Federation*, Halstead Press in association with Australian National Maritime Museum, Sydney.

Burgmann, Verity (1985) *'In Our Time': Socialism and the Rise of Labor, 1885-1905*, Allen & Unwin, Sydney.

— (1995) *Revolutionary Industrial Unionism: The Industrial Workers of the World in Australia*, CUP, Melbourne.

Cameron, Clyde (2001) 'Henry Ernest Boote: It's Wrong to be Right', *Labour History*, 80, May, pp. 201-14.

Cannon, Michael (1975) *Life in the Cities: Australia in the Victorian Age: 3*, Thomas Nelson, Melbourne.

— (1981) *That Damned Democrat: John Norton, an Australian Populist, 1858-1916*, MUP, Melbourne.

Cain, Frank (1983) *The Origins of Political Surveillance in Australia*, Angus & Robertson, Sydney.

Davitt, Michael (1898) *Life and Progress in Australasia*, Methuen and Co., London.

Docker, John (2001) 'Arabesques of the Cosmopolitan and International: Lucien Henry, Baroque Allegory and Islamophilia', http://www. australianhumanitiesreview.org/archive/Issue-June-2001/docker3.html.

Ebbels, R.N. (1965) *The Australian Labor Movement 1850-1907*, Cheshire-Lansdowne Press, Melbourne.

Fanning Discontent's Flames: Australian Wobbly Poetry, Scurrilous Doggerel, and Song, 1914-2007 (2007) Corrosive Press, Albany WA.

Fitzgerald, Ross (1994) *"Red Ted": The Life of E.G. Theodore*, University of Queensland Press (UQP), Brisbane.

Frame, Tom and Baker, Kevin (2000) *Mutiny! Naval Insurrections in Australia and New Zealand*, Allen & Unwin, Sydney.

Franklin, James (1999) 'Catholics versus Masons', *Journal of the Australian Catholic Historical Society*', 20, pp. 1-15.

Fry, Eric (ed.) (1983) *Rebels and Radicals*, Allen & Unwin, Sydney.

— (1994) 'Sydney's Republican Riot', *The Hummer*, vol. 2, no. 3, Summer.

— (1965) *Tom Barker and the I.W.W.*, Australian Society for the Study of Labour History, Canberra.

Gathercole, Peter, Irving, Terry and Melleuish, Gregory (eds) (1995) *Childe and Australia: Archaeology, Politics and Ideas*, UQP, Brisbane.

Harris, Joe (1970) *The Bitter Fight*, UQP, Brisbane.

Hearn, Mark (1990) *Working Lives: A History of the Australian Railways Union*

(*NSW Branch*), Hale & Iremonger, Sydney.

—— (2003) 'A Wild Awakening: The 1893 Banking Crisis and the Theatrical Narratives of the Castlereagh Street Radicals', *Labour History*, 85, November, pp. 153-72.

Hearn, Mark and Knowles, Harry (1996) *One Big Union: A History of the Australian Workers Union, 1886-1994*, CUP, Melbourne.

Irving, Terry and Taksa, Lucy (2002) *Places, Protests and Memorabilia: The Labour Heritage Register of New South Wales*, Industrial Relations Research Centre, University of New South Wales (UNSW), Sydney.

James, Bob (1986) *Anarchism and State Violence in Sydney and Melbourne, 1886-1896: An Argument About Australian Labor History*, published by the author, Newcastle NSW; online at http://www.takver.com/history/indexbj.htm.

Johnson, Audrey (1990) *Bread and Roses - A Personal History of Three Militant Women and Their Friends, 1902-1988*, Left Book Club, Sydney.

Lang, Jack (1980) *I Remember*, McNamara's Books, Katoomba NSW.

Lawson, Olive (1990) *The First Voice of Australian Feminism: Excerpts from Louisa Lawson's 'The Dawn 1888-1895'*, Simon & Schuster, Sydney.

Lawson, Sylvia (1983) *The Archibald Paradox: A Strange Case of Authorship*, Allen Lane, Melbourne.

Love, Peter (1984) *Labour and the Money Power: Australian Labour Populism, 1890-1950*, MUP, Melbourne.

Macintyre, Stuart (1998) *The Reds: The Communist Party of Australia from Origins to Illegality*, Allen & Unwin, Sydney.

McInerny, Sally (ed.) (1977) *The Confessions of William James Chidley*, UQP, Brisbane.

McKenna, Mark (1996) *The Captive Republic: A History of Republicanism in Australia, 1788-1996*, CUP, Melbourne.

McNair, John and Poole, Thomas (eds) (1992) *Russia and the Fifth Continent: Aspects of Russian-Australian Relations*, UQP, Brisbane.

Markey, Raymond (1994) *In Case of Oppression: The Life and Times of the Labor Council of New South Wales*, Pluto Press, Sydney.

O'Farrell, Patrick (1986) *The Irish in Australia*, UNSW Press, Sydney.

Pearl, Cyril (1965) *Wild Men of Sydney*, Cheshire-Lansdowne, Melbourne.

Radi, Heather (1986) 'Lawson, Louisa (1848-1920)', *ADB*, vol. 10, MUP, Melbourne, pp. 23-25.

Rodd, Lewis C. (1975) *A Gentle Shipwreck*, Thomas Nelson (Australia), Melbourne.

Ross, James A. (1993) 'The Genesis of *Hard Cash*', *The Hummer*, 35, January-June, pp. 9-12.

Scalmer, Sean (2001) '"A Co-Fraternity - Not Merely a Few Sheets of Famine-Prices Paper": Reading as a Labour Movement Community Practice in Australia', in Raymond Markey (ed.), *Labour and Community: Historical Essays*, University of Wollongong Press, Wollongong NSW, pp. 242-60.

Scates, Bruce (1997) *A New Australia: Citizenship, Radicalism and the First Republic*, CUP, Melbourne.

Scott, Ernest (1989) *Australia During the War*, UQP, Brisbane.

Shillingsburg, Miriam Jones (1988) *At Home Abroad: Mark Twain in Australasia*, University Press of Mississippi, Jackson.

Spence, William Guthrie (1909) *Australia's Awakening: Thirty Years in the Life of an Australian Agitator*, The Worker Trustees, Sydney.

Stephen, Ann (ed.) (2001) *Visions of a Republic: The Work of Lucien Henry - Paris - Noumea - Sydney*, Powerhouse Publishing, Sydney.

Svensen, Stuart (1995) *Industrial War: The Great Strikes 1890-94*, University of Wollongong, The Ram Press, Wollongong NSW.

Syson, Ian (1996) 'Henry Ernest Boote - Putting the Boot into the Australian Literary Archive', *Labour History*, 70, May.

Turner, Ian (1965) *Industrial Labour and Politics: The Dynamics of the Labour Movement in Eastern Australia, 1900-1921*, Australian National University (ANU), Canberra.

Van den Broek, Diane (1995) 'The 1929 Timber Workers' Strike: The Role of Community and Gender', Occasional Paper 104, School of Industrial Relations and Organisational Behaviour, UNSW, Sydney.

Walker, Bertha (1972) *Solidarity for Ever*, The National Press, Melbourne.

Windle, Kevin (2006) 'A Troika of Agitators: Three Comintern Liaison Agents in Australia, 1920-22', *Australian Journal of Politics and History*, vol. 52, no. 1, pp. 30-47.

1930 TO 1959

Amos, Keith (1976) *The New Guard Movement, 1931-35*, MUP, Melbourne.

Antony, Ernest (1930) *The Hungry Mile And Other Poems*, Sydney.

Arrow, Michelle (2002) *Upstaged: Australian Women Dramatists in the Limelight at Last*, Pluto Press with Currency Press, Sydney.

Barcan, Alan (2002) *Radical Students: The Old Left at Sydney University*, MUP, Melbourne.

Beasley, Margot (1996) *Wharfies: A History of the Waterside Workers' Federation*, Halstead Press in association with Australian National Maritime Museum, Sydney.

Blake, Audrey (1984) *A Proletarian Life*, Kibble Books, Malmsbury VIC.

—— (1989) 'Notes on the Development of the Eureka Youth League and its Predecessors', published by the author.

Bloodworth, Sandra and O'Lincoln, Tom (eds) (1998) *Rebel Women in Australian Working Class History*, Interventions, Melbourne.

Broeze, Frank (1998) *Island Nation: A History of Australians and the Sea*, Allen & Unwin, Sydney.

Cameron, Clyde R. (1996) 'When Incompetence and Corruption Merge: The AWU and *The World* Newspaper', *Labour History*, 70, May, pp. 169-81.

—— (2001) 'Henry Ernest Boote: It's Wrong to be Right', *Labour History*, 80, May, pp. 201-14.

Cahill, Rowan (2009) '"Of the Things I Know I Sing": The "Lost" Working Class Poet Ernest Antony (1894-1960)', in Bobbie Oliver (ed.), *Labour History in the New Century*, Black Swan Press, Perth, pp. 41-49.

—— (1987) 'Return of the Sea Devil: Von Luckner in Australia, 1938', presented at the Reaction in Australia Between the Wars Conference, Sydney, 27 June (unpublished paper).

Chang, Arthur Locke (1999) 'Anecdotes of CYL - Down Memory Lane', *Chinese*

Youth League of Australia - 60th Anniversary Magazine, Sydney, p. 51.

Cottle, Drew (2002) *The Brisbane Line: A reappraisal*, Upfront Publishing, Leicester UK.

—— (2000) 'Unbroken Commitment: Fred Wong, China, Australia and a World to Win', *The Hummer*, vol. 3, no. 4, pp. 1-13.

—— (2001) 'Forgotten Foreign Militants: The Chinese Seamen's Union in Australia, 1942-46', in P. Griffiths and R. Webb (eds), *Work, Organisation, Struggle: Papers From the Seventh National Labour History Conference*, ASSLH Canberra Region Branch, pp. 104-09.

Cottle, Drew and Keys, Angela (2008) 'Anatomy of an "Eviction Riot" in Sydney During the Great Depression', *Journal of the Royal Australian Historical Society*, vol. 94, part 2, December, pp. 186-200.

—— (2007) 'Danger from Below: Anti-Eviction Struggles in Sydney, January to July 1931', in Scott Poynting and George Morgan (eds), *Outrageous! Moral Panics in Australia*, ACYS Publishing, Hobart.

Darby, Robert (2001) 'New Theatre and the State: The Ban on *Till the Day I Die* 1935-41', *Labour History*, 80, May, pp. 1-20.

Day, Marele (1988) *The Life and Crimes of Harry Lavender*, Allen & Unwin, Sydney.

Deery, Phillip (2001) 'Community Carnival or Cold War Strategy? The 1952 Youth Carnival for Peace and Friendship', in R. Markey (ed.), *Labour and Community: Historical Essays*, University of Wollongong Press, Wollongong NSW.

Fitzgerald, Shirley (1996) *Red Tape, Gold Scissors: The Story of Sydney's Chinese*, State Library of NSW Press, Sydney.

Fitzpatrick, Brian and Cahill, Rowan J. (1981) *The Seamen's Union of Australia, 1872-1972: A History*, Seamen's Union of Australia, Sydney.

Gray, Oriel (1985) *Exit Left: Memoirs of a Scarlet Woman*, Penguin Books, Melbourne.

Hewett, Dorothy (1990) *Wild Card: An Autobiography, 1923-1958*, McPhee Gribble, Melbourne.

—— (1976) *This Old Man Comes Rolling Home*, Currency Press, Sydney.

—— (1999) *Bobbin Up*, 40th Anniversary Edition (ed. Ian Syson), The Vulgar Press, Melbourne.

Hogenkamp, Bert (1997) '*Indonesia Calling*: A Film on the Crossroads of Four Continents', *Labour History*, 73, November, pp. 226-31.

Horner, Jack (1994) *Bill Ferguson, Fighter for Aboriginal Freedom*, 2nd edition, published by the author, Canberra.

Irving, Terry and Taksa, Lucy (2002) *Places, Protests and Memorabilia: The Labour Heritage Register of New South Wales*, Industrial Relations Research Centre, UNSW, Sydney.

Johnson, Audrey (1992) 'Reminiscences of an Old Leftie', *The Hummer*, 34, April-August.

Jones, Paul (2001) 'Chinese Seamen and Australian Labour: the Mass Desertion from the S.S. *Silksworth* at Newcastle, October 1937', in P. Griffiths and R. Webb (eds), *Work, Organisation, Struggle: Papers From the Seventh National Labour History Conference*, ASSLH, Canberra Region Branch, pp. 162-67.

Lockwood, Rupert (1975) *Black Armada*, Australasian Book Society, Sydney.

—— (1987) *War on the Waterfront: Menzies, Japan and the Pig-iron Dispute*, Hale & Iremonger, Sydney.

Love, Peter (1984) *Labour and the Money Power: Australian Labour Populism, 1890-1950*, MUP, Melbourne.

McCarthy, Barbara (interviewer) (2003) 'Ted Egan and the History of the Tuckiar Case', on 'Stateline Northern Territory', Radio National, 27 June, http://www.abc.net.au/stateline/nt/content/2003/s890106.htm, accessed 25 March 2009.

McDonald, Tom and Audrey (1998) *Intimate Union*, Pluto Press, Sydney.

Macintyre, Stuart (1998) *The Reds: The Communist Party of Australia From Origins to Illegality*, Allen & Unwin, Sydney.

McNair, John and Poole, Thomas (eds) (1992) *Russia and the Fifth Continent: Aspects of Russian-Australian Relations*, UQP, Brisbane.

Manwaring G.E. and Dobree, B. (1937) *Floating Republic - An Account of the Mutinies at Spithead and the Nore in 1797*, Penguin, London.

Markey, Raymond (1994) *In Case of Oppression: The Life and Times of the Labor Council of New South Wales*, Pluto Press, Sydney.

Matthews, Brian (1987) *Louisa*, McPhee Gribble, Melbourne.

Maynard, John (2007) *Fight For Liberty and Freedom: The Origins of Australian Aboriginal Activism*, Aboriginal Studies Press, Canberra.

Milner, Lisa (2003) *Fighting Film: A History of the Waterside Workers' Federation Film Unit*, Pluto Press, Melbourne.

Mitchell, Winifred (1977) 'Home life at the Hungry Mile: Sydney wharf labourers and their families, 1900-1914', *Labour History*, 33, November, pp. 86-97.

Moore, Andrew (1989) *The Secret Army and the Premier: Conservative Paramilitary Organisations in New South Wales, 1930-32*, UNSW Press, Sydney.

—— (2005) *Francis De Groot: Irish Fascist, Australian Legend*, The Federation Press, Sydney.

Muirden, Bruce (1968) *Puzzled Patriots: The Story of the Australia First Movement*, MUP, Melbourne.

Munro, Craig (1984) *Wild Man of Letters: The Story of P.R. Stephensen*, MUP, Melbourne.

Nelson, Tom (1957) *The Hungry Mile*, Waterside Workers' Federation, Sydney Branch, Sydney.

Poynting, Scott (1989) 'The Youth Carnival for Peace and Friendship, March 1952', *Labour History*, 56, May, pp. 60-68.

Poynting, Scott, and Morgan, George (eds) (2007) *Outrageous! Moral Panics in Australia*, ACYS Publishing, Hobart.

Redfern, Lea (producer) (1999) 'Forever Striking Trouble', *Hindsight*, ABC Radio National, March, http://www.abc.net.au/ourplace/national/striking.htm, accessed 7 September 2009.

Rühen, Carl (1988) *The Sea Devil: The Controversial Cruise of the Nazi Emissary von Luckner to Australia and New Zealand in 1938*, Kangaroo Press, Kenthurst NSW.

Spearitt, Peter (1978) *Sydney Since the Twenties*, Hale & Iremonger, Sydney.

Tennant, Kylie (1943) *Ride on Stranger*, Angus & Robertson, Sydney.

—— (1986) *The Missing Heir: The Autobiography of Kylie Tennant*, Macmillan, Melbourne.

Walker, Robin (1980) *Yesterday's News: A History of the Newspaper Press in New*

South Wales from 1920 to 1945, Sydney University Press, Sydney.

Walshe, R.D. (1947) *Student Work for Progress*, The Acacia Press, Annandale NSW.

Wheatley, Nadia (1980) 'Meeting them at the door: Radicalism, militancy, and the Sydney anti-eviction campaign of 1931', in Jill Roe (ed.), *Twentieth Century Sydney - Studies in Urban and Social History*, Hale & Iremonger, Sydney.

—— (1984) *The House That Was Eureka*, Viking/Kestrel, Melbourne.

—— (1975) 'The Unemployed Who Kicked: A Study of the Political Struggles and Organisations of the New South Wales Unemployed in the Great Depression', unpublished MA thesis, Macquarie University.

1960 TO 1989

Anon (no date) 'The Juanita Nielsen Case', http://www.milesago.com/features/nielsen.htm, accessed 21 August 2009.

Anderson, Tim (1985) *Free Alister, Dunn and Anderson: The Ananda Marga Conspiracy Case*, Wild & Woolley, Sydney.

—— (1992) *Take Two: The Criminal Justice System Revisited*, Bantam, Sydney.

Armstrong, Mick (2001) *1, 2, 3, What Are We Fighting For? The Australian Student Movement from its Origins to the 1970s*, Socialist Alternative, Melbourne.

Baker, A.J. (no date) 'Sydney Libertarianism', http://www.takver.com/history/sydney/indexsl.htm, accessed 30 July 2009.

Bloodworth, Sandra (no date) 'Aboriginal Rights and Trade Unions in the 1950s and 60s', *Socialist Alternative* website, http://www.sa.org.au/index.php?option=com_content&task=category&sectionid=16&id=57&Itemid=124, accessed 20 June 2009.

Bramble, Tom (no date) 'War on the Waterfront: The MUA Dispute', *Socialist Alternative* website, http://www.sa.org.au/index.php?option=com_content&task=category&sectionid=16&id=57&Itemid=124, accessed 24 August 2009.

Burgmann, Verity (2003) *Power, Profit and Protest: Australian Social Movements and Globalisation*, Allen & Unwin, Sydney.

Burgmann, Meredith and Burgmann, Verity (1998) *Green Bans, Red Union: Environmental Activism and the New South Wales Builders Labourers' Federation*, UNSW Press, Sydney.

Clancy, Meg (no date) memoir, http://www.pramfactory.com/memoirsfolder/, accessed 5 November 2009.

Coombs, Anne (1996) *Sex and Anarchy: The Life and Death of the Sydney Push*, Viking, Melbourne.

Edwards, Peter (1997) *A Nation at War: Australian Politics, Society and Diplomacy during the Vietnam War, 1965-1975*, Allen & Unwin in association with the Australian War Memorial, Sydney.

Faro, Clive, with Wotherspoon, Garry (2000) *Street Seen: A History of Oxford Street*, MUP, Melbourne.

Foley, Gary (2001) 'Black Power in Redfern, 1968-1972', *The Koori History Website*, Essay 1, http://www.kooriweb.org/foley/essays/essays_page.html, accessed 20 July 2009.

Franklin, James (no date) 'The Push and Critical Drinkers', http://www.maths.unsw.edu.au/~Jim/push.html, accessed 24 July 2009.

Gorman, Clem (2009) 'Beyond the Fringe - Australian Experimental Theatre in the

60s', unpublished.

Hall, Richard (1978) *The Secret State: Australia's Spy Industry*, Cassell Australia, Sydney.

Hamel-Green, Michael E. (1983) 'The Resisters', in Peter King (ed.), *Australia's Vietnam: Australia in the Second Indo-China War*, Allen & Unwin, Sydney, pp. 100-28.

Harris, Alana (1988) *Australia's Too Old To Celebrate Birthdays*, Aboriginal Studies Press, Canberra.

Hickie, David (1985) *The Prince and the Premier*, Angus & Robertson, Sydney.

Hocking, Jenny (1993) *Beyond Terrorism: The Development of the Australian Security State*, Allen & Unwin, Sydney.

James, Bob (1985) 'Bulgarian Anarchists in Sydney', http://www.takver.com/history/aia/aia00028.htm, accessed 2 September 2009.

Jiggens, John (2007) 'The Banker & The Killer Kop: The Murder of Don Mackay', http://drjiggens.com/the_banker_and_the_killer_kop.html, accessed 20 August 2009.

—— (1991) *The Incredible Exploding Man: Evan Pederick and the Trial of Tim Anderson*, Samizdat Press, Brisbane.

Langley, Greg (1992) *A Decade of Dissent: Vietnam and the Conflict on the Australian Home Front*, Allen & Unwin, Sydney.

Lee, Martin A. and Shlain, Bruce (1985) *Acid Dreams: The Complete Social History of LSD: The CIA, the Sixties, and Beyond*, Pan Books, New York.

Louis, Les (1992) '"Operation Alien" and the Cold War in Australia, 1950-53', *Labour History*, 62, May, pp. 1-18.

McCoy, Alfred W. (1980) *Drug Traffic: Narcotics and Organised Crime in Australia*, Harper & Row, Sydney.

Molomby, Tom (2000) *Spies, Bombs and the Path of Bliss*, Potoroo Press, Sydney.

Murphy, Peter (2008) video interview, http://www.news.com.au/story/0,23599,23284448-5016087,00.html, accessed 20 May 2009.

Ormesher, Patricia (interviewer) (2002) 'Oral History Interviews About The Block-2002': 'Roberta Sykes Remembers Mum Shirl [Shirley Smith]'; 'Ted Kennedy'. Redfern Oral History, http://redfernoralhistory.org, accessed 20 August 2009.

Pemberton, Gregory (ed.) (1990) *Vietnam Remembered*, Lansdowne, Sydney.

Scalmer, Sean (2002) *Dissent Events: Protest, the Media and the Political Gimmick in Australia*, UNSW Press, Sydney.

Watson, Don (2002) *Recollections of a Bleeding Heart: A Portrait of Paul Keating, P.M.*, Knopf, Sydney.

Willett, Graham (2000) *Living Out Loud: A History of Gay and Lesbian Activism in Australia*, Allen & Unwin, Sydney.

Wotherspoon, Garry C. (1993) 'Delaney, Colin John (1897-1969)', *ADB*, vol. 13, MUP, Melbourne, pp. 610-11.

York, Barry (2001) 'Looking Back at Oz Magazine', *National Library of Australia News*, vol. 11, no. 8, May, pp. 10-12.

INDEX

Numbers in **bold** indicate illustrations.

Aboriginal History Committee 222
Aboriginal Legal Centre (Redfern) 332
Aboriginal Legal Service 331
Aboriginal Medical Service 331
Aboriginal resistance 9, 10 *see also* Black
 Power
Aboriginal Worker, The 329
Aborigines 8-12, **143**, 163, 217, 266, 270,
 271, 272, 280-81, 283, 328-34 *see also*
 Metropolitan Local Aboriginal Land
 Council
Aborigines' Progressive Association 218-220,
 219, **220**
Acid Dreams (Lee and Shlain) 297
Active Service Brigade 90, 93, 110-12
Adelphi Hotel xvi, 54 *see also* Royal
 Australian Equestrian Circus
Adyar Hall xvi, 241, **242**
Alexander, Hal 260
Alexandria 59, 266
Alexandria Spinning Mills 269
Allen, George 43
Allen, Norm 308
Amalgamated Railways and Tramways
 Service Association 183
American War of Independence 17, 57
A Nameless Concern (John Romeril) 297
Ananda Marga 306, 314-320
anarcho-syndicalism 299
Anderson, James 308
Anderson, John 296
Anderson, Maybanke 94
Anderson, Tim 315-16, **317**, 318, 319
Andrade, Will 145
Angel Place xvi, 186
Anglican, The 287-88
Annandale 120, 170, 172, 199, 306
anti-conscription *see* conscription
anti-communism 194, 200, 213, 237, 249,

278, 279, 284, 316 *see also* Communist
 Party of Australia and New Guard and
 secret armies
anti-semitism 228, 239
Anti-Transportation League 55, 57-58
anti-war movement *see* peace
Antony, Ernest 343, 345
 'The Hungry Mile' (poem) 345
Archibald, J.F. 100-01
Argyle Place 98
Arnold, Vic 213
Armstrong, David 260
Armstrong, Mick 259
Arthur Street 161
Ashfield 283
Asian Airlines Ltd. 248-49
Askin, Robin 308
Alister, Paul 319, 320
Astley, William ('Price Warung') **102**, 103-04
Australasian Chronicle 36
'Australia First' 239, 241, **242**, 243
Australian Aboriginal Progressive Association
 163-67
Australian Alps 30
Australian Free Theatre Troupe 297
Australian Hall xvi, 216-220, **221**, 222
Australian Highway 184
Australian Labor League of Youth 150
Australian Labor Party 185, 191, 227, 298,
 301, 308, 329 *see also* Labor Party
Australian Patriotic Association 28, 31
Australian Performing Group (Melbourne)
 297
Australian Protective League 194
Australian Railways Union 227
Australian Security Intelligence Organisation
 (ASIO) 213, 281, 294, 317, 318, 319
Australian Socialist League/Party 79, 90, 93,
 119, 157
Australian Women's Weekly 179-80
Australian Workers' Union 175-77, **182**,

184–85
Australian Workman 90, 102, 181
Australasian Star 183

Bacon, Wendy 296
Bakunin, Michael 299
Balmain 4, 119, 170, 199, 306
Bankstown 4, 170, 197, 199, 283
Barangaroo 343
Barcan, Alan 257-58
Barker, Tom 116, **117**
Barrack Street 106-107, 112-13
Barrington, Joy 171, 173
Bass, Tom 285
Bateman, George 207, 209
Bathurst Street 41, 119, 120, 175, 216
Baume, Eric 288
Bear's Freethought Book Depot 90, 94, **95**
Beasley, Jack 267
Bebel, August 94
Bellamy, Edward 94
Bellear, Bob 331
Belmore 170
Berrima Gaol 195
Besant, Annie 94
Bialoguski, Michael 295
Birchgrove Park 336
Black, George 89-90, 117-18, **119**
Black, Harry 274, 275
Black Panther Party (USA) 330
Black Power 6, 329, 330, 331, **332**
Blackwattle Bay 49, **169**, 171
Blake, Audrey **280**, 281
Bligh, Governor William 98
Bligh Street xvi, 212, 238, 242
Blue Mountains 8
bodgie gangs 3
Bolshevism *see* Communist Party of Australia
Bombo 336
bonneting 37, 59
Bonney, Roseanne 296
Boote, Henry E. 184-185, **185**
Botany 4, 170
Botany Bay 9
Botany Road 265
Brady, Edwin 92-93
'Brains Trust, The' 274
Bramble, Tom 340
Bridge Road 139, 141
Bridge Street 151
British General Strike of 1926 191
British Union of Fascists 195

Broeze, Frank 341
Broken Hill Pty. Ltd. (BHP) 341
Brookfield, Percy 134
Bruce, Lenny 288
Buchenwald concentration camp 227
Builders Labourers *see* New South Wales
     Builders Labourers' Federation
Bull, Tas 337
Bulletin Place xvi, 97-98
Bulletin, The 75, 78, 81, 82, 86, 88, 98, **99**,
     103, 100-04, 107
Burchett, Wilfred 224
Burns, Jocka 196
Burns, Robert 26, 57
Burrows, Claude 39, 40
bushranger 25, **26**
Bushwhackers Band, The 293
Byron, Lord 30

cabbage tree hat 3, 58-59
Cabramatta 125
Callan Park 183
Cameron, Clyde 184
Cameron, Robert 320
Campbell, Clarence 248-49
Campbelltown 27, 50
Camperdown 136, 139
Cannon, Michael 336
Cantrell, Leon 297
Carbonari 30
Carousel Club 313
Carpenter, Edward 94
Carrington Hall 216
Casey, William (Bill) 337-38
     Bump Me Into Parliament 338
Castlebrook Lawn Cemetery **19**, 20
Castle Hill 16, 19
Castlereagh Street 54, 79, 157, 162, 181, 182,
     188, 213, 214, 216, 234, 283, 285
Casula 122-24
Catholic Club 157
Central Intelligence Agency (US) 292-93
Central Railway Station xvi, 24, 119, 121-28,
     140
Chang, Arthur Locke 247
Chartism 31, 55, 62-63
Chidley, W. J. 183
Childe, Gordon 130, **132** 133-35
China 16
Chinese Seamen's Union 244-248, **248**
Chinese Youth League 246, 247, **250**, 283
Chippendale 4, 49, 120, 138

Christian socialism 5
Church of England 323
Circular Quay 48, 97, 98, 126-27, 171, 335, 342
City Recital Hall 186
Clancy, Meg 297
Clarence Street 54
Clark, Dave 295
Cleveland Paddocks 328
Cleveland Street 187
Clontarf 198
Cockatoo Island 41, 42
Coghlan, Daniel 55
Cold War 213, 215, 237, 260, 287, 294, 339
College Street 5
Colonial Observer, The 52
Coloured Progressive Association 162, **165**
Comber Street, 293
Comintern *see* Communist International
Communist International 145, 148, 205
Communist Party of Australia 3, 120, 147-49, 152, 157-59, 170, 186, 190, 212, 213, 218, 227, 248, 267, 268, **269**, **270**, 273, 279-80, 283, 294, 329
Communist, The 158
Commonwealth Investigation Branch 230
Concordia Hall 157, 158, **160**, 217
conscription
  World War I 184
  Vietnam War 287, 300-01, 304
Constitutional Association 44, 55, 186
convict revolt of 1804 16-20
convict system 13-14, 21, 22-23, 40-1, 48, 100-04
Cook, Captain James 67, 335
Cook, Ken 231, 235-236, **235**, 237
'coolies' 49
Cooper, Robert 48-52, **51**
Cooper, William 218
Cottle, Drew 199, 235
Cousens, Charles 234
Craig-y-Mor 234, 237
crime *see* organized crime
Crown Street 164
Crucible, The (Miller) 215
cultural rebellion 6
Cumberland Street Watch House xvi, 36, **38**, 53
Cunningham, Philip 18
Curtin, John 185
Customs House, Circular Quay xvi, 46, **48**, 53

Daily Mirror 263
Daily Post 102
Daily Telegraph 127, 129, 226, 229
Daking House 145, **146**
Dark, Eleanor 281
Darling Harbour 3, 24, 54, 341, 342
Darling Point 187
Darlinghurst 4, 120, 306, 321, 323
Darlington 4, 6, 138, 296
Davidson, Morrison 94
Davitt, Michael 267
  Life and Progress in Australasia 267
Dawes, Lieutenant William 7-12
Dawes Point xvi, 7-8, **11**
Dawn Club, The 93-94
Dawn, The 85-88, **87**, 90
Day, Marele 1
Day of Mourning 216-222
De Groot, Francis 188, **189**
Delaney, Colin 323
democracy 5, 20, 31, 58-59
Democrat, The 90
Deniehy, Daniel 58
Desmond, Arthur 107, **111**, 112
Devanny, Jean 208, 212
Devine, Tilly 268
Dhakiyarr Wirrpanda 204, 209
Dharma 314, **315**, **318**
Dibbs, Sir George 108
Disher, Norma 276, 277
Disloyal Organisations Act 204, 207
Dispatch, The 41, 44
Dixon, Chicka 329
Dixon Street 152, 250
'Document J' 237
Domain, The xvi, 5, 6, 83, 85, 91, 111, 112, 126, 151, 154-55, **158**, **159**, 187, 283, 332
Donahue, 'Bold' Jack, **26**, 27
Double Bay 189
draft resistance 301-02, 304
Druitt Street 39, 54
Dunn, Ross 319, 320
Dwyer, Bill 295, 297

Earsman, William (Bill) 147-49
Edmond, James 100-01
Educational Workers' League 150
eight-hour day 61-66, 155
Eight Hour Day Committee 152
election riots of 1843 49-52
Elizabeth Bay 187
Elizabeth Street 37, 45, 157, 217, 239

Elkin, A. P. 209
Elliott, E. V. 253, 254, **255**, 339
Empress Hotel, Redfern xiv-xv, 329, **330**, 331 *see also* Regent Hotel
Enmore 140, **170**
Erskine Street 273
Erskineville 170, 196-203
Essex Street 36
Eureka Stockade 20, 195
Eureka Youth League 260, 280
Evatt, H.V. (Bert) 135, 149, 169, 185, 279
Evatt, Mary Alice 169-70
Eveleigh Railway Workshops 140, **143**, **190**, 227, 266, 329
evictions 149, 196-203, **197**
Exhibition Building xvi, 75, 78, 80, **80**

Fairfield 282
Farrar, Adam 332
Female Factory 41
Ferguson, William 167, 218
Fell, Liz 296
Festival of Light 323
Finey, George 212
FitzRoy, Governor Sir Charles 43
Five Dock 170
Flanagan, Merv 136, 138, **139**, 140-142
Flaus, John 295
flogging 19, 21, 23, 27
Foley, Gary 167, 329, **332**
Fort Phillip 3, 13, **14**, 20
Fowler, Mick 308, 311, 312, **312**, 313
Foy, Mark 226
Franklin, Miles 94, 241
'Frank the Poet', *see* MacNamara, Frank
Fraser, Malcolm 317
Free University, The (Sydney) 296, 297
French Revolution (1789) 14, 50, 57
Friends' Meeting House xvi, **131** *see also* Religious Society of Friends
Friends of the Soviet Union 150
Fry, Eric 2

Galahs, The 293
Game, Governor Sir Philip 195
Garden, John Smith (Jock) 147-148, **149**, 157, 171, 172, 202
Garrison Church xvi, **64**
Garvey, Marcus Aurelius 161, 162, 163, 164
Gay Freedom Day Committee (San Francisco) 323
Gay Mardi Gras 323-27

General Post Office, Martin Place xvi, 251, **252**
General Strike *see* NSW General Strike
'gentrification' 306-07
George, Henry 96, 182
George's River 10
George Street 36, 39, 150, 218, 248, 251, 294
Gibbs, Pearl 167, 218
Gipps, Governor Sir George 40-41, 42, 47, 52
Glebe, 5, 6, 49, 140, 168-69, 170, 171-74, 199, 283, 306
Glebe Island Bridge 141
Gloucester Street 36, 43
Glynn, Tom 155
Goebbels, Dr. Joseph 226
Gordon, Sir Thomas 235
Gorman, Clem 297
Goulburn Street 119, 140, 152, 283
Government House 4
Gow, Keith 276, 277
Grace Building xvi, 231, 232
Grancharoff, Jack 295
Granville 199
Gray, Oriel 210, **211**
Great Depression (1929-32) 186, 190, 198, 210, 231
Greer, Germaine 296
Green Bans 1, 6, 307, 313
Greens, The *see* New South Wales Greens
Greenway, Francis 21, 39
Grenfell (NSW) 83
Grenville, Kate 8
Grosvenor Hotel 267
Guardian, The 51, 55

Hall, Richard 294
hanging 18, 19
'Happy Valleys' 198
Hard Cash 105, 108-12
Harold Park 281
Harpur, Charles 57
Harrington Street 36, 37, 39
Hawkesbury River 16, 17, 18
Hawksley, Edward J 55-60
Haymarket 54
Hay Street xvi, 119, 244, **249**
Healy, Jim ('Big Jim') 273, 339
Hellenic Herald 293
Henry, Juliette xvi, 67, 73-74
Henry, Lucien xvi, 67-74, **69**

Hewett, Dorothy 265, 268, 269, **271**
  Bobbin Up 270
Hickey, T. J. 272
Hickson Road 342
Higgins, Esmonde 171
Hilton bombing (1978) 317-18, 319, 320
Himmler, Heinrich 226
History Council of New South Wales 222
Hitler, Adolf 223, 226
  Mein Kampf 223
Holland, Sekai 304
Holman, William 183
homosexuality 23
Honi Soit 296
Howard, John 340
Hudson's Timber Yard xiv-xv, 168, **169**,
  172-73
Hughes, William Morris (Billy) 89-90, 93,
  95-96, 130-31, 144
Hulett, Alistair 196
Hungry Mile, The xvi, 3, 342, 343, **346-47**
  The Hungry Mile (Nelson) 344
Hunter Street 291
Hyde Park 5, 23, 41, 50, 83, 151, 187, 326
Hyde Park Barracks xvi, 21, **22**, 23, **24**, 40,
  41, 52

Imperial Service Club 188
India 316
Indonesia 244, 253, 256
Indonesian Seamen's Union 254
Industrial Workers of the World 114, 116,
  117, 119, 123, 146, 155, 184, 207
Ingelburn 198
Innes, Captain 36-37
intellectuals 30, 35, 41, 44, 58
International Labour Defence 204-209, **205**,
  206
International Socialist Club 119
International Trade Union Congress (Paris)
  77
Irish 3, 13-16, 17, 28, 44, 50, 54, 144
Irish Rebellion of 1798 14-15, 17, 19, 20
Ironworkers' Building xvi, 283
Iron Chieftan 341
Iron Crown 341
Iron Knight 341
Ivens, Joris 244
  Indonesia Calling 244

James, Francis 287-88
Japan-Australia Society 233, 235

Japanese collaborators 231, 234, 237
Japanese Consulate 188, 231-33
Johnson, Audrey 172
Johnson, Dr Hewlett (The 'Red Dean') 217
Johnson, Jack 162, **165**
Johnston, Major George 17, 18
Johnston Street, Annandale 173
'Jolly Miller' pub 36, 43, 44
Jones, C. Lloyd 233
Judd, Ernest 156, **159**
Juniper Hall 49

Keating, Paul 270-/1
Kembla Building xvi, **259**, 260, 261
Kelly's Bush 307
Kennedy, Father Ted 329, 330
Kent Street 36, 42, 54
Kerr, John 290
Keys, Angela 199
Khaki Legion 195
Kiama 336
Killara 189
King and Empire Alliance, The 154, 158,
  194, 195
King, Arthur 308
King, Governor Philip Gidley 3, 10, 13, 17,
  19, 20
King's Cross 6, 187, 236, 305, 308, 320, 326
King Street 54, 55, 57
Kisch, Egon 149, 224
Klugman, Dick 261
Knatchbull, John 23
Kogarah 283
Krahe, Frank 308
Kruta, Vadislav 30
K'tut Tantri ('Surabaya Sue') 260

Labor Choir 152
Labor College, 134, 147, 152
Labor Council of NSW 134, 148, 151, 152,
  154-55, 169 *see also* Unions NSW
Labor Daily, The 168-69, 173, 177
Labor News, The 156-57, 158
Labor Party 3, 82, 110, 117, 130, 134-35,
  144, 145, 152, 156-57, 170, 176-77, 179
  see also Australian Labor Party
Labor Research and Information Bureau 152
Labour Heritage Register, The 266
labour movement 4
Lai, Stanley 247
Lakemba 199
Lamm, Mary 171, **172**, 174

Land and Environment Court (NSW) 222
Lang, John Thomas (Jack) 90, 93, 151, 183,
    188, 189-91, **190**, 195, 217
  I Remember 183
Lang, Reverend John Dunmore 52, 55
La Perouse 198, 283
Lashwood, Hal 287
Lawrence, D.H. 153, 191, 239
  Kangaroo 191, 194
  Lady Chatterley's Lover 239
Lawson, Henry xvi, 82, 83, **84**, 85, 184, 266
Lawson, Louisa 83, 85-88, **86**, 93
Lawson Square xiv-xv 265, 266, 272
Lawson, Sylvia 104
League of Liberators 52
League of National Security 195
Leary, Timothy 293
Left Book Club 150
Legislative Assembly 100
Legislative Council 44, 47, 51, 52
Leichhardt 4, 120, 170, 199
Leigh House 162
Leigh, Kate 268
Levine, Justice Aaron 289
Levy, Jock 276
Lhotsky, Johann 28-35
Liberty Hall 294
Lilley, Merv 266, 267, 268
Lilyfield 119
Liverpool 122-25, 127, 128
Liverpool Street 140, 158, 160, 216
Locke, G. A. (Magistrate) 288, 289
Longford, Raymond 276
Loyal Orange Institution 181
LSD 292-93, 296-97
'Lucy in the Sky with Diamonds' (Beatles)
    296
Lyons, Joseph 223, 228

MacArthur, General Douglas 231
Macdonnell House xvi, **176** 177, **178**
MacNamara, Frank 23-27
Macquarie, Governor Lachlan 10, 21, 22,
    23, 97
Macquarie Street 5, 41, 45
Malcom X 161, 162
Maloney, Monty 329
Mann, Tom 63
Margaret Street xvi, 257, 260, 263
Mariners' Church xvi, **64**
Maritime Strike of 1890 181
Maritime Union of Australia (MUA) 278,

336-37, 340
  'War on the Waterfront' (1998) 340
Market Street 150
Marrickville 4, 140, 283
Marriott Street, Redfern xiv-xv, 268, **270**
martial law 17
Martin Place 113, 252
Martin Plaza 326
Marx Hall 216
Marx, Karl 94
Marylebone Cricket Club 194
Mascot 170
mass media 6
Matteson, Michael 298-302, **303**, 304
Matthias, Betsy 171
May Day 107, 154-55
Mayer, Henry 294
Maynard, Fred 161, 162, 163-166, **167**
Maynard, John 167
Mazzini, Giuseppe 34
McCoy, Alfred W. 307
McCurtayne, William 44, 55
McGowen, J. ('Honest Jim') 267
McIntyre, John 9
McKell Building 145
McKell, William (Bill) 134, 267
McLaughlin, James 241-42
McNamara, Bertha 84
McNamara's Bookshop xvi, 79, 90, **90**,
    92-93, 109
McNamara, William 79, 84, 109, 112, 181,
McPhail, John 54
Meissner, Joe 308
Melbourne (Victoria) 27, 50, 62-63, 259,
    263
Menzies, Robert ('Pig-Iron Bob') 254, 268,
    279, 285
Metherell, Terry, 296
Metropolitan Local Aboriginal Land Council
    222
Metternich, Chancellor Prince 30, 35
MI5 230
middle-class radicals 6
Miles, Bee 239
Miles, W. J. 218, 239
Militant Women's Movement 150, 152
military 40, 42-43, 44, 121-129, **122, 125**
Military Intelligence (Australian Army) 234
Millers Point 3, 98
Milperra 198
Miners' Federation 177
Modern Publishers 150

Mohr, Rick 296
Molnar, George 296, 304
Monk, Albert 251
Mooney's Club 218
Moore Park 269
Moorhouse, Frank 294
Mortuary Station xvi, 136, **137**
Mountbatten, Lord Louis 251
Movement against War and Fascism 150, 227
Mrs Macquarie's Chair xvi, 218, 332, **333**
Mudgee, NSW 27
Muir, Thomas 15
Mundey, Jack 307
Munn Street 343
Murphy, John 296
Mussolini, Benito 191, 223
mutiny 121, 128, 265, 272
Mutual Protection Association 46-53, 55

Napoleonic Wars 13
Napoleon Street 343
National Farmers' Federation 340
National Front 319, 320
National Maritime Museum xvi, 276, 335, 341, **342**
National Trust (NSW) 222
Nation Review 291
Naval Intelligence (RAN) 230
Nelson, Tom 344
Nestor, Cecil 293
Nestor, Grivas 293, 294
Nestor's Cellar 292-94, **295**, 296-97
Netherlands East Indies (NEI) 253-55, 257
  NEI Boycott 253-56, 257
Neutral Bay 225
Neville, Richard 287, 288, 290
New Caledonia 68, 71-73
New Guard 160, 186-195, 207, 226
New Left 290, 292, 294, 297, 307
New South Wales Builders Labourers'
  Federation 304, 307, 308, 311, 313
New South Wales Corps 16, 17
New South Wales Council of Reconstruction
  Trainees 261
New South Wales General Strike of 1917
  136-142, **143**, 145, 152, 183, 194
New South Wales Greens 313
New South Wales Legal Rights Committee
  150
*New South Wales Literary, Political and
  Commercial Advertiser* 31, **32**

New South Wales Teachers Federation 283
New Theatre xiv-xv, 210-215, 276, 283, 293
Newtown 120, 138, 170, 196, 197, 198, 199, 283, 297, 314
Newtown Bridge 114
New Zealand 62
Nicholls, Doug 218
Nielsen, Juanita 309, 312, 313
Noongah 336
Norfolk Island 17
North Shore 189
North Sydney 170
Norton, John 76-78, **79**, **81**, 118
Now 311, 313
nuclear disarmament 6

Oatley 170
Observatory Hill xvi, 13
O'Connell, Daniel 44, 54
O'Connell Street 188
Odets, Clifford 212
  Till the Day I Die 212-213
  Waiting for Lefty 212
Old Guard 195
Omnibus and Sydney Spectator 39
One Big Union 120, 145, 152, 183
Onus, Bill 167
Opera House 299
organised crime 129, 307-08, 323
Owen, Robert 61
Owens, Joe 307
Oxford Street xvi, 5, 49, 293, 292, 326
Oz (London) 290
Oz (Sydney) 284, 285-91, **286**

Packer, Frank 179
Paddington 4, 6, 170, 187, 283, 292, 293, 306
Paddington Town Hall xiv-xv, 326
Paddy's Market 247
Paine, Thomas 14
P&O Building, Hunter Street xvi, 285
  P&O fountain-sculpture 285, 286, 291
Papadoulos, Viron 278
Paris Commune 67-73
Parkes, Henry 58-59, 78-79, 100, 182
Parliament 4, 5
Parramatta 8, 10, 16, 17, 19, 125
Paterson 50
Paterson, A. B. (Banjo) 98
Patrick James R. 189, 226
Patrick Stevedores 340

Patten, Jack 167, 218, 220, **220**
Patyegarang 8
peace movement 6, 130-134, 208, 217
Pearl Harbour 236
Peckham, Ray 283, 329
People's Advocate and New South Wales Vindicator 55, **56**, 57-59
People, The 114
Perkins, Charles 331
Petrie, Larry 181
Petrov Royal Commission 237
Petrov, Vladimir 294
Phelan, Edward 42
Phillip, Governor Arthur 8-10, 97, 218, 332, 335
Picton 25
Pig Iron Dispute 246, 254, 276, 337
Pioneer Bookshop 150
Pitt Street 37, 39, 40, 97, 98, 104,176, 210, 251
Pittwater 9
Plebs League 150
police 5, 36-37, 39, 41, 42, 44, 110-121, 127, 151, 199-201, **200**, **201**, 208, 241, 268, 272, 276, 288, 308, 318, 319, 320, 321, **322**, **324 -25**, 326, 327, 329, 330, 331, 332, 333, 334
   21 Squad 261, 330
   Commonwealth Police 300, 302, 304, 317
   Darlinghurst Police Station xvi, **322**, 323
   NSW Special Branch 281, 302, 317, 318, 319
   verbals 261, 318
Political Association, The 55, 57-59
Political Labor Leagues 183
Port Arthur, Tas 25
Port Jackson 7
Potts Point 187, 305
Powerhouse Museum, Sydney 74
Prince Alfred Park 75, 328
Prince Charles 333
Princess Diana 333
Pringle, Bob 304, 307
Prospect Hill 10
Protestant Hall 181, 182, 183, 184, 216
Public Library of NSW 184
Publicist, The 218, 239, 240
Push, The 309
Pybus, Cassandra 12
Pyrmont 3, 119, 170
Pyrmont Bridge 140
Pyrmont Bridge Road 169, 173

Quakers *see* Religious Society of Friends
Queen's Square xvi, 41, 79, 91, 110, **115**
Queen Street, Newtown xiv-xv, 314

race relations 7
Racial Hygiene Association 186
Radio 2KY 152, 227
Rae, Arthur 147
Railway Square 119
Rawson Chambers 144-145, **146**, 150
Rawson Place xvi, 144-145, **146**, 150
Redfern 1, 4, 5, 6, 83, 120, 170, **197**, 199, 265, 266, 267, 268, 269, 270, 271, 272, 283, 328-34
Redfern, William 265-66
Red Flag **122**, 126, 154, 158-59
Red Flag Riots 194
Reedy River (musical) 214, 293
Rees, Lloyd 227, 281
Rees, Nathan 343
Regent Hotel (Redfern) 333
Regent Street 266, 328, 329, 330, 331, 333
Religious Society of Friends xvi, 130
Republican, The 85
Republican League, The 89
resident action 6, 196-203
Returned Soldiers and Sailors' Imperial League 186
Revolutions of 1848, The 43, 56
Rhiannon, Lee 196
Roach, Ted 253, 254, **255**, 260, 339
Rocks, The xv, 3, 5, 13, 23, 36, 37, 43-45, 54, 65, 119, 167, 339
Robeson, Paul 275
Rodd, Lewis 5
Roderick, Colin 181
Rogerson, Roger 318
Roland Betty 276
Roma House, George Street xvi, 207
Rosa, Sam 109, **111**, 112
Roseberry 170
Rosenthal, Major General Sir Charles 153, **154**, 156, 194
Rose Street, Darlington 108
Rouse Hill 20
Rozelle 199
Royal Australian Equestrian Circus, York Street xvi, 54, 58, **60**
Royal Foresters' Hall 216
Royal Hotel, George Street xvi, 28, **29**
Royal Sydney Yacht Squadron 225
Russian Revolution of 1905 145

Russian Revolution of 1917 146, 152
Ryan, Edna 170-71
Ryde 170

Saffron, Abe 308, 313
Sandringham Hotel 196
Sarkar P. B. (Baba) 316
Sato, Ken 234, **235**
Saving's Bank, Barrack Street xvi, **106**, 112-13
Sawtell, Mick 209
scabs *see* strike-breakers
Schellenberg, Joe 112
Scott, Ernest 122
Scott, Jack 194, 234
Scott, Rose 94
Scottish and Australian Land Company 266
Seeadler 225
seamen 36, 110
Seamen's Union of Australia (SUA) 212, 246, 251, 253, 283, 283, 293, 336, 337
Seary, Richard 320
'secret armies' 160, 191, 194 *see also* New Guard and Old Guard
secret ballot 4
Secularist Society 76
Seeteufel 224-226
sexual liberation 6
Sharp, Martin 287, 288, 290
Shaw, Rod 275
'Shire', The 1
Silk, Cooper 278
Simonoff, Peter 145-50, **148**
Sinclaire, Frederick 130, 147
Single Tax League 92
Sinn Fein 154, 194
slave trade 10
Smith, Christian Jollie 147, 149
Smith, Sue 203
   In the Violet Time 203
Socialist Labor Party 114-15, 116, 119, 156-57
Society for the Protection of Life and Property 3, 43
soldiers *see* military
Southern Cross Hall 157
South Sydney 'Rabbitos' 329
speakers' corners *see* street-corner meetings
St Andrew's Place 175
Star and Workingman's Guardian 42-43
Station House 145, **146**, 147, 150
St David's Hall, Surry Hills xvi, 161, 164, 166

Stephensen, Percy ('Inky') 218, 239-43, **240**
Stevens, Joyce 332
St James's Watch House xvi, 37, **38**, 39, 43
Stonemason's Society 62-63, 65
Stonewall Riots (New York) 326
Storey, Premier John 134-135
St Peters 188
street-corner meetings 4, 114-20
strike-breakers 139-141
student protest 259, 260-63, **262**, **263**
Subianto, Tuk 254
Sun, The 179, **192-193**, **200**, **201**, **289**
Surry Hills 4, 5, 45, 120, 130, 161, 164, 166, 187, 199
Survival Day 328-34
Sussex Street 42, 54, 108, 119, 150, 238, 273, 278
Swift, Jonathan 26
Sydenham 4
Sydney Anarchist Group 293, 294
Sydney Cove 8, **11**, **14**
Sydney Cricket Ground 139-140, 141
Sydney Free Press 40
Sydney Gazette 25
Sydney Harbour Bridge 7, 188
Sydney Libertarians 294, 296, 309
Sydney Morning Herald 48, 50, 65, 78, 80, 109, 124, 126, 141, 155, 156, 234, 238, 249, 262, 303, 304, 327, 333
Sydney Push 293
Sydney Stadium 162
Sydney Technical College 74
Sydney Town Hall xvi, 4, 67-68, 75, 78, 126, 223, 227-29
Sydney University xiv-xv, 80, 133, 135, 258, 269, 294, 299, 302
   front lawn *298, 299*
Sydney Workers' Art Club 210
Sykes, Bobbi 329
Syson, Ian 184
Szabados Academy 283

Tank Stream 97-98, 104, 108
Taronga Park Zoo 140
Taylor Square 187, 326
Tench, Lieutenant Watkin 9, 10
Tennant, Kylie 205, **206**
   Ride on Stranger 205
Textile Workers' Union 269
Thälmann, Ernst 226-27
Theeman, Frank 308, 311, 312, 313

Theodore, E.G. (Ted) 179-80
Thomas, Lowell 225
Thorburn, Jim 294
Thoreau, H. D. 94
Thorpe, Billy 302
Timber Workers' Relief Depots **170**, 171
Tong, K. Y. 247
Trades and Labour Council 77 *see also*
    Labor Council and Unions NSW
Trades Hall, Goulburn Street xvi, 136, 151,
    152, **153**, 160, 207, 283
trades societies 29, 41, 48
treadmill 24, 33
'Tree of Liberty' 57, 59
Tribune, The 150, 268, 332
tricolour ribbon 58-59
Truth 77, 107
Tucker, Margaret 218
Twain, Mark 182-183
Twyford House 188

Ultimo 4, 5, 49
Underwood Street, Paddington 108
unemployed workers 41, 46-47, 48, 50, 52,
    110-11
Unemployed Workers' Movement (UWM)
    196-203
Union of Democratic Control 133
Unions NSW 160
Union Street, Erskineville xiv-xv, 196-203
Universal Negro Improvement Association
    161-62, 164

Vernon 341
Victoria Barracks 3
Victoria Street, King's Cross xvi, **73**, 187,
    305, 308, **309**
Victoria Theatre 37
Vietnam War 264, 287, 288, 290, 291, 292,
    298, 300, 301, 314
Village Voice 290
Vinegar Hill 3, 13, 15, 17, **19**, 20
Von Luckner, Count Felix 224-230, **225**

Wai, Stanley 247
Walker, Margaret 281
Walsh, Adela Pankhurst 159-60, 241
Walsh, Richard 287, 288, 290
Walsh, Tom 159, 241
Walshe, R. D. (Bob) 261-264
    Student Work for Progress 263

Ward, Eddie 173
Warner, Denis 234
Warragamba Dam 247
watch houses 36, **39**
Waterloo 59, 138
Waterside Workers' Federation 162, 214-15,
    251, 253, 260, 273, 336, 337
    WWF Cultural Committee 274-75
    WWF Film Unit 276-78, 277
Watson, Chris 267
Wells, H. G. 223
Wentworth Avenue 5
Wentworth Park **169**
West Bengal 316
West's Bush, Paddington 108
Wharfies' Hall, Sussex Street xvi
Wharf Labourers' Union 140 *see also*
    Waterside Workers' Federation (WWF)
Wheatley, Nadia 203
    The House That Was Eureka 203
White Australia Policy 244, 245
Whitlam, Gough 298, 301, 304, 331
Whitman, Walt 109
Wilberforce, William 10
William Street 326
Willis, A.C. 145
Windschuttle, Keith 296-97
Windsor 50, 58
Wingello House 186
Womanhood Suffrage League, The 88, 181
Woman's Voice, The 94, 181
women 171, 172
Women's Literary Society 94
women's rights 85-86, 93-94
Woolloomooloo 4, 5, 45, 50, 120, 187, 254,
    305, 339
Wong, Fred 244, 245, 246, 247, 248, 250
Worker Building, The xvi, 181, 216
Worker, The 90, 142, 147, 175, 184-85
Workers' Educational Association 134, 184
Workers' Weekly, The 150
working-class culture 45
World, The 175, 177-79, **180**
World War I 5, 122, 184, 217
World War II 238, 240, 243, 244, 245, 246,
    253, 257, 258, 259, 288, 293, 336, 343
Wright, Tom 218

Yagoona 319
York Street 42, 54, 231
Youth Carnival for Peace and Friendship
    (1952) 279-84, **282**, **284**